Seeing Red

Seeing Red

Russian Propaganda and American News

SARAH OATES AND GORDON NEIL RAMSAY

OXFORD
UNIVERSITY PRESS

Oxford University Press is a department of the University of Oxford. It furthers
the University's objective of excellence in research, scholarship, and education
by publishing worldwide. Oxford is a registered trade mark of Oxford University
Press in the UK and certain other countries.

Published in the United States of America by Oxford University Press
198 Madison Avenue, New York, NY 10016, United States of America.

© Oxford University Press 2024

All rights reserved. No part of this publication may be reproduced, stored in
a retrieval system, or transmitted, in any form or by any means, without the
prior permission in writing of Oxford University Press, or as expressly permitted
by law, by license, or under terms agreed with the appropriate reproduction
rights organization. Inquiries concerning reproduction outside the scope of the
above should be sent to the Rights Department, Oxford University Press, at the
address above.

You must not circulate this work in any other form
and you must impose this same condition on any acquirer.

CIP data is on file at the Library of Congress

ISBN 978–0–19–769643–9 (pbk.)
ISBN 978–0–19–769642–2 (hbk.)

DOI: 10.1093/oso/9780197696422.001.0001

Paperback printed by Marquis Book Printing, Canada
Hardback printed by Bridgeport National Bindery, Inc., United States of America

Contents

Acknowledgments	vii
1. Introduction	1
2. American News in the 21st Century	27
3. Strategic Narratives: What Do the Russians Want?	53
4. U.S. 2020 Presidential Campaign Narratives and Russian Propaganda	81
5. Curating Chaos: Election Fraud Claims and the Capitol Insurrection	115
6. Russian Strategic Narratives and the War in Ukraine: From Neo-Nazis to NATO	142
7. Conclusions	172
References	183
Index	201

Acknowledgments

This book has spanned several years, many paper presentations, workshops, seminars, and literally hundreds of conversations with colleagues, collaborators, students, friends, and sometimes complete strangers. When we were both at the University of Glasgow, the late Bill Miller used to give the sage advice that scholarship was always a "conversation." And we acknowledge that these conversations—and the time and wisdom given so generously by others—were a critical part of writing this book.

For Sarah Oates, a fellowship at the Wilson Center in Washington, D.C. was critical to the foundation of the book. Activities at the Kennan Institute at the Wilson Center provided connections to key experts and expertise in Russia. In addition, the Philip Merrill College of Journalism at the University of Maryland supported the efforts with both research funding and teaching release.

Gordon Neil Ramsay would like to thank Martin Moore and Ben Campbell for the help in devising, testing, and refining Steno across many research projects and many time zones. Sam Robertshaw was instrumental in the development of methods to trace Russian disinformation in UK media, and the Open Society Foundations in Brussels and Texty.org.ua in Kyiv provided research funding and support in the Weaponising News project that laid the foundations for some of the research in this book. Thanks also to colleagues at the University of Akureyri for the time, space, and support while writing.

We are grateful to our very patient Oxford University Press editor Angela Chnapko for her insight and support throughout this process. Without her, this book would not have happened.

We would also like to thank the following people for their support and contributions to our research for this book: Jesse Anderson, Joseph Barrow, James Bilsland, Scott Brown, Lucy Dalglish, Danielle Deibler, Valentina Feklyunina, John Gray, Sam Greene, Olya Gurevich, Abby Jones, David Knickerbocker, Doowan Lee, Wei-Ping Li, Rafael Lorente, Josh Macleder, Gillian McCormack, John McQuaid, Wendy W. Moe, Sean Mussenden, Rachel O'Hare, William Pomeranz, Philip Resnik, Tom Rosenstiel, David

viii ACKNOWLEDGMENTS

Rubenstein, Regina Smyth, Christopher Walker, Derek Willis, and the late Catherine Schuler.

Finally, we would like to thank our families for their support: Sarah would like to thank David, Laura, and Emma Cross; Gordon would like to thank Kirsty Twidale for her patience, invaluable companionship, and support.

1
Introduction

Donald Trump could be the greatest gift to the Russians in the history of propaganda. This is not because of evidence that Russians held secret information on him or manipulated him through some undetected network. Trump became a foreign asset because he produced both words and actions that could be used to attack democracy, a key strategic goal of the Russians. Trump consistently denies reality, vilifies the free media, and broadcasts disinformation. This opens the door for foreign disinformation to flow into the U.S. news, hidden in plain sight by Kremlin-style rhetoric from a U.S. president and amplified by the right-wing media. Through the 2020 election, the Stop the Steal conspiracy, and the Capitol insurrection, Russians found myriad ways to publicize the end of American democracy and the rise of Russia.

The convergence of strategic narratives from a U.S. president and the Kremlin created historic opportunities for Russian information warfare. While Russian propaganda may have less opportunity to profit from the war in Ukraine, the struggles of U.S. democracy and traditional media empowered Russia's global narrative for the massive invasion in 2022. This elevation of Russian soft power could not have happened without Trump, who has been aided and abetted by politicians and U.S. outlets that favor propaganda over information.

The threat of Russian disinformation is real, and it played a significant role in the 2016 U.S. elections. Despite knowledge of the risk and resourceful work by analysts and journalists in tracking down Russian propaganda in the United States, the problem of foreign disinformation continues to this day. As this book will demonstrate, this is in part due to exploitation of the American tradition of free speech and the open nature of the U.S. media system. The much more dangerous menace lies not in how foreign governments attempt to manipulate the media but in how our media system has been compromised by domestic actors who follow an authoritarian playbook. When it is hard to tell the difference between what the Russians are saying about the Democrats and how Fox News is covering Joe Biden, it is time to realize that some U.S. outlets have crossed the line from news to propaganda.

Seeing Red. Sarah Oates and Gordon Neil Ramsay, Oxford University Press. © Oxford University Press 2024.
DOI: 10.1093/oso/9780197696422.003.0001

2 SEEING RED

These forces came to a head again on January 6, 2021. Trump's manipulation of the media, honed over years of creating narratives that resonated more with myth-making than democratic reality, played a central role in the assault on the U.S. Capitol by Trump supporters seeking to overturn his loss in the 2020 election. Just as the Russians learned to seed disinformation narratives over the years, Trump deployed classic tactics of propaganda. He began projecting the narrative of a stolen election in 2020 months before the vote as his support in the polls fell amid the expanding COVID pandemic, taking the extraordinary step of pre-emptively refusing to accept election results that were not in his favor. With his powerful pulpit, unquestioningly supportive right-wing media, and devoted following, he summoned his supporters to Washington and told them to march to the Capitol and "fight much harder" (Associated Press 2021).

Trump's post-election propaganda campaign had one immediate goal: to keep him in office. But its deeper, more important purpose was to delegitimize his opponent's victory, establishing a tactic adaptable to any future election and thus undermining American democracy. A crucial element of this strategy was vilifying and disempowering the media because journalists had the duty and responsibility to report on and expose Trump's lies. This matches a central goal of Russian propaganda to take power away from the media.

These tumultuous events, as well as Russian propaganda's recurring role in them, have come at a time when the U.S. media is consumed with its own deepening crisis. With the power of the Trump presidency and much of the Republican Party allied against the press, public trust in the media has declined. At the same time, the economic struggles of the U.S. media make them increasingly vulnerable to Russian attacks. The strategy many U.S. outlets adopted to survive—and indeed profit—in this period was to abandon the notion of objectivity and the independent monitoring of power to work in the service of Trump and propaganda. This is an exceptionally dangerous trend. Without professional news outlets, there is no truly free press. Without a free press, there is no democracy worthy of the name.

The Fusion of Russian and Republican Propaganda in the News

This book illuminates how Russian disinformation, Russian propaganda themes, and tactics adopted by Republicans have come to colonize the

INTRODUCTION 3

information environment of the United States. It may seem like U.S. democracy successfully weathered its recent storms. The Capitol was cleared of the armed mob in a matter of hours, Trump left office in early 2021, Biden was sworn in peacefully, and candidates who echoed Trump's conspiracy theories about a stolen presidency largely failed in the 2022 midterm elections. The electoral system withstood an enormous test under a president who desperately deployed massive resources to try to overturn an election. He failed in large part because the courts, some with judges appointed by Trump, chose the law over political favoritism. But the threats to democracy have not gone away.

As a society, we need to know our enemy. Russia is a classic foe of U.S. democracy. That's not only due to the historic rivalry and enmity between the two countries, but also because the U.S. serves as the primary target for Russian outrage over Western dominance in global political and economic affairs. The United States is Russia's Enemy Number One in its ongoing global information war. But the deeper danger to U.S. democracy is internal: Propaganda tactics that we recognize and understand from foreign information wars are now routinely deployed by domestic politicians on their own population. Yet, once we recognize these tactics, we can work to take away their power.

This book addresses this ongoing threat. We demonstrate how our free media systems are infected with both Russian propaganda and U.S. news that echoes Kremlin talking points—from the appearance of Russian-generated text on the U.S. alt-right website Infowars to the amplification of crucial Russian narratives that resonate with the Trump administration on Fox News—and suggest ways to counter this danger. We also highlight where journalistic norms of balance and objectivity can sometimes work to amplify Russian propaganda.

Why the U.S. Media Is Vulnerable

At the center of this issue lies the peculiar institution that is the U.S. media. Both uniquely vulnerable and particularly powerful compared to counterparts in other liberal democracies, the U.S. media function under a commercial model that is quite different from corresponding systems in other countries. Almost all nations have significant state-funded media sectors, including major national television channels that are paid for with government funding. In theory, if not always in practice, these act to counterbalance media organizations that follow strictly commercial logics. U.S. media rely strongly on advertising to fund their operations, making the profession and practice of journalism far more vulnerable to market forces.

This independence from a state-run media sector is viewed as critical to American democracy because it means the media can serve its citizen-customers and not the powerful governments who fund state media. But this decentralized, liberal system with almost no government control and a strong tradition of free speech is also susceptible to manipulation. This is especially the case now that the audience engagement that draws advertising dollars is increasingly separated from high-quality journalism that functions in the public interest.

The First Big Warning

The U.S. media's growing vulnerabilities, as well as the ability of both Trump and Russia to exploit them, came into sharp focus during the 2016 U.S. presidential campaign. Democratic contender Hillary Clinton was dogged by wave after wave of negative news coverage. Much of it came from the orchestrated release of her hacked emails that were published by WikiLeaks, news that directly competed with the *Access Hollywood* video that showed Trump bragging about assaulting women. In the fog of campaign coverage, it would seem that journalists were simply following the news. But later investigations revealed that Russian propaganda played a role in shaping coverage of Clinton and, by extension, influenced an American election.

This was a glorious moment for Russians, who have felt marginalized by their country's loss of global status since the collapse of the Soviet Union in 1991. It was a more confusing moment for Americans. Older citizens could remember dire warnings about Russian disinformation, but this was a distant memory mixed up with "red scares" and cartoonish propaganda from decades ago during the Cold War. For younger generations, it was just a puzzling part of a much broader political storm as Trump swept into the presidency against the odds. Why were Russians posing as Americans on Facebook and other social media? Why did the Russians appear to support Trump? Why did Trump appear to support the Russians? And what exactly was this Russian propaganda, and did it reach many Americans?

It was clear that a Russia-influenced information war was now embedded in American politics. Yet U.S. action on this challenge was elusive. During

INTRODUCTION 5

the crowded and contentious 2016 Democratic primaries and into the general election, there was no organized response from the U.S. government to Russian propaganda. From 2017 on, despite an outcry against Russian meddling, congressional hearings, the Mueller investigation, and increased U.S. sanctions on Russian interests, there was little clarity or action on identifying and countering Russian messaging as it leached into the U.S. media system.

A key feature of this information war was an attack on the notion of traditional American democracy and the amplification of a central strategic narrative that democracy is flawed and failing. This was the most successful convergence between Russian and Republican narratives, although the Kremlin also is able to use political division and right-wing media outlets to push its narrative that the West and NATO, with their unreasoning hatred of Russia expressed in what Russians call rampant "Russophobia," are out to destroy Russia.

This convergence sometimes makes it hard to distinguish Russian propaganda from U.S. right-wing rhetoric. Indeed, when doing research for this book, often we either could not tell the messages apart or discern whether Russian propaganda was recycling and amplifying Republican messaging. Was this a deliberate alliance in information warfare? No. While there are parallels between Russian and U.S. right-wing narratives, it's not particularly useful to search for a direct, conspiratorial link between the two; the reality is more complicated and far-reaching. It's much more beneficial to analyze scientifically how narratives from the Kremlin and narratives from the U.S. right align and dynamically influence one another.

We began our research by using tools for identifying foreign propaganda hiding in plain sight in the U.S. media system. We found resonance between Russian and Republican narratives in campaign coverage of Biden, in the Stop the Steal conspiracy, and in the Capitol insurrection. In these cases, the Russians were pushing at an open door, as Trump's rejection of traditional news and democratic values amplified propaganda narratives. We found that some important Russian propaganda campaigns, particularly against NATO and the Western military, found little traction in U.S. news until the Russian invasion of Ukraine in 2022. However, we detected a pattern in elite U.S. media outlets of repeating Putin's talking points that blamed NATO for the invasion of Ukraine without always countering them by showing the Russians are the aggressors.

As a deeply divided American public struggled to navigate political and social challenges under Trump, Russian propaganda attempted to disinform,

6 SEEING RED

disengage, and disillusion U.S. citizens. As this book will demonstrate, this strategy is part of a major information war aimed at weakening the United States as the primary enemy of Russia. Foreign propaganda is most effective at driving wedges into existing political and social fissures. That's much easier if the domestic media are recycling and amplifying the messages. As Marlene Laruelle points out, it is not that Russia can transform American society, but Russia can act as "an echo chamber" for American society's "own doubts and transformations" (2019, 198). In this scenario, it is often difficult to know if the negative coverage about American democracy is coming from RT (formerly Russia Today) or from Fox News.

Our research shows how Trump's constant attacks on the free press, embraced by many on the U.S. right, gave an unprecedented opportunity for foreign adversaries to attack the country at a vulnerable time. This book analyzes the Russian influence on U.S. national news narratives at four crisis moments in American and global politics: the divisive 2020 U.S. presidential election campaign, the Stop the Steal conspiracy, the 2021 Capitol insurrection, and the Russian invasion of Ukraine in February 2022. Russia is not the only foreign adversary infiltrating U.S. media, as China in particular actively carries out propaganda campaigns. However, by using our in-depth knowledge of Russian propaganda, we outline an effective way to detect and deter foreign propaganda in the U.S. media in general.

Americans *can and should* know if the source of what we read, watch, or listen to is coming from Washington or Moscow. We show how to track disinformation back to its source to identify, deter, and even counter a key element in the erosion of American media freedom. Rising above the usual debates over "fake news" or attempts to claim foreign propaganda is easily isolated from U.S. journalism, this book uses powerful analytical tools to define and demonstrate where Russian-based narratives appear in the U.S. news. It also shows where Russian propaganda tactics are deployed by the U.S. right-wing media by looking at news narratives, which characterize how stories are told to support end goals.

Understanding the History of Russian Propaganda

Why—and how—would Russia make the United States its primary global target for propaganda more than three decades after the U.S.-Soviet superpower rivalry came to an end? This is both an echo of the Cold War and a

INTRODUCTION 7

reflection of current Russian realpolitik. During the Cold War, both nations had active propaganda campaigns aimed at championing their ideological values. All Soviet media was saturated with pro-communist propaganda. Indeed, the central purpose of the Soviet media was to support and promote the Communist Party of the Soviet Union (Siebert et al. 1956). The United States spent lavishly on American-produced "public diplomacy" aimed at the Soviet Union. This included Voice of America and Radio Liberty.

The Soviet Union's collapse just two years after the fall of the Berlin Wall was seen at the time as a permanent global victory for Western ideals and way of life. Russia, however, did not embrace Western-style democracy despite some flirtation with free elections and media. Rather, power was quickly consolidated in the hands of a group of oligarchs, who also seized control of national assets to amass staggering personal wealth. Today, Russia is an authoritarian state that relies heavily on media messaging to control its population under the popular figurehead of President Vladimir Putin. He has been elected, with no viable opposition, enough times to have now ruled Russia for more than two decades, and a 2020 change to Russian law will allow him to stay in office until 2036.

Putin's domestic influence is boosted by his response to external threats, both real and imagined. The founding of the Russian Federation in 1991 was marked by economic instability, rampant inflation, insecurity about neighboring states, and a long civil war in Chechnya. Russia was deeply angered by the NATO bombings of Yugoslavia during the Kosovo War in 1999, as the Western alliance proceeded with the strikes without authorization from the United Nations Security Council to evade a Russian veto. This was a significant signal to Russians about their lack of influence in their own neighborhood of Eastern Europe. Although Russians like to tell an uncomplicated narrative about NATO as a historical threat to Russia, there were times when Russian and American leaders even broached the idea that Russia could join NATO. But for Russia, NATO has come to represent its failure to find a dominant role in the world. Although NATO is technically a defensive alliance, for Russia it stands as an existential threat.

Inculcating fear about foreign threats is a useful method to bolster public support of a regime that is unable to offer democratic choices to citizens or build a society free from rampant corruption. It is more expedient to manufacture consent by framing Russia as an encircled, embattled state that must protect the Russian motherland and her people from being overrun. At the same time, demonstrating the power of the Russian nation through limited wars in places as diverse as Georgia and Syria is a powerful driver of positive domestic public opinion. A "rally-round-the-flag" syndrome is certainly not new or limited to Russia: Ratings for U.S. President George W. Bush soared after the 9/11 attacks and allowed his White House to craft a "War on Terror" frame and launch the second Gulf War. This changed U.S. politics and policy in ways that resonate to this day.

So, if using foreign threats or even limited invasions is not new, what is different about Russia's 21st-century information strategy? It combines three elements that significantly amplify its traditional projection of power. First, Russia has shown it will savagely punish neighboring countries for even appearing to side with the West. This was seen in Russia's invasion of Ukraine. Second, Russia uses its formidable media presence in the post-Soviet region to engage in massive propaganda campaigns. Third, Russia is leveraging current opportunities in the global media ecosystem, notably the lack of regulation of online and social media, to wage an aggressive propaganda campaign against a range of countries in the West. Its efforts in the information war against America are the focus of this book.

While Russia can wield military threats or other forms of power in its own region, the object of its propaganda in the West is much more about undermining the narratives of U.S. superpower dominance and the virtues of liberal democracy. While it is willing to invade other countries, Russia also finds it effective to manipulate American hearts and minds to get a useful outcome to support the Putin regime. This can take the form of sowing chaos in an enemy state or even managing to manipulate elections to get a candidate more sympathetic to the Russian viewpoint elected. In the case of Trump, Russia may have gained both in 2016.

The 2016 U.S. Elections: What the Russians Learned

The Russian propaganda campaign in the 2016 U.S. elections must have exceeded the wildest expectations of its organizers. Although Americans were alarmed by the revelations that Russians had posed as Americans and bought political ads on social media, the evidence that the Russian-backed leak of Democrat emails may have influenced the U.S. news agenda at a critical time in the election is perhaps more worrying (Jamieson 2018). At the same time, Trump was much friendlier to Russia, apparently easier to

INTRODUCTION 9

manipulate, and did not conform to the usual presidential caution in dealing with Russia (or indeed any foreign country). While it was unclear whether he didn't understand why he should be prudent with Russia or he just didn't care, it benefited Russia to have a rogue president with a clear affinity for authoritarian leaders.

Even the direct benefits of a Trump presidency, however, were not the greatest gains for Russia from the 2016 elections. With a relatively small investment in social media advertisement and a hack-and-dump operation that targeted the Democrats, the Russians were able to spook both American leaders and the public with an idea of a malevolent enemy with superior information-warfare skills. It didn't matter that evidence remains very much mixed as to the exact impact of the Russian social media campaign on the U.S. vote (Jamieson 2018; Eady et al. 2023). What matters is the specific fear that it inspired of Russia, which is inferior to the United States in both conventional military strength and global economic clout, as well as the idea that electoral democracy could be so easily subverted. To help get Trump elected over Clinton was a short-term win; to demonstrate that U.S. democracy is dangerously vulnerable is a far bigger victory.

But looking at social media messaging alone or a single operation targeting the Democrats is far too narrow a lens through which to view Russian propaganda. It is neither just a few messages on social media nor a vastly powerful influence engine. Rather, Russian propaganda is funneled into broad and diverse media systems in the United States, sometimes resonating with a story but mostly getting lost in the vast sea of media messages or overtaken by the next big moment in the news cycle. Although we often see Russian propaganda as attempting to influence specific opinions or events in the West, it's more productive to understand it from the Russian point of view. We need to view Russian propaganda as part of broader Russian strategic narratives that define and transmit the Kremlin's foreign policy objectives.

At the same time, it's critical to understand the nature of the current U.S. media system so we can see how foreign messages enter our information sphere, how they are spread, and whether they resonate effectively in American society. The traditional mass media, online media sites, and social media networks all play a role. While Russian narratives have not been particularly compelling over time for the U.S. audience, America's current political polarization offers Russian propaganda a promising vector into the

10   SEEING RED

U.S. media ecosystem. Even foreign propaganda can be welcome if it supports your point of view. An asymmetric media situation between the West and Russia—one open with few restrictions, one much more controlled—also helps favor Russian information warfare over Western civil discourse.

Trump's approach to information control is closer to Russian tactics than to traditional American political messaging. Classic Russian propaganda tactics include obfuscating, denying facts, lying, attacking critics, defaming others, and illogically shifting blame to specific groups in society (such as immigrants or liberals, etc.). An additional central element of the Russian propaganda playbook is attacking the media and journalists. A quality that both Putin and Trump share is the ability to play on conservative fears and values, to promise that traditional values matter and will triumph over liberalism. Trump stood apart from previous U.S. presidents—many who did reprehensible things while in office—by fully embracing propaganda over reputable political communication.

Plan of the Book

This book examines three critical parts of the foreign propaganda equation. On the one hand, we document the efforts by Russians to project their national needs and desires onto the U.S. media ecosystem through their international outlets such as RT and Sputnik. We analyze the stories the Russians wish to tell and the image they seek to construct about Russia, namely, a strong and resurgent nation that rejects Western models of governance. Even more importantly, we analyze the image that Russia constructs of the West as a weak, failing, and venal system that seeks to destroy the Russian motherland. These messages may penetrate the mainstream media agenda in the United States, although they are more likely to feed into anti-democratic echo chambers, such as those on the right.

We also need to consider the news environment into which these 'Russia First' and 'Evil America' messages are projected: a flawed and challenged American media system. The problems that have left democratic media systems particularly vulnerable to disinformation campaigns range from the collapse of the commercial model for traditional journalism to a lack of regulation of the online sphere to how social media algorithms reshape news distribution. In many ways, it's the perfect storm for propaganda, and just what

INTRODUCTION   11

Russia needed to overcome decades of dislike and distrust from Western audiences.

Finally, we found through the course of writing this book that Trump's messaging and Russian propaganda often seem to be singing from the same hymn book. When our coders encountered difficulties trying to differentiate between Russian propaganda and U.S. media content, we had to consider what this meant for the content and motivations of different media organizations. A significant part of the U.S. media system, mostly anchored around Fox News, used what Yang and Bennett (2021) term "interactive propaganda" in which the news organization actively promoted Trump's disinformation. These tactics echoed Russian propaganda campaigns.

The active participation of U.S. media outlets in supporting propaganda is a chilling and dangerous moment in American democracy. That is not to say that U.S. news organizations have not rather blindly supported pro-American messages in the past—such as during world wars or after 9/11—but Fox News reached levels of collusion with the Trump administration that crossed the line from patriotism to propaganda. The Russians took note: By 2022, Russian domestic television was using clips from Fox News as propaganda to support its invasion of Ukraine (Thompson 2022). At the same time, the logics of U.S. media that promote balance and objectivity meant that outlets such as *The New York Times*, *The Wall Street Journal*, and *The Washington Post* often echo Putin's talking points about the war in Ukraine.

This is not a "whodunnit" book that reveals how a particular Russian information operation led to specific voting patterns or protests in certain cities. There are studies that examine the influence of propaganda on this level, although it's difficult to prove its exact effects. Media messages are part of a complex phenomenon that can inspire people to action, ranging from reconsidering their beliefs to voting to even rioting. Instead, the research in this book establishes both how to identify foreign propaganda and the pathways that bring that propaganda into the news consumed by the American audience. This is about how to be a disinformation detective rather than solving a specific disinformation 'crime.'

To that end, this book will use a trio of powerful tools to more precisely define, track, and assess the spread and influence of Russian propaganda content and techniques: strategic narrative theory, content analysis, and computational analysis.

Strategic Narrative: What's the Goal of a Message?

How does Russia define its propaganda goals for the West? In other words, what does Russia want Americans to believe about Russia? Russian propaganda is aimed at shaping attitudes toward Russia in a particular way while undermining faith in democracy itself (Pomerantsev 2014). Russia wishes to impose its version of world events and perceptions on a global audience through the promotion of strategic narratives. A strategic narrative is the intersection of communication and power: "tools that political actors employ to promote their interests, values, and aspirations for international order by managing expectations and altering the discursive environment" (Miskimmon et al. 2017, preface). For Russia, strategic narratives have both reflected and justified their military incursions, including in Ukraine (Szostek 2017; Hinck et al. 2018).

The United States is a prime target for the propaganda created to support Russian strategic narratives, although Russia has active media-influence campaigns around the globe (Herd 2016; Helmus et al. 2018; Bradshaw and Howard 2019). Russian strategic narratives seek to define and project Russian power in specific ways, in particular by framing NATO as an opportunistic tool of American global ambitions; Ukraine as the rightful territory of the Russian state; and Russia as a resurgent power in the world.

If that's what Russia wants, did Trump and his allies want the same things? There were times during the Trump administration when it was hard to decode Trump's policy intent, although he was predictable about his messaging to his core constituency of right-wing voters as well as his overt admiration of authoritarian leaders. Trump also was reliable in the way he deployed disinformation consistently throughout his presidency, choosing to rely more heavily on lies as his term continued (Kessler et al. 2021). This was apparent from his first day in office when he broadcast disinformation about the size of his inauguration crowds in January 2017, and he reached a new level of obfuscation with a refusal to publicly condemn violent White supremacists in Charlottesville, Virginia, seven months later. By the time he refused to accept his defeat in 2020, the pattern was familiar although his levels of disinformation increased until he was documented making 503 false or misleading claims in a single day on November 2, 2020 (Kessler et al. 2021).

Trump's strategic narratives came into even sharper focus in early 2020 due to the twin challenges of COVID and reelection. His approach to the COVID epidemic was to consistently downplay the crisis. A charitable interpretation would be that he was concerned with the economic and social damage that widespread panic or shutdowns could cause. In an unprecedented health crisis, leaders around the globe were presented with massive challenges in a fast-moving and frightening situation.

A less generous explanation would be that Trump was unable to understand the magnitude of the problem or that he was more concerned with looking good—and re-electable—than he was with rational policy in a global emergency. At any rate, his narrative of dismissing the dangers of the epidemic led to several worrying tactics, including ignoring scientific evidence, denigrating his own health specialists, promoting false cures such as hydroxychloroquine, and fighting against public health measures such as masks and closures (Yang and Bennett 2021). Once it became clear that COVID could not be dismissed or downplayed, Trump began to warn against early voting and absentee ballots, falsely claiming these were not valid. This narrative set him up to challenge a narrow result, although it ultimately did not work. However, this narrative did play a large part in the Capitol insurrection on January 6, 2021.

Content Analysis

As media consumers, we observe the ebb and flow of news coverage. We come to expect and understand how certain stories get covered and why some stories get little or no attention (Boczkowski and Mitchelstein 2013; Harcup and O'Neill 2017). As content analysis specialists, we are interested in measuring and analyzing this coverage to understand its underlying meanings. In particular, how are stories organized around specific themes or narratives, and how do these differ among various outlets and over time? Why do some stories endure and others fade? How and why do certain media narratives change over time?

In this book we use content analysis to explore these questions. Content analysis is the systematic evaluation of texts. At its most fundamental, content analysis can provide simple measures of the characteristics of texts, such as the number of words in an article, the publication in which the text appears, the date it appears, and even how many times a specific word or words are used. Content analysis of Russian state media sites in English such as RT and Sputnik allow us to analyze how Russia frames and articulates its central strategic narratives. In turn, content analysis of American news

14   SEEING RED

allows us to see how these narratives resonate in the U.S. media. We look at a range of evidence, from specific keywords to actors who are quoted to what is cited to amplify their claims.

The authors of this book have, between us, more than forty years of experience in carrying out content analysis projects. The technique can be good at finding the signal in the noise, but it's complicated and time-consuming. It's complicated because you need to find a way to define and quantify media coverage, whether it is assessing the central topic in the story or establishing the tone of the coverage. It's time-consuming because unless you can automate the process, humans need to read, listen to, or watch all the content (usually more than once) to apply a coding frame.

If content analysis was complex before the internet, the rise of the digital age has created significantly more challenges. To be fair, there are more opportunities as well. The changes to traditional media content are not as profound, and, indeed, the online distribution of media content makes it easier for scholars to gather material. But understanding media content is no longer about merely knowing the nature of the text. It's now possible to study how the news is shared, commented upon, liked, re-appropriated, and so forth. Much of this distribution and commentary takes place on social media. Our study focuses on the content of news itself, although it is important to acknowledge the relevance of how news is both produced and distributed.

Computational Analysis

As the last of the three central research elements of this book, computational analysis allows us to translate specific verbal patterns into digital codes, making it possible to tag and trace particular narratives as they move from the Russian sites into the U.S. media. In this way, we see the echoes (and sometimes the exact words) from Russian propaganda sources appear in American media. Through our research, we also found that U.S. news content is sometimes recycled into Russian English-language propaganda.

As discussed above, while it's not difficult to find what narratives Russians want to project—not least because they go to considerable efforts to broadcast these narratives via their international outlets—it's somewhat more challenging to find specific linguistic markers of Russian propaganda in the U.S. media. We want to see whether ideas rooted in Russian propaganda

INTRODUCTION 15

make it into mainstream U.S. media discourse. During our research, we also came to see which U.S. messaging was incorporated into Russian strategic narratives. To measure these incursions (both into and out of Russian propaganda), we use computational methods combined with traditional media content analysis for this book.

This is where computational linguistics, which applies computer science to the analysis and synthesis of language and speech, can augment human content analysis. Computational linguists have developed ways of codifying text such as news stories and political messages that make it possible for a reliable link to be established between the original story and its retelling in other formats (Card et al. 2015). Leskovec et al. (2009) detailed how to use computational linguistics to isolate unique elements of statements and narratives, which they call verbal memes, so that these components can be tracked across social media platforms. For example, in the U.S. 2016 presidential campaign, one verbal meme was "nasty woman"—originally uttered by Trump during a debate to castigate Clinton but then picked up as a riposte by liberals. One of the most famous catchphrases from the election was "build a wall," popularized by Trump as a hardline response to immigration issues.

The ability to visualize how specific narratives travel across a media system greatly enhances our capacity to use narrative to understand how stories spread. There is compelling and useful work that has measured the content of Russian propaganda, including Orttung and Nelson's (2019) examination of online RT content, but it's not feasible to conduct in-depth coding in real time or at the volume necessary to track Russian or other propaganda. This book offers a way forward in terms of understanding the nature and spread of propaganda by building on existing scholarship and carrying out the research with the help of automated tools.

Analyzing the Health of U.S. Media Discourse

It's important to point out that this research does not study the effect of Russian propaganda on individual Western *citizens*. Rather, this book is interested in identifying and isolating the effect of Russian propaganda on U.S. media *discourses*. How does Russian propaganda and disinformation seep into daily news content in the United States? This means our unit of measurement is the content itself—the stories as they are defined by linguistic tools and how they fit into strategic narratives. We are focusing on the detection of propaganda because we want to know how vulnerable Western media systems are to foreign propaganda writ large. At issue here is not the hearts and minds of individuals but the overall health and resilience of democratic media systems.

This approach demonstrates that social media messages linked to Russian trolls are often at the end of a long chain of events that starts with the construction of Russian communication strategy at the highest levels. If we want to gauge the relevance and power of evidence such as the spread of a particular story, we need to start much closer to the origin of the propaganda and examine how Russians construct their global propaganda aims. At the same time, we need to follow the trail of propaganda breadcrumbs through the media ecosystem. Which stories with roots in Russian propaganda resonate in U.S. news? Which stories become part of a national news discourse? And which stories fail to gain any attention?

Understanding Russian Propaganda: What Do Russians Want?

Every country works to project its image onto the world stage. Indeed, the study of national strategic communication, or "public diplomacy," has become a field in its own right, linked to the broader concept of soft power (Nye 1990). In this sense, Russia is in no way unique in wishing to project a powerful and meaningful image globally. The difference with Russia—and some would say with world powers in general—is that this image projection is linked to military strategy. This is often referred to as "hybrid warfare," in which traditional military measures go together with communication strategy (Hoffman 2007).

A Russian international image-branding campaign in the United States would seem to be an uphill battle. The one thing that most Americans know about Russia is that they don't like it (Letterman 2018). While one might expect that to be the case in recent years after extensive reporting on Russian disinformation aimed at the United States, this dislike had been consistent over many decades. This antipathy made sense during the Cold War, which lasted from the end of World War II until the collapse of the Soviet Union in 1991. Dislike for Russia increased to record highs in 2022, with 92 percent of Americans reporting an unfavorable view of the country (Wike et al. 2022).

INTRODUCTION   17

Given the distance Russia has traveled from its communist era and the Cold War, why would Russia still wish to carry out an information war with the West? The answer lies in combining a critical internal and external factor: rallying domestic support, and the need to reclaim its Soviet era influence in the world. Russia found itself in an existential crisis after the collapse of the Soviet Union. Once a mighty state power perceived to be on par with the United States, post-Soviet Russia struggled with basic social services and internal chaos. Blaming the problems of the Russian state on the West, particularly the United States, is more politically useful to the Kremlin than acknowledging the weakness of its own policies and rampant corruption. For Russia, anti-Western rhetoric is a win-win: It increases domestic support for leaders and gives Russia a more powerful voice in the world as an avowed enemy of the United States, NATO, and the European Union.

The strategic narratives that Russia would like to project are that the West is out to destroy Russia, Russia is resurgent as a great nation, Russia will protect Russians outside its boundaries, and Western liberal democracy is corrupt and failing (Oates and Steiner 2018). These narratives overlap to a degree, weaving into a compelling and coherent story for the country. At the same time as Russia promotes its nationhood, it denigrates Western systems as corrupt and failing, a narrative that has been particularly resonant with Trump's election, political conflict in the United States, and the surprising 2016 vote by the United Kingdom to exit the European Union.

Where do Russian narratives originate? While this is discussed in more depth in Chapter 3, it's important to highlight the strong hand of the state in Russian media. While there are commercial media in Russia, all media outlets must be loyal to the Kremlin. Media outlets that challenge the Kremlin, ranging from the commercial television network NTV in the 1990s to the Dozhd (Rain) cable channel in 2011, find themselves subject to forced changes in ownership or even lose their ability to broadcast. The Kremlin sets regular "themes" to be covered on state-run television that specify what can be covered, how it can be covered, and what should be ignored. Full censorship and control, such as during Soviet times, is not necessary given the ability of the Kremlin to make examples of media outlets and journalists who do not toe the line. Tactics ranging from intimidation to violence to even murder of journalists remain relatively common in Russia (Committee to Protect Journalists n.d.). Control and censorship have been markedly more severe since the 2022 invasion of Ukraine.

18   SEEING RED

Thus, the Kremlin has formidable control of a large and lively media sphere in Russia, ranging from news to entertainment. This control is extended to Russian international media, notably RT and Sputnik News. But it's not as if Russian media outlets just have sections entitled "Why Russia Is Better Than Other Countries" or "How Democracy Is Failing." Much of the material on these sites is breaking news and feature stories. However, our analysis of the content shows a pervasive framing of events, ranging from discriminatory reporting of facts to highly selective quotes, that provide persistent support of the Russian key narratives: the West hates us, Russia is a resurgent power, we protect Russians worldwide, and democracy is failing. We will discuss the creation of Russian strategic narratives in more depth in Chapter 3.

By knowing the central narratives, the pieces of the media coverage puzzle fall into place for Russia's international propaganda. While stories are occasionally completely falsified or grossly misreported (as with Russia's seizure of Crimea in 2014 or the Russian military shooting down of Malaysia Airlines Flight 17), the strength of the international propaganda really lies on a consistent fidelity to telling stories in ways that support the central Russian strategic narratives.

Trump's Narrative

If we can identify Russian strategic narratives, what were Trump's strategic narratives? It probably makes more sense to call them campaign narratives, as they were less focused on Trump's ambitions for America than his goal of getting reelected in 2020. As noted above, it was difficult to establish meaning from many of Trump's statements, which were often unclear and contradictory (Oates and Moe 2017). But through an analysis of his statements and news coverage during the COVID crisis, the 2020 campaign, and his insistence that the election was stolen despite no evidence, clear themes emerge.

Trump consistently blamed the "fake media" or "liberal media" for lying, whether this was his claims that they were telling untruths about him or exaggerating the COVID threat to undermine him. Throughout his presidency, he complained about "Russiagate" and "Russophobia," that the Democrats exaggerated the threat of Russia and its interference in the 2016 elections to challenge his legitimacy as president. He warned that the widespread protests that followed the police killing of Black victim George Floyd in Minneapolis in 2020 were leading to chaos on the U.S. streets. For this, he

INTRODUCTION 19

blamed Black Lives Matter, Antifa, and "socialist Democrats," and he talked of deploying the U.S. military and shooting protestors. He constantly said that Biden was too old and too corrupt to be president. He started to sound an alarm that mail-in ballots were not secure during the 2020 election campaign, a narrative that became dominant as soon as it was clear that he would lose the election once the mail-in ballots were tallied.

Playing Field or Battlefield? The U.S. Media Ecosystem

What is the media system in which this conflict among narratives—whether from Russians or a U.S. president—is taking place, and what makes it such a fertile environment for propaganda? The digital age has brought great innovation to news, but it has come with the twin challenges of money and trust.

In terms of money, the online sphere has undermined the traditional financial model of the news. In the past, the more popular coverage of sports, weather, and entertainment would draw in readers, allowing media outlets to fund newsrooms big enough to publish the generally less popular reporting on political and economic affairs (Boczkowski and Mitchelstein 2013). There was little concern about exactly what attracted people to buy a newspaper or watch a television news program—as long as there were enough readers or viewers to keep advertising dollars flowing, it wasn't critical. However, as the media became more stratified with the expansion of cable television, major networks started to face serious competition.

If media outlets in the West were challenged by a broader choice in content by the 1980s, much deeper financial problems emerged with the rise of the internet (Pickard 2020). Newspapers relied on income from essentially local advertising monopolies for marketing everything from goods in classified ads to home sales to political campaigns. The online sphere, as a more effective and personalized way to deliver advertising to consumers, has captured much of the marketing revenue. At the same time as media were losing advertisers to the digital sphere, they were failing to maintain their (paying) audience as well. Not only did media outlets hemorrhage revenue and advertisers through declining subscription rates, but they also lost control of their content monopoly and even their brand as their work was distributed for free online (either by accident or design). Online advertising revenues are only a fraction of previous advertising dollars for traditional media outlets.

20 SEEING RED

While losing control of the distribution network for their content, media outlets also struggle with trust and authority. When there were relatively few media outlets in the United States, trust in media was higher. As the market has fragmented, trust in the media has declined. From 2016 to 2022, trust in national news organizations fell from 76 percent of the population in the United States to just 61 percent (Liedke and Gottfried 2022). This is a very worrying development for a liberal democracy that relies on the free media to inform and mobilize citizens. The Reuters Institute for the Study of Journalism reported that trust in the U.S. news overall was just 26 percent in 2022 (Newman et al. 2022). As will be discussed in Chapter 2, a particularly disturbing trend is a sharp gap in trust between Democrats and Republicans, with Republicans far less likely to trust the media.

As both money and trust dwindle, so do the number of professional journalists employed in the United States. The Pew Research Center reported that U.S. newsroom employment has fallen 25 percent since 2008, with the steepest decline at newspapers (Walker 2021). In just sixteen months between January 2017 and April 2018, a third of large U.S. newspapers laid off workers (Grieco et al. 2018). While most of U.S. media are experiencing financial pressure, the cuts at newspapers are particularly concerning as the print media traditionally has pursued more in-depth reporting than other news formats. Fewer reporters mean less investigative reporting, and, in many cases, the financial woes have led to the closure of media outlets altogether. This has created "news deserts" in many parts of the United States that no longer have any local media outlets (Bucay et al. 2017).

As the model of the traditional commercial news media collapsed in the United States, digital outlets entered the marketplace and further fragmented the audience. As a study by Benkler et al. (2018) found, different segments of the audience responded in varying ways to the new media environment. They analyzed millions of media stories and links shared on social media sites to find that a sizable minority of U.S. citizens have become enmeshed in information echo chambers. Citizens who opposed Trump were much more likely to have a varied media diet of reliable sources. However, Trump supporters were more likely to rely on right-leaning Fox News and far-right news outlets (Gottfried et al. 2017; Benkler et al. 2018).

Problems with the news are exacerbated by journalists acting as political mouthpieces rather than as professionals who strive to give balanced and impartial news to citizens. The research by Benkler et al. (2018) noted that politicized media outlets such as Fox News fail to live up to the standards of

INTRODUCTION 21

objectivity or balance that is part of traditional U.S. journalism ethics. Many Americans now consume news that is designed to persuade rather than to inform (Gottfried et al. 2017). When news is transformed into persuasion campaigns, it is more likely that foreign propaganda will be used as a source, as long as it resonates with the political views of the outlet. This is particularly apparent on alt-right websites that label themselves as news but exist solely to propagandize a point of view.

These fissures in the American news media—the collapse of the viable newsroom, segmentation of the audience, the rise of commentary over news—all provide a nurturing environment for both foreign and domestic disinformation. In an atmosphere of increasing suspicion and distrust of the news media, it is easy to appeal to segments of the audience who are disenchanted with mainstream news narratives. As Starbird (2017) found, conspiracy theories have wide and enduring appeal, including conspiracies such as the 2012 mass shooting at Sandy Hook Elementary School was staged by "crisis actors" and that Navy Seals were behind the 2013 Boston Marathon bombings. With news values and trust at a low ebb, there is more appeal for outlets such as Breitbart and Infowars that cater to political extremes. For many, the distinction between quality journalism outlets and disinformation sites is blurred, making it easier for foreign propaganda such as RT and Sputnik to pose as news.

Arguably even more important than how the online sphere enables the publication of material is the way information is circulated via social media. As argued by Siva Vaidhyanathan in *Antisocial Media* (2018), the logic of social media undermines the logic of quality news consumption. Rather than being encouraged to consume professional journalism that attempts to present all sides of complex issues, social media typically funnels users, via recommendations and algorithmic prioritization, into consuming ever-narrower content that resonates with one's own opinions and beliefs. More ominously, evidence from within Meta (parent company of Facebook, Instagram, and WhatsApp, among other platforms) has demonstrated how the company knows that divisive and dangerous content is more popular yet continues to allow it to spread virtually unchecked to foster growth on its platform (Horwitz 2021).

According to the Pew Research Center, two-thirds of Americans report that they get at least some of their news on social media (Shearer and Matsa 2018). As social media platforms encourage like-minded people to stay within information bubbles, disinformation can become

22   SEEING RED

powerfully resonant within these relatively closed and trusted communication circles. In an environment in which people typically value information that matches their own convictions over informed debate, foreign disinformation can find acceptance and even popularity with the targeted audience.

Fear and Loathing on the Campaign Trail

The 2016 U.S. presidential campaign rang a warning bell about problems with the American media system and the threat of foreign propaganda. By the 2020 campaign, these fissures had grown into a deep cleavage across the American media landscape, led by a president who routinely attacked specific outlets and journalists as well as denigrated the entire concept of a free press. The two sides of the political landscape are unequal, however, in terms of their orientation to the media. Trump supporters are far less likely to engage with journalism that strives toward unbiased and objective reporting. Truth becomes secondary to whether the information corresponds to an existing worldview, particularly on social media (Schradie 2019). This means that Trump supporters are routinely exposed to more disinformation. In a choice between using media that produce news and those that put ideological needs to the forefront, Trump supporters often choose the latter.

How did we wind up here? Journalists have long tended to focus on the "horse race" aspects of presidential elections, framing the contest as a race to be won rather than a time to inform the voters on critical issues (Patterson 1993, 2016). This has eroded the value and tradition of talking about policies and democratic ideals in an election. Barack Obama rose to the top of a crowded Democratic pack in 2008, beating out a formidable challenge from Hillary Clinton and showing superb control of the media message. Obama's 2008 campaign demonstrated the asymmetric power of the media over political party traditions and institutional barriers. It was a lesson others were to learn.

The power of the media was particularly important in 2016 as both political parties were in relative disarray. The Republicans were still struggling with the legacy of the Tea Party movement, which moved some Republicans too far right for many centrists. The Democrats were involved in a bitter split of their own, between a left wing that supported Bernie Sanders and a more centrist wing that supported Clinton. There was also an unprecedented

INTRODUCTION 23

amount of dislike in the race for both final candidates, and, by extension, discord and disillusion among the voters themselves.

While in the 2016 elections both parties had intensely competitive and antagonistic primaries, the 2020 election took place in an unprecedented era of distrust and dislike in modern times between the left and right in the United States. A 2019 survey shows the depth of divide, as more than 42 percent of those surveyed viewed the opposition as "downright evil" (Kalmoe and Mason 2019). Almost 20 percent of the respondents agreed with the statement that their political opponents "lack the traits to be considered fully human—they behave like animals." Slightly more Democrats (20 percent) than Republicans (16 percent) thought the United States would be better off if "large numbers of the opposing party in the public today just died."

This divisiveness, indeed irrationality, fosters an excellent environment for disinformation as many people prefer partisanship over truth. Unlike in Soviet times, Russian propaganda no longer needs to convince Americans of the evils of capitalism and the benefits of communism. Soviet communism is long gone, but since democratic societies are experiencing new forms of social unrest and division, Russian propaganda can be used to help widen the divides. This should have the intended effect of weakening democracy and augmenting the power of authoritarian regimes such as Russia. The Russians are playing a zero-sum game: The worse things are in America, the better things will be for Russia. Viewed through this perspective, it is clear why recent American history has created the current promising environment for foreign propaganda.

Chapter Summaries

We need to identify the overarching narrative that the Russians project, find specific messages in Russian propaganda aimed at the West, and then measure how these messages traveled in the U.S. media system. We are interested in key markers of foreign message penetration: Do U.S. media outlets echo Russian strategic narratives, particularly about the demise of democracy? We analyze Russian strategic narratives in four critical political events: the 2020 U.S. presidential elections, the Stop the Steal conspiracy, the Capitol insurrection, and the 2022 Ukrainian invasion.

Chapter 2 will explore in more depth the vulnerabilities of the American media system to propaganda through a discussion of national media norms,

24 SEEING RED

laws, ownership, and journalistic standards. America has a virtually unique media system, in that there is almost no state funding of the mass media and relatively little regulation. As a result, the media remain particularly wedded to corporate structures and the attendant economic pressures. While this has been traditionally seen as healthy for American journalists by most analysts, newsmaking had been under significant financial pressure for decades before the digital revolution created an existential challenge to how news is produced, distributed, consumed, and even defined in the United States.

The chapter argues that several factors in the U.S. media environment, including shrinking newsrooms, the rise of populist media such as Fox News, and the increasingly personalized coverage of candidates, have created significant problems for the U.S. media. At the same time, fragmentation of the audience into separate filter bubbles—some of them deliberately disengaged from quality news—has led to a dangerously misinformed, but highly engaged, electorate. It is against this background that Russian propaganda has found an environment in which to flourish, especially as Trump spent much of his first term in office attacking the media as an institution as well as subverting trust in political reporting through constant falsehoods.

The goal of Chapter 3 is twofold: to discuss the concept of strategic narrative in more depth as well as explore more fully the key strategic narratives that Russia wishes to project onto the United States. Strategic narratives are how countries construct and project their preferred image and destiny on the world stage (Miskimmon et al. 2017). While there are echoes of Soviet propaganda in Russian strategic narratives, contemporary Russian strategic narratives are more dynamic and responsive to world events. The chapter explores the rationale behind these four narratives: Russia is resurgent as a great nation; Russia will protect Russia and Russians no matter where they live; the West is against Russia; and democracy is a corrupt and dying system. Within each of these narratives, one can identify stories in English-language propaganda sources such as RT and Sputnik. This specific text can then be coded to tag and trace these markers of central narratives as they are deployed in the U.S. media system.

In Chapter 4, we compare campaign news in the 2020 U.S. presidential election in Russian English-language sources such as RT and Sputnik with six U.S. news outlets. We analyze the campaign news through the lens of narratives that presented the acrimonious election in ways that promoted a particular view of the world. How did Russian outlets characterize the U.S. 2020 presidential campaign for its English-speaking audience? How did this converge with—or diverge from—how *The New York Times*, *The Wall Street*

Journal, USA Today, The Washington Post, CNN, and Fox News presented important campaign issues and their implications to the American audience? The analysis finds a strong resonance between Fox News and Russian propaganda due in large part to a shared interest in attacking democracy, although Russian outlets were less enthusiastic about Trump than Fox News.

Chapter 5 presents an in-depth analysis that compares coverage of Stop the Steal and the Capitol insurrection on RT, Sputnik, Fox News, and the rightwing online outlet Newsmax. Unsurprisingly, electoral fraud and the resulting violence were of great interest as both news and propaganda showcased the alleged failures of American democracy. We found that Russian propaganda sites enthusiastically covered the election conspiracy narrative along with the violence, using a challenging moment in U.S. politics to bolster a significant Russian strategic narrative. This allowed the Russian outlets an unprecedented opportunity to build their propaganda.

In Chapter 6, we consider the nature and meaning in the shift of Russian strategic narratives by Putin from long-standing narratives to more mythic anti-Ukrainian conspiracies on the eve of the 2022 invasion. This demonstrates that tracking narratives can provide useful signals in understanding planned military actions from Russia. In addition, we demonstrate that Russian conspiracy stories about Nazism in Ukraine were reported by the mainstream media, but there appeared to be little serious engagement with this false assertion. Conversely, the Russian claim that NATO—as opposed to Russian aggression—was the cause of the 2022 invasion found more traction and engagement in a review of *The New York Times, The Washington Post,* and *The Wall Street Journal.* This raises questions about how a media system that strives for balance and objectivity can effectively deal with foreign disinformation.

Chapter 7 offers conclusions to the following questions addressed in the book: How effectively do Russian narratives penetrate the U.S. media ecosystem? Where and when are they evident? Who are the "fellow travelers" with the Russians in terms of narrative? What methods work for tagging and tracking Russian narratives in the U.S. news? What does this mean for American freedom and democracy?

Why This Matters

The American media system is under attack. Much of the hostility has come from domestic partisan struggles, notably Trump and his allies, but Russia

26 SEEING RED

is attempting to weaponize the U.S. media to undermine American democracy. We must know the nature, scope, and scale of those attacks that attempt to turn our political institutions against us. When you view the state of the American political communication system through this lens, it is unsurprising that Trump and his circle rarely criticized Russia and Putin. They are fellow travelers in disempowering the free media to reduce it from the watchdog of power to a lapdog who serves political elites.

Both research and investigative journalism have uncovered many incidents of Russian disinformation, especially as it was designed to aid the Trump campaign. But this is looking at the problem in the rearview mirror. We need a faster and better way to reliably track and understand just how much Russian disinformation shapes our media discourse on a daily basis. Disentangling the threads of Russian disinformation from American news is complicated—but possible. By defining Russian strategic narratives and deploying automated coding seeded by human insight, we can code and track how Russian messages migrate through Western media systems. This is a crucial step toward protecting media freedom in democratic nations.

2

American News in the 21st Century

It's common to view hostile propaganda as a communication attack, in which enemies bombard us with aggressive messaging in a kind of information carpet bombing. Yet, this us-against-them scenario fails to show how modern propaganda really works by exploiting and influencing narratives already present in domestic media. The successful modern propaganda campaign is carried out through a form of information guerilla warfare, detecting and leveraging the vulnerabilities of a national news system and its audience. The contemporary U.S. media landscape provides an increasingly favorable environment in which foreign propaganda can flourish.

This chapter will explore the vulnerabilities of the American media system to propaganda. While all national media systems are unique to a degree, the U.S. system has some characteristics that set it apart from its democratic peers, in that there is almost no state funding of the mass media and relatively little regulation. As a result, media remain particularly wedded to commercially oriented corporate structures and the attendant economic pressures. While this has traditionally been seen as generally healthy for American journalism, newsmaking had been under significant financial pressure for decades before the digital revolution created an existential challenge to how news is produced, distributed, consumed, and even defined in the United States.

This chapter argues that several dynamics in the U.S. media environment, including shrinking newsrooms, the rise of populist approaches in some established media, the emergence of highly partisan digital news sites, and the increasingly personalized coverage of candidates, have complicated the relationship between the news media and its performance of the traditional civic function of journalism. At the same time, increasingly individualized information diets—with many citizens deliberately disengaged from mainstream media or exposed to narrow, self-reinforcing flows of political information—have led to a dangerously misinformed, but highly engaged, electorate. Trump's 2016 campaign and presidency accelerated the crisis in U.S. journalism. It did this directly by attacking the media's historic role as an external

Seeing Red. Sarah Oates and Gordon Neil Ramsay, Oxford University Press. © Oxford University Press 2024.
DOI: 10.1093/oso/9780197696422.003.0002

monitor of political power and abandoning communication for coercion in dealing with journalists. It did this indirectly by incentivizing partisan coverage at the expense of scrutiny or verification.

It is in this context that Russian propaganda has found an environment in which to flourish. Elite political figures—Trump foremost among them—have routinely attacked the media as an institution and subverted trust in political reporting. They have pursued these attacks decrying all scrutiny as politically motivated and therefore invalid while at the same time making constant false statements that filter through news reporting. Traditionally, the American media have been seen as a watchdog for the political process: a critical, albeit separate, component of a functioning democracy. In contrast, the media are seen primarily as a political weapon by Russia. In recent years, this view has been adopted by actors in the American political communication environment.

This is not to suggest that any significant part of the U.S. media system has become a direct tool of the Russian government. Nor is there widespread support for Russia or Russian policies on the U.S. right, despite some isolated U.S. individuals or groups who have expressed support or a convergence in some conservative values (Laruelle, 2019). However, this chapter identifies some significant warning signs and problems for U.S. media outlets and audiences that give reason for grave concern about the ability of the American media to fulfill its critical function in upholding democracy. In particular, this chapter considers the conundrum of one country with two media systems. One U.S. system ascribes to traditional norms of journalism within democracy. The other favors propaganda over news as well as allegiance to political movements and their belief systems over scrutiny and good governance. What opportunities does this offer to vigilant foreign adversaries waging disinformation campaigns against U.S. citizens and institutions?

The U.S. Media System: Uniquely Strong or Fatally Fragile?

The U.S. media system is unique among powerful nations for its lack of a large publicly funded media sector. While there is some federal funding of media—the Corporation for Public Broadcasting received $465 million from Congress in 2022 (Corporation for Public Broadcasting 2023, 6)—the U.S. news landscape is dominated by commercial providers. For example,

U.S. federal funding for public broadcasting amounts to about $1.35 per American per year and has remained level for almost a decade. In contrast, in the United Kingdom the BBC received approximately $4.6 billion (£3.8 billion) of license fee income from the British public in 2021–22 (British Broadcasting Corporation 2022, 214), a figure that amounts to about $74 per person or more than fifty times the public media funding per citizen in the United States.

Though the U.S. media has been subject to some modest financial support better attuned to an analog age, such as postal subsidies, received wisdom has been that public media subsidy is antithetical to American values and to the self-perception of news organizations (Pickard 2020). The U.S. media system rests on two premises: The market will support effective journalism, and journalists must be independent of the state. The landmark study *Four Theories of the Press* (Siebert et al. 1956) introduced descriptive models of how the media operate in different political systems. They identified the media in the United States in the mid-20th century as having traditionally a "libertarian" or commercial model, tempered by growing advocacy of a "social responsibility" model that acknowledged the obligation of journalism to serve the public good.

Under the libertarian model, the ability of the U.S. media to support democracy derives from its financial independence from the state. Instead of state support, media are mostly funded by citizens through direct subscription payments and advertising. In other words, consumers were willing to pay for the 'product' that is quality news and advertisers would support the media as they marketed their products. Siebert et al. acknowledged that this was not a strictly commercial arrangement as there were strains of social responsibility that put public interest before profits within the U.S. media. Siebert et al. also defined the Soviet communist media model as being in direct opposition to the U.S. system, in the sense that it did not require journalism to engage in a search for truth, but instead to tell citizens how they were expected to behave in service of ruling powers (1956, 5).

Though the typology of models in *Four Theories* has been criticized and replaced by more nuanced comparative models of media systems (Hallin and Mancini 2004), the identification of media systems as reflections of unique national cultures, histories, and norms is still important. In particular, this establishes what is considered best practice for media in one country may be considered abnormal or even dangerous in another. Under the libertarian model, U.S. media are subject to relatively few legal

30   SEEING RED

controls. This is good in the sense that it allows the U.S. media to fulfill its historic function as a "watchdog" or "fourth estate" to check the power of the U.S. president, legislature, and courts. It leads to difficulties as the U.S. media is particularly vulnerable to market forces, including investors who buy media companies with little interest in the quality of journalism. On the one hand, this puts economic pressure on traditional newsrooms, where the norms of U.S. journalism are generally upheld and transmitted to new generations of journalists. On the other hand, it means profit often trumps the pursuit of journalism in the public interest. With little state funding or legislation, U.S. journalism is particularly vulnerable to shifting economic pressures.

In particular, two changes have weakened the American media's ability to function as a pillar of democracy. One issue is the end of the Fairness Doctrine by the Federal Communications Commission (FCC) in 1987. The other is the explosion of media outlets, first on cable television and later via the internet, that broadened and diluted the information market so that journalism professionalism no longer controls broadcasting and the news market in the United States.

The Fairness Doctrine, enacted after World War II and enforced by the FCC, was designed to guarantee that major television networks (ABC, CBS, and NBC) could not misuse their broadcast licenses to support political parties or factions with biased reporting. The doctrine mandated that broadcast networks had to devote airtime to contrasting views on issues of public importance. By the 1970s, the FCC called the doctrine the "single most important requirement of operation in the public interest or the sine qua non for grant of a renewal of license" (Federal Communications Commission 1974). However, in 1985 the FCC released a report claiming that the doctrine violated free speech, and the commission repealed the doctrine in 1987. Although Congress attempted to reinstate the Fairness Doctrine, this was vetoed by President Ronald Reagan.

U.S. broadcast licenses began to proliferate due to the advent and growth of cable television with the launch of Cable News Network (CNN) in 1980. Just as outlets were beginning to multiply and challenge the information dominance of the three major U.S. networks, the law supporting informed debate ended. This was combined with the market forces of segmentation, in which many more extreme political commentators, such as radio host Rush Limbaugh, found reporting with a strong conservative bias filled a popular— and profitable—niche in the market. In the American media market, combining popularity with profits is the desired outcome. Sustaining journalistic standards often make these twin goals harder to achieve.

U.S. Media Laws, Ownership, and Journalistic Standards

In the absence of the Fairness Doctrine, what laws regulate the U.S. media? The short answer is very few. The right to free speech is enshrined in the U.S. Constitution, and the U.S. Supreme Court has ruled that speech must incite "imminent lawless action" in order to violate the principle of free speech (*Brandenburg v. Ohio* 1969). While speech can be limited in times of war and other national emergencies through both overt censorship and patriotic press self-regulation (Entman 2003), in general the ability of U.S. media to publish is not circumscribed by laws or compulsory regulation.

Even through the rise of politicized broadcast and online media outlets, journalistic professionalism has had relatively clear norms well into the 21st century. The Society of Professional Journalists has a detailed code of ethics that encourages accuracy and verification, as well as advancing the accountability of the powerful and the exchange of competing views (Society of Professional Journalists 2014). Kovach and Rosenstiel's survey of U.S. journalists at the beginning of the century generated an inventory of fundamental elements of journalism, foregrounding an obligation to truth, loyalty to citizens, independence from those they cover, and the essential status of verification in the journalistic process (2001, 12–13). Separate theoretical accounts defined journalism's role in U.S. democracy in similar terms, including the provision of information to allow citizens to make sound political choices, the importance of scrutiny and investigation, and the distillation of complexity into coherent frameworks to help citizens understand the world in which they live (Schudson 2008, 12).

U.S. journalistic norms dictate that news outlets should adhere as best they can to principles of objectivity in reporting the news, confining opinion to clearly demarcated segments of shows or publications. In practice, news organizations often fell short of this ideal and attracted significant criticism prior to Trump's campaign, particularly over concern about consistent political bias at certain networks (Morris 2005). This was especially apparent in Fox's coverage of the Iraq War and during the first presidential elections after 9/11 (Oates et al. 2010). On matters of public policy, critics have focused on uneven coverage of critical problems in society, where incident-led coverage

32 SEEING RED

or "episodic" reporting obscures public understanding of the importance of issues, their underlying causes, and those responsible for alleviating them (Iyengar 1996; Patterson 2000).

Another shortcoming has been observed in the tendency of news organizations to focus on political actions in terms of their success or failure as strategic gambits rather than an appraisal of their appropriateness, effectiveness, or their moral implications (Patterson 1993). This game frame approach makes sense from a procedural perspective, as it sidesteps the consequences of making evaluative judgments of policy positions and insulates journalists from accusations of bias (Tuchman 1972). The pure form of the game frame in political journalism occurs in what has been termed "horse race" journalism, where political contests—most notably elections—are covered in terms of opinion polling shifts and electoral outcomes as the main mechanism of judging political actions (Aalberg et al. 2012, 167). This form of journalism has been observed in U.S. political coverage over several decades and has been linked to editorial decision-making as well as the broader political communication context (Cappella and Jamieson 1997; Lawrence 2001; Dunaway and Lawrence 2015).

The framing of politics as a game in this way has been identified by Bennett (2016) as one of the four information biases endemic in American political journalism due to the primacy of the commercial imperative and the need to maximize audience attention. The other three he notes are: the tendency to personalize complex social, economic, and political phenomena and boil them down to contests of interpersonal competition at the expense of political process; the dramatization of events through an emphasis on crises rather than continuity; and the fragmentation of information through the isolation of events from the wider context.

Despite these criticisms—grounded in careful studies of news production, content, and audience response—objectivity and balance are found as core principles within journalistic organizations such as the Society of Professional Journalists. They remain at the heart of journalism degree programs, which are a key factor in transmitting and maintaining journalism standards in the United States. Hearns-Branaman (2016) notes that journalistic objectivity as a complete lack of favoritism or freedom from bias is impossible, but objectivity is still a powerful journalistic norm when held up as a goal toward which to strive. However, given that many U.S. journalists did not study in journalism programs and relatively few belong to professional organizations, the status of journalist was traditionally conferred by working for a news organization. This is distinct from many other professions in the United States, ranging from doctor to lawyer to certified public accountant, where professional status is attained through both specific qualifications and formal accreditation.

A major problem facing journalism is that newsrooms, the central hub through which these professional journalistic norms are upheld, are disappearing in the United States. Newsroom employment has fallen by 26 percent since 2008, according to a study by the Pew Research Center (Walker 2021). This reflects a long, steady decline in employment for traditional journalists. The economic reality is that even though news outlets transitioned to the online sphere, the revenue obtained from online advertising has not come close to offsetting losses from print advertising. Since 2005, 2,500 newspapers—around a quarter of all U.S. titles—have closed or merged with other outlets (Carnevale and Wenzinger 2022, 8–9). During the COVID pandemic, when demand for news was particularly strong, 360 newspapers closed (Abernathy 2022).

While it is difficult to meet any journalist—broadcast, print, or online—who has not either experienced unemployment or worked at an outlet that has either closed or implemented wide-scale layoffs, newspaper journalists are particularly hard hit. Since the 1980s, average employment by newspaper publishers has fallen by 63 percent (Carnevale and Wenzinger 2022, 10). Employment in broadcasting has grown over the same period, as have jobs in internet publishing and online search portals (Carnevale and Wenzinger 2022, 10). But these organizations and jobs rarely echo the same journalistic professionalism as found in U.S. newsrooms in the 1980s. Unsurprisingly, the number of bachelor's and master's degrees in journalism awarded at U.S. universities has declined as well. Interest in education and careers in journalism remains strong, but early-career jobs that pay a living wage are relatively scarce (Carnevale and Wenzinger 2022).

Judged on the status of professional accreditation and a shrinking number of jobs, U.S. journalism would seem to lack power and authority. Yet the opposite is true in that a free media is a critical element of American democracy in particular and democratic governance in general. There are specific, high-profile ways in which U.S. journalists hold power to account. For example, the listing of Pulitzer Prize winners for public service journalism reveals reporting that has highlighted injustice and led to significant social change. This includes constant exposure of the corruption of elected and government officials, abuses by the police, racial injustice, mistreatments in the immigration system, environmental contamination by companies complicit with local authorities, military cover-ups of preventable deaths in service, Watergate, and more (Pulitzer.org n.d.).

While journalists have been accused of perpetuating the status quo in a gravely unequal capitalistic society (Herman and Chomsky 1988), it's important to reflect on how the media augments democracy and promotes social justice. This includes exposing abuses of power such as those committed by wealthy and influential sexual predators who operated with impunity for decades but were brought to wider public attention by reporting in the *New Yorker*, *The New York Times*, and elsewhere. At the local level, the impact of journalism in incentivizing good governance can be even more pronounced. For example, cutbacks in local journalistic capacity have led to reduced political competition in municipal politics (Rubato and Jennings 2019), less efficient spending of public money at the local level (Gao et al. 2018), and less effective oversight of corporate misconduct (Heese et al. 2022). The rollback of journalistic capacity due to economic and political pressures affects vital Fourth Estate functions.

The Rise of the Online Sphere and the Decline of Traditional Journalism

The status of the American journalist became much more precarious and ill-defined with the rise of the digital information environment. As the online sphere exploded, print newsrooms imploded. Driving this was a shift of advertising revenue from print to digital, and legacy media largely did not recognize online opportunities in time to effectively exploit them. Publications lost important monopolies on classified ads as sites such as Craigslist, Zillow, and Indeed rose to become billion-dollar companies offering platforms for transactions in goods, real estate, and jobs. At the same time, consumers showed less interest in paying for subscriptions to news publications, given what they considered comparable content could be accessed online for free. While the U.S. performs comparatively well internationally when it comes to paying for online news, the proportion of the public willing to do so is still only 19 percent (Newman et al. 2022, 19). As noted by Boczkowski and Mitchelstein (2013) in their study of what news consumers value on news sites, people are typically more interested in sports, entertainment, and the weather. Absent a national crisis, large segments of the audience are generally uninterested in news and disinclined to pay for it.

As the economic struggle for survival of media outlets worsened as the 1990s progressed, another change in federal law had a significant effect on the sector. The 1996 Telecommunications Act relaxed rules about the monopoly ownership of media outlets in a single broadcast market. This was in part a reflection of the reality that cable, satellite, and the internet had broadened the availability of news everywhere. The changing rules accelerated the acquisition of media outlets by major corporations, many of which were more interested in profit than the quality of news (Pickard 2020, 118). This also raised questions about the influence of owners on media content, a constant concern in the libertarian model of the media. While there have been many accounts on the effect of owners on media content (Bagdikian 2004; Wolff 2008), lately more concern has turned to the way outlets such as Fox favor sensation and commentary over hard news to attract and engage audiences. In other words, it's not so much the views of the owner; rather, it is how the owner does or does not support traditional journalistic values while claiming to run a news outlet.

One note of hope from Boczkowski and Mitchelstein (2013) was their finding that in times of national crises, audiences are very interested in political and economic news. Following 9/11, audience consumption of news content increased (Lachlan et al. 2016). In 2020, Americans were highly attentive to news throughout the COVID pandemic and the contentious presidential elections (Nelson and Lewis 2022). That interest dropped off precipitously in 2021. While Boczkowski and Mitchelstein suggest that this type of selective attention means that citizens are still engaged at critical times, they acknowledge that the general lack of interest and engagement in serious news makes it difficult for newsrooms to pay for consistent quality journalism.

While traditional news organizations continue to maintain a relatively high profile in the online era, a sizable part of the U.S. population has shown much more interest in partisan news and analysis (Benkler et al. 2017). Even prior to the symbiotic relationship between Trump and Fox (Yang and Bennett 2021), Fox News created a successful and profitable product with a more partisan, nationalistic slant on American events (Oates et al. 2010; Iglesias 2018). For decades, the American media sphere was dominated by the "Big Three" television networks. In the 1970s, the nightly news programs of ABC, CBS, and NBC together attracted 90 percent of the national audience

36 SEEING RED

(Morris 2005, 58). Figures from the Pew Research Center (2004) show that viewership of network news and cable news was starting to converge by 2004, with about 33 percent of Americans watching network television news regularly, compared with about 20 percent for CNN and 23 percent for Fox News. In particular, the fortunes of Fox News were bolstered by its jingoistic coverage of the second Gulf War (Collins 2004, cited by Morris 2005, 60).

Studies show variation in news coverage, including framing, story selection, and who is given voice, among media outlets. For example, Groeling (2008, 634) found significant disparity in how ABC, CBS, NBC, CNN, MSNBC, and Fox presented information about presidential approval ratings from 1997 to 2008. All the networks except Fox emphasized poor results for Republican presidents and good results for Democratic presidents when reporting polling results, while Fox did the opposite. Even within the networks that exhibited the same pro-Democrat bias, the reporting varied. This demonstrates that while objectivity may be a standard, as Hearns-Branaman argues, there is ideological slant and variation even within similar news formats.

But is this type of variation the type of bias that many on the right accuse the media of? Groeling (2008) highlights two issues with the blanket accusation of systematic bias in the news media. While some studies, such as his, have found variation in mainstream media coverage that suggests support for candidates or particular points of view, the results of many studies are mixed. It is also typically difficult to ascertain the reason for the variation: "Perceiving an ideological slant in media content is one thing; attributing such a slant to politically biased editorial judgment by the media is another" (p. 633). He notes that while 90 percent of coverage that suggests a president (such as Trump or Biden) is doing a bad job might not be biased as "it may simply reflect the president only doing a good job 10% of the time" (p. 638).

Sutter (2001) makes a compelling argument against systematic liberal bias from the view of the market as opposed to the view of objective journalistic standards: If media outlets are biased toward liberal views, then they will lose a significant part of the market. He also argues that media owners, rather than using their outlets to express political preferences, are far more interested in maximizing profits. While Sutter notes studies that showed journalists were overwhelmingly more likely to hold liberal views, he argues that the need to attract a wide audience would mitigate a liberal slant in the coverage. As he wryly noted, Republicans won the presidency for twenty-eight of the forty years between 1952 and 1992 (p. 448), an unlikely event if the "liberal" media had significant power to influence the electorate. Sutter rather presciently argues that while it appeared the average media user was more liberal than the average voter, there was room in the market for a product that more overtly supported conservative viewpoints and he cited the then-nascent Fox News as an example of an outlet that could attract this audience.

As Sutter predicted, there was indeed a ready market for conservative news, which Fox caters to very successfully and opened the way for others. Launched in October 1996 to seventeen million cable subscribers, it now reaches seventy million households in the United States (Fox Corporation 2022, 3). This is less than CNN, which reaches approximately eighty million (CNN 2023), and comparable with MSNBC, which reaches around seventy-four million households (Comcast Corporation 2022). Fox News has a consistent, measurable pro-Republican bias; what some observers have deemed a "patriotic" or "nationalistic" approach to the news (Seib 2004, cited in Barnett and Roselle 2008, 13). Supporters of Fox would argue that this merely balances a more covert liberal bias found in other major networks, but Fox coverage is qualitatively different, as has been demonstrated in analyses of the nightly news shows, while political analysis shows such as those hosted by Tucker Carlson and Laura Ingraham routinely used disinformation and propaganda to support their points (Yang and Bennett 2021). This practice exposed Fox to significant legal jeopardy in the aftermath of the 2020 presidential election, as shown in Chapter 5 of this volume.

The structures of ownership in media industries have changed over the past half-century, from the era of media outlets as vehicles to advance the personal and business interests of owners, to media conglomerates, to financial portfolio diversification with reduced intervention into content production by owners (Noam 2018). Rupert Murdoch, the long-time owner of Fox News, has been a key player in broadcast and print media throughout that period of evolution. Perhaps as a result of this longevity, in many ways his style of management encompasses all three of the periods Noam describes. On the one hand, he has been viewed as one of the last of the interventionist media moguls, with a string of news brands in different countries exhibiting similar right-of-center ideological positions and a track record of pressuring political figures to further his own interests (Wring 2012). On the other hand, while he has shown a sentimental attachment to print, he has ruthlessly sought to grow and consolidate into different, more profitable markets, including abandoning his Australian citizenship and broadcasting licenses (at that time) to expand into the United States (Gaber and Tiffen 2018).

38 SEEING RED

Under Murdoch's ownership, Fox's conservative slant throughout many of its programs can be said to be driven by consolidating an audience rather than political machinations. Is this merely the market segmentation that Sutter predicted, or is it something fundamentally different? However, the effect on news content is the same, regardless of the motivation. As projects such as AllSides demonstrate (AllSides n.d.), crowd-sourced perceptions of bias or slant on media outlets demonstrate a significant variation in political orientations within the U.S. media system. Such pluralism of political viewpoints in media content is generally a sign of a healthy and diverse information environment (Picard and Pickard 2017, 21), but observable political allegiance does not tell the whole story of how bias operates in contemporary media.

If political slant were the only dimension relating to news quality, there would be a binary distinction between newsgroups such as CNN on the left and Newsmax on the right. As the Ad Fontes Media project suggests, however, news sources cannot be assessed on a single axis of political leanings. A critical dimension is the contrast between news sources that show evidence of adherence to journalistic professionalism versus those that manifest characteristics of propaganda or disinformation. Ad Fontes Media contrasts original factual reporting as its highest standard with content that contains inaccurate or fabricated information as the lowest rating. At the same time, it scores outlets on a political spectrum from "Most Extreme Left" to "Most Extreme Right" (Ad Fontes Media n.d.). On this two-dimensional ranking system, many stories from the CNN website are designated as "Middle or Balanced," but many are also placed in the "Skews Left" category. Some are in "Strong Left" and a few in "Hyper-partisan Left" categories (from the Ad Fontes website https://adfontesmedia.com/interactive-media-bias-chart/, accessed October 22, 2023). On the same date, the pattern is paralleled on the right for stories from the Fox News website, with many in "Skews Right" or "Strong Right" category. A larger number of online stories from Fox are in the "Hyper-partisan" category than stories from CNN on the chart. In addition, more CNN stories are classified as having better news value and reliability than those on the Fox News website.

In addition to this, the Ad Fontes Media analysis compares different products within the same media group. While the Fox News website is not that far away from the CNN news website in terms of reliability on the chart, the Hannity Fox talk show is ranked as falling into "selective or incomplete story, unfair persuasion or propaganda." But for CNN, its flagship talk show with Anderson Cooper is rated on the same levels (both in terms of reliability and bias) as the general CNN News network. Quality and reliability are the key factors rather than bias.

That is not to say there aren't news sources on the left with poor reliability or significant individual failings on the part of journalists. There are, but there is more evidence of low commitment to journalistic standards of reliability and verification in many prominent, right-leaning media outlets such as Fox News (and even more so on Fox talk shows). If we return to the comparison of bias between CNN and Newsmax that we find on AllSides, Ad Fontes Media highlights the difference: While CNN still skews left and Newsmax skews right, Newsmax scores far lower on reliability, which marks a qualitative difference in the journalistic content each source produces.

Given that the United States has functioned under a market-driven media model, in which the consumers make their own decisions, we could trust American consumers to ignore poor-quality news or at least use it with caution. Evidence suggests this is not effective. First, while professional journalists know how to define quality news, this mindset is not necessarily shared by their audience. When given the opportunity to select news, consumers often choose low-quality news over quality information. At the same time, some of the key factors in quality news, such as journalistic standards of accuracy, verifying information, and attempting to portray an approximation of the truth based on limited information, are not the factors that many prefer in content.

Instead, as Benkler et al. (2018) suggest, many prefer a "hyperpartisan" news style with its divergence from traditional standards by the rejection of objectivity, open ideological bias, and clear allegiance to political candidates and movements (Rae 2021, 1118). It also includes attacks against both other views and authoritative sources of information. This toxic combination of assaults on reliable, professional journalism with the simultaneous promotion of propaganda (or what one could more charitably call poor-quality news) has significantly damaged the ability of U.S. journalism to fulfill its function as the Fourth Estate. It also creates an excellent opportunity for the infiltration of foreign propaganda.

Another key point is that Fox, while the most prominent right-wing media outlet in the United States, is only one part of what Benkler et al. termed a "right-wing media ecosystem" (2018, 13). Benkler and his colleagues analyzed 1.25 million news stories published in 25,000 sources online between April 1, 2015, and November 8, 2016 (i.e., Election Day). They found

40   SEEING RED

a distinct and insulated media system on the right, which used social media as a conduit to transmit hyper-partisan content. Breitbart, despite not being a mainstream media outlet, was found to be the "anchor" in a pro-Trump media sphere that set the agenda for the conservative media realm and strongly influenced the broader media agenda. Subsequent research has shown that Breitbart exemplifies the new model of highly partisan, populist news media on the right, where traditional norms of journalism are subordinate to ideological positions and attacks on opponents (Davis 2019; Rae 2021). The research by Benkler et al. (2018) also highlights the growth of sources in the right-wing media ecosystem and how hyper-partisan sites differ from traditional outlets that still adhere to historical journalistic ideals.

These findings suggest that there are two new elements within the U.S. media system. The U.S. media sphere could no longer be described as a libertarian system, in which professional news organizations compete for audiences on a level playing field of providing information (albeit sometimes somewhat biased). Rather, there is now one country with two distinct media systems: a liberal-leaning media that adheres to traditional journalistic values, and a right-wing system that often emphasizes populism and propaganda over facts. By the eve of Trump's election, a significant segment of the U.S. media audience was not consuming mainstream news. Rather, a large part of the right-wing audience preferred content that reflected their views rather than informed them about both sides of the political spectrum. It was into this arena that Trump entered and triumphed in 2016.

The Trump Effect: Deepening Fractures in the Libertarian News System

While analysts had been concerned about the quality of election coverage for decades, Trump ushered in a new era in political communication by rewriting the campaign handbook. Work by Patterson (2016) highlights how political reporters struggled to cover Trump's constant lies, attacks on immigrants and minority groups, appeals to White supremacy, as well as his overt sexism. Distracted by these techniques and falling into a well-established pattern of marginalizing female candidates, the U.S. media highlighted real and perceived issues within Hillary Clinton's campaign to create a false equivalency between her significant lapses of good judgment and his scandals (Patterson 2016). At the same time, key national newspapers failed to explore Trump's widespread popular appeal to voters (O'Hare 2020). In essence, most of the national media did not take Trump seriously, but enough American voters did to elect him in 2016.

Decades of warnings about the failures of the U.S. media in political campaigns could have predicted Trump's success. The concerns are linked to the broad problem that the news either ignores, trivializes, or personalizes national political and economic concerns. As a result, important issues such as healthcare costs and the increasing marginalization of blue-collar workers are rarely discussed and debated. Crime tends to be framed episodically, suggesting that individual moral failings rather than social laws and norms drive illegal activities. The personalization of news—the overreliance on a narrow set of mostly White male elites as experts—means many voices go unheard. In multiple studies of U.S. election campaigns over many decades, it is clear that personality has come to dominate over policy (Patterson 1993, 2016; Oates et al. 2010; Bennett 2016).

Yet, U.S. elections still work to translate the preference of American voters into their electoral choices. Barack Obama also benefited from a media that sought evocative sound bites and images. Although he had little of the traditional experience expected of a national candidate for president, Obama gained extraordinary attention in the traditional media while also inspiring broad popular engagement on social media. While doing fewer formal press conferences than many previous U.S. presidents, Obama was able to continue to use the traditional media as an effective platform. He was the first U.S. president to have a meaningful and influential presence on social media as well. Obama was a central figure in changing the terms of engagement with the mass media both as a candidate and a president: Although he had a well-articulated platform, his coverage often focused on his character more than his policies.

The 2016 presidential campaign between Trump and Clinton highlighted the contrast between the new and traditional ways of campaigning. Trump relied on sound bites and slogans, notably "Build a Wall" as an anti-immigrant rallying cry and "Lock Her Up" to express his conviction that Clinton was corrupt. Indeed, Trump's official website featured no specific policy platform, unlike the detailed policy documents found on Clinton's website during the campaign (Oates and Moe 2017). As Patterson (2016) notes, the media responded in the expected way given the patterns of electoral coverage that had evolved: The colorful, populist Trump who no one expected to win was covered as political spectacle, while front-runner Clinton with a traditional

42   SEEING RED

party platform and long experience in politics was held accountable and negatively framed.

Matt Carlson identified the key problem with covering Trump in 2016 by using Daniel Hallin's sphere theory of journalistic coverage (Carlson 2016). Hallin conceptualized journalists as sorting events into three spheres: consensus, legitimate controversy, and deviance. At any moment in history, journalists generally agree that some issues fall into the sphere of consensus, such as the sanctity of motherhood or the value of a thriving economy. At the other end of the spectrum, there are issues that are considered universally deviant, such as child abuse and terrorist attacks. In between lies the sphere of legitimate controversy, in which journalists should objectively report the facts to allow citizens to make their own judgments. Over time, issues move from one sphere to another. For example, while at one point in American history segregation fell into the zone of consensus, it moved over time into the sphere of legitimate controversy and finally into the sphere of deviance.

The problem with Trump in 2016, according to this conceptualization, is that some journalists identified his behavior and rhetoric as outside the accepted scope of political debate and argued that he should be covered as deviant (O'Hare 2020). However, treating a candidate for the U.S. presidency as deviant, and therefore unworthy of objectivity, was a major departure for the media. When established journalists suggested that Trump be treated as deviant, it threatened long-held journalistic norms. Carlson quotes Jim Rutenberg of *The New York Times* and Jorge Ramos of *Time,* who each pondered the validity of the traditional practices of political journalism during elections, that is, a position of neutrality and the objective portrayal of candidates on equal terms, in covering Trump (2016, 11). Given Trump's behavior and language during the campaign, it is not surprising that many journalists began placing the candidate in the sphere of deviance.

Yet an elected president—unlike a brash and outspoken candidate— cannot be placed in the zone of deviance for his entire administration. Trump's election launched an uncomfortable relationship between the media and the White House, which deteriorated over time and reached a crisis stage by late 2020 (Carlson et al. 2021). The twin challenges of the COVID epidemic and Trump's failure to get reelected accelerated this process, but eventually pushed even the president into the deviance zone by late 2020. Trump told more than 500 documented lies in a single day alone on November 2, 2020 (Kessler et al. 2021). Abandoning any pretense at responsible communication, Trump was fully engaged in a propaganda war by the time of the

2020 election, one he continued to carry out long past polling day with his conspiracy theory that Biden did not win the presidential election.

American Chaos, Russian Opportunity

Russia does not embrace freedom of the press in theory or practice. After the collapse of the Soviet system, a nascent free media system was soon coopted by political and economic forces in Russia (Oates 2007). A sustained campaign against media freedom from the late 1990s to the present day in Russia means that the Kremlin elite control virtually all the major media outlets and narratives (Walker 2016; Ramsay and Robertshaw 2019). At the same time, Russia is one of the most corrupt countries in the world, with an increasing lack of freedom for its citizens (Transparency International 2023). Absent a media to tell truth to power, oligarchic elites have much more latitude for repression and corruption. For example, Putin's personal wealth is estimated at $200 billion by the former head of Hermitage Capital, an investment firm that was once a large portfolio investor in Russia (Morrow 2022). Yet, Russian journalists are not allowed to report on Putin's personal fortune or the staggering wealth of his circle.

While media freedom has been constantly eroded in Russia since Putin came to power, repression of the media accelerated significantly when Russia launched its large-scale invasion of Ukraine in February 2022. Indirect pressure and targeted attacks on journalists who challenged Putin directly on key issues switched into widespread censorship and repression. Notably, all remaining media that challenged the state messaging in any meaningful way were banned as was any mention of a "war" or "invasion" of Ukraine. Independent outlets were banned or declared "foreign agents," multiple journalists were imprisoned, and amendments led to deliberately vague legislation applying penalties of up to fifteen years in prison for publishing "false information" about the armed forces or other Russian state bodies operating abroad (Reporters Without Borders 2023a).

The United States and Russia (including its time as the Soviet Union) have been locked in a propaganda war for more than one hundred years. The Soviet Union sought to "destabilise other political systems during the Cold War through disinformation campaigns" (Moore and Colley 2022, 4) and through what Thomas Rid has identified as "active measures" (2020). Active measures are secret, organized deception campaigns, which include operations such as planting disinformation that AIDS was created in a U.S. laboratory (Moore 2018). While there was somewhat of a hiatus in the covert information campaigns as Russia underwent a transition from a communist to an authoritarian state in the late 1990s and early 2000s, Putin's regime has continued to prioritize international information warfare. Russia Today (later renamed RT) was established in 2005, while the online video platform Ruptly.tv began in 2013 and Sputnik in 2014.

RT describes itself as "an autonomous, non-profit organization that is publicly financed from the budget of the Russian Federation." The website states that "RT creates news with an edge for viewers who want to Question More" and that RT covers "stories overlooked by the mainstream media, provides alternative perspectives on current affairs, and acquaints international audiences with a Russian viewpoint on major global events." In 2013, as the Russian portfolio of international media was expanding, RT's budget was increased to $400 million, with additional funding to ensure its availability in hotels and via satellite and cable broadcasting across the world (Elswah and Howard 2020, 634). RT broadcasts in English, Arabic, Spanish, French, German, Serbian, and Russian, and while it is currently a banned organization in the United States and the European Union, its content is still accessible via YouTube despite an attempt by the platform to ban Russian state-funded media (Paul 2023).

Russians made their first serious foray into attempting to influence Americans in a presidential election in 2016 (Jamieson 2018). There is still debate about the extent of the influence of Russian propaganda in the 2016 U.S. campaign, as Russia illegally bought political ads to support both candidates on social media (Jamieson 2018). Although the planted Trump content did reach some popularity on social media and did influence a limited number of real-life meetings (Abrams 2019), the more disturbing part of the 2016 Russian disinformation campaign was how it was able to influence critical U.S. news coverage of Clinton in the closing days of the campaign (Jamieson 2018). A phishing scheme that has been traced to Russian security services obtained internal emails from the Democratic National Committee, sparking coverage of a damaging story for Clinton in the final days of the campaign.

The Obama administration was aware of the Russian interference but chose to remain silent during the 2016 campaign to avoid the appearance of partisanship (Higgins 2020). As Jamieson shows in her analysis of the 2016 election, it is impossible to assess the exact effect either of the Russian-sponsored social media campaign or the email leak on vote choice in 2016. However, the clear evidence of Russian meddling and the marginal victory of Trump that might have been possible only due to Russian influence both made for a worrying moment for U.S. election security.

More to the point, there was a natural resonance between Trump's messaging and Russian attacks on democracy, which will be discussed in more detail throughout the book. For Russia, the most effective propaganda strategy has been to push at existing cleavages in U.S. society to advance Russian strategic narratives (Howard et al. 2018; Ramsay and Robertshaw 2019). In Chapters 4, 5, and 6, we will use three in-depth case studies to show which specific stories and frames that Russian propaganda chose to try to advance its narrative in the United States: Election 2020, the Stop the Steal conspiracy that led to the Capitol insurrection, and the Russian invasion of Ukraine.

What Americans generally don't recognize is that it is not awkward social media posts with poor English grammar, such as those documented in 2016, that are the real problem with Russian propaganda. Indeed, studies suggest that there was little actual influence from social media posts, particularly as they only reinforced attitudes among a small number of dedicated right-wing social media users (Eady et al. 2023). Rather, Russia uses a "partisan parasite" model that "seeks credibility by impersonating a partisan media outlet within another country's media ecology" (Moore and Colley 2022, 3). We push that point further, demonstrating that there is a convergence of propaganda on the U.S. right with Russian propaganda.

From a Moment of Reckoning to Years of Reckoning

The 2016 election created an intense period of self-reflection and reckoning for U.S. journalists, although they were unaware that this was just the beginning of the most significant challenge to their profession in modern American history. As noted by O'Hare (2020), dozens of U.S. journalists engaged in a public debate immediately after the 2016 results to analyze their inability to predict the outcome and how they had covered the election.

O'Hare analyzed how eighty-five members of the media explained their failure in taking Trump or his supporters seriously, finding the idea that his election was "unthinkable" was a leading reason. Another reason they gave was that many reporters were "out of touch" with the broad swath of the

46 SEEING RED

American public who supported Trump (2020, 177). In addition, journalists attributed their poor coverage of Trump as a serious candidate to reliance on polls; newsroom practices that meant routine election coverage that lacked little reflection on broad social shifts; lack of reporting capacity due to budget cuts; lack of ideological diversity in the newsroom; and staffing cuts at local media outlets. O'Hare's research found that local newspapers in Pennsylvania were less likely to stereotype Trump voters and more likely to incorporate vox populi in a meaningful way about the candidate than national outlets such as *The New York Times* and *The Washington Post*. But as noted previously, local newsrooms are dying off at a critical rate, exacerbating the problem of a disconnect between journalists and local audiences.

While journalists were examining their own shortcomings, Trump demonstrated a historic switch in presidential communication tactics. While it is sometimes difficult to define a central narrative in Trump's messages (Oates and Moe 2017; Carlson et al. 2021, 13), Trump immediately embraced propaganda over traditional presidential communication. There is often a false equivalence in comparing Trump with former presidential communication tactics. U.S. presidents have frequently manipulated the media, omitting facts or even outright lying in ways that cross party lines. For example, Richard Nixon lied about attempts to spy on the Democratic Party, and Bill Clinton lied about having sex with an intern in the Oval Office. Both presidents were impeached, although the process only led to a loss of office when Nixon resigned.

The critical difference is that lying was supposed to have consequences for the president, but Trump immediately demonstrated he was more interested in optics than facts. His "first lie as president," as Carlson et al. phrased it (2021, 145), was to falsely claim that crowds at his inauguration ceremony were larger than those at Obama's inauguration. It was plain from aerial photographs and other metrics that this was false, yet Trump and the White House refused to accede the point. This launched a presidency in which deliberate lies and attacks on the media (for refusing to believe or to uncritically republish the lies) defined the White House strategy. Trump adviser Kellyanne Conway infamously called the false statements about the attendance numbers "alternative facts," a position that attracted much ridicule but that simultaneously signaled the lengths to which the administration was prepared to go to justify a policy of airing deliberate falsehoods.

This policy continued throughout Trump's presidency. A *Washington Post* investigation identified more than 30,000 false or misleading claims during the four years of his presidency, with the rate increasing over time from around six claims per day in his first year to an average of thirty-nine each day in the final year (Kessler et al. 2021). This peaked on the final day before he lost reelection, with 503 false claims in a single day (Kessler et al. 2021). Trump consistently made false statements about healthcare, Russia, the economy, trade, immigration, Ukrainians, COVID, and education. PolitiFact's scorecard for Trump notes that just 11 percent of his claims were "true" or "mostly true," compared with 74 percent that were "mostly false," "false," or their lowest rating, "pants on fire," where a statement makes ridiculous claims (PolitiFact n.d.).

Trump's constant and escalating campaign of disinformation challenged journalists because they felt they had a civic duty to report on the president, even if he was making false claims. Although much of the media would contextualize what the president said as incorrect, his disinformation still had power given that presidential communication—inherently imbued with newsworthiness—historically can set media agendas and ensure the circulation of the claims, true or false (Entman 2003). At the same time, Trump continually and openly attacked media outlets, individual journalists, and the rights of the free press during his presidency. As journalists were already dealing with economic survival and a fragmented audience, Trump's assaults on the media as a profession were particularly dangerous. His rhetoric encouraged and led directly to physical attacks on journalists, including at the Capitol insurrection in January 2021 (Bauder 2021).

Trump's actions and attacks on the media did not destroy U.S. journalism. Rather, it led to an even greater divide between supporters and opponents of a free press in the United States. Just as a divergence has grown in the U.S. media sphere between fact-based journalism that adheres to traditional journalistic standards and media outlets that favor propaganda over facts, so has the electorate diverged on their expectations of what news media should be and do. Overwhelmingly, Trump supporters preferred U.S. outlets that were more propagandistic in nature in the run-up to the 2016 election. In a survey of 4,183 adults soon after the election, the Pew Research Center found that Fox News dominated for Trump voters, with 40 percent claiming Fox as their main source for election news. At the same time, no single news source even came close to the same dominance for Clinton voters. CNN was the most popular source for Clinton voters at 18 percent, followed by MSNBC at 9 percent (Gottfried et al. 2017).

Trump's attacks on the press were much more than attempts to denigrate and disempower specific reporters and media outlets. Trump's power largely derived from his ability to dominate mainstream media narratives (Patterson 2016), and it became increasingly clear through his administration that he preferred populism to democracy. Media criticism was unacceptable to him, as it directly challenged his ability to weave narratives or just reinterpret inconvenient facts. For his type of populism to succeed, Trump either had to control the media narrative or he had to destroy trust in the media that questioned his authority. He worked at doing both.

Trump's relationship with the media appears paradoxical but has a certain logic. Trump relied on the right-wing media to connect with and energize his supporters. However, this relationship was different from the traditional one in which a politician relies on media outlets for endorsement or support: Trump had such unusually deep and fervent support from many of his voters that media outlets benefited from their coverage of Trump rather than Trump needing the media outlets to maintain support. Supporting Trump and right-wing causes ensured a much more stable, engaged audience than attempting to cover news in a more traditional manner. Trump's ability—unique for a U.S. president—to drive news coverage through his posts on Twitter has attracted much attention and is relevant to understanding his appeal and relationship with the media (Wells et al. 2020) However, this study takes a broader view by focusing on Trump's coverage in the news in general.

While Trump won the presidency with the help of the U.S. media—both in terms of the failure of the mainstream media to cover Trump with the same critical lens as Clinton and a staunchly pro-Trump right-wing media sector—he increasingly attacked the free press during his presidency. Although his attacks on individual journalists or media outlets (often on Twitter) attracted coverage, it was his growing campaign against a free press in general that was the most disturbing. In fact, Trump appointed a close ideological ally as head of state-run Voice of America, which provides U.S.-focused news to foreign countries, to try to ensure a more positive framing of his presidency from the outlet. The move was met with an enormous backlash, not least from the journalists at Voice of America who refused to accede to demands that they produce propaganda rather than news (Borger 2020; Edmondson and Wong 2020). It should be noted that funding for Voice of America, along with other outlets that provide America-focused news to foreign countries, is not considered a subsidy to domestic media.

AMERICAN NEWS IN THE 21ST CENTURY   49

This book delves into more detail about Trump and the media, particularly in his wildly divisive end game of promoting the "Stop the Steal" disinformation narrative, in Chapters 4 and 5.

The U.S. Media After Trump

This chapter has discussed the libertarian and commercial underpinnings of the U.S. media system as well as the drawbacks and benefits of this system in a democracy. There have been changes and challenges to this system, notably growing economic pressures on traditional forms of journalism. Changes in federal oversight and the explosion of online sources have significantly shifted the flow of political information in the United States. A large portion of the U.S. electorate is more heavily engaged with right-wing opinion rather than mainstream news. Social media further challenges information integrity while allowing selective exposure to information and the erosion of a shared discursive space.

This was the American political arena in 2016 that both Trump and Russian interference entered. Both benefited from the developments in the U.S. media system that favored the circulation of conspiracies and populism over democratic deliberation. While the U.S. media and most of the political elite (and apparently even Trump himself) were caught off guard by Trump's election, it might have been expected that Trump would embrace a more traditional approach to presidential communication. Instead, Trump acted as a propagandist, with disregard for truth or tradition in American politics. It's beyond the scope of this book to consider why Trump did not choose to act as a more traditional president. It may have been beyond his abilities and those of the team he picked. It also may have reflected the pragmatic view that his power derived from this propagandistic style and that he could not afford to change it. No matter what the reason, the evidence shows that he increasingly embraced disinformation and deception as his first administration progressed.

Chaos is a friend to propaganda. In their crisis theory of communication, Doris Graber and Johanna Dunaway (2005) note that the worst reporting and the greatest amount of misinformation appear in the first phase of a crisis. This is not because journalists suddenly lose their minds or their abilities; rather it is how a crisis challenges the institution of journalism. Using 9/11 and Hurricane Katrina as examples, Graber and Dunaway note that in the first phase of a crisis,

50   SEEING RED

there is a huge demand for news, but very little information is available. As a result, journalists often fill the large and urgent news hole with rumors, speculation, or interviews with people who have little knowledge of the situation. As a result, incorrect information is often broadcast and repeated, until it becomes difficult to correct later. While journalists will correct and update with better information as they gain access to officials and events on the ground, it is often difficult to fix first impressions or early misinformation.

The United States weathered three huge crises within a single year, from early 2020 through early 2021 with COVID, the refusal of Trump to accept valid election results, and the Capitol insurrection. In each case, the mainstream media struggled with crisis reporting yet performed their journalistic duties well by any measure. The COVID epidemic is unprecedented and was exacerbated by Trump's propaganda (Yang and Bennett 2021). In addition, Fox News entered an extraordinary alliance with Trump and the White House to downplay the effects of the virus and blame the Democrats for exaggerating the threat (Yang and Bennett 2021). But, as Graber and Dunaway's theory would predict, Fox News eventually switched to a more realistic portrayal of the virus and its effects. Early reporting on the virus was chaotic across the media spectrum, reflecting the nature of the situation. However, reporting quickly moved toward a frame of resilience, with an emphasis on social compliance to stop the spread of the virus.

U.S. election campaigns are always huge media events, but the 2020 elections were extraordinary in part because the usual campaigning that provided the visuals and the coverage points was disrupted due to COVID. The Democrats canceled their August 2020 in-person convention and traditional 'coronation' of their presidential candidate. The Republicans had a scaled-back convention to showcase Trump the following week. Fears over the unknown course of the pandemic continued, particularly with a lack of a vaccine. Trump and his family had COVID in the final weeks of the campaign, with Trump ill enough to be briefly hospitalized.

As with all recent U.S. elections, personality issues dominated the 2020 election campaign, with Biden calling Trump unfit to hold office and Trump calling Biden senile and corrupt. This left a dilemma for journalists; while they could discuss policies ranging from trade to healthcare to immigration, the election hinged almost completely on the personal assessment of the two candidates. Obsession with polls, especially because they were inaccurate in

2016 in favor of the Democrats, reached a new high among the population and in the news.

It would be easy to criticize journalists for a dearth of discussion of the deeper issues affecting Americans, particularly at the height of the worst health crisis in modern history. But as Graber and Dunaway suggest, journalism is inevitably a mirror of society; while journalists may construct news based on professional norms or in line with the organizational rules in their newsroom or even because of political preferences, reality has a way of setting the news agenda. Thus, the 2020 election evoked strong emotions, not so much pro-Trump and pro-Biden but rather pro-Trump or anti-Trump. At the same time, as sitting president, Trump was judged through the lens of the COVID pandemic and the lack of a clear exit strategy for it. As Trump bitterly noted, the first vaccine was not announced until just after the 2020 election.

Biden's victory triggered the most significant manifestation of the effects of a crippled U.S. libertarian media system. While the mainstream media, including the main Fox News broadcast, called the election for Biden, Trump refused to concede as he claimed there was widespread electoral fraud. Here, the power of the audience became apparent, as Fox viewership dropped, and the network scrambled to reconfigure its coverage of the fraud issue to prevent viewers from switching to smaller right-wing outlets such as Newsmax or One America News that more enthusiastically pushed Trump's conspiracy theories (Serwer 2023). After four years of covering Trump as the president-elect or president, major networks ceased transmission of his live press conference the day after Election Day as Trump groundlessly claimed widespread fraud. This marked a shift of placing Trump back in the "sphere of deviance" as defined by Hallin.

But in a system reliant on audience preferences to support quality journalism, a significant portion of the audience sought out 'news' that supported their point of view rather than fact-based reporting. As shown in documents from the libel case brought by Dominion Voting Systems, which was falsely accused by Fox talk show hosts of being complicit in election fraud, Fox chose to continue broadcasting lies about election fraud to maintain audience share. This again highlights the central weakness of the libertarian media system given that it is neither funded nor directed by anything except the market for the most part. Infowars, the conspiracy site that presents itself as news and sits at the extreme edge of the Ad Fontes Media matrix in terms of hyper-partisanship and unreliability of content, has at times generated income of $800,000 per day (Hsu 2022). Clearly, there is a market for news-like content that deliberately eschews traditional journalistic standards and processes. If the audience will not—or cannot—distinguish between propaganda and journalism, why shouldn't outlets capitalize on the market for disinformation? It is precisely what our foreign adversaries, such as the Russians, would prefer that we do.

3

Strategic Narratives

What Do the Russians Want?

For years, Russia has broadcast four key strategic narratives through speeches, statements, and state-run media: Russia is resurgent as a great nation; Russia will protect Russians no matter where they live; the West is out to destroy Russia; and democracy is a corrupt and dying system. This chapter will explore how these narratives play out in the U.S. media system, revealing how Russian propaganda both penetrates the U.S. system and echoes attacks on democracy from American voices themselves. This chapter will discuss the concept of strategic narrative and demonstrate how it allows us to understand more clearly—and even measure—how Russia carries out information operations aimed at the United States.

Strategic narratives are employed by countries to construct and project their preferred image and destiny on the world stage (Miskimmon et al. 2017). This chapter reflects on how Russian history and politics have come to define a set of core goals for the Russian state to project its image globally. The definition of Russian strategic narratives is a core component of this book, as they provide the linguistic anchors for identifying Russian messaging in the U.S. media ecosystem. Within each of these narratives, one can identify linked stories in English-language propaganda sources such as RT and Sputnik. It is these specific texts that can then be coded to tag and trace these markers of Russian narratives as they are deployed in the U.S. media system. We can then address various questions, for example: Which stories convey messages within Russian narratives? Which media outlets are most likely to spread these messages? Which Russian narratives resonate most closely with U.S. news in moments of crisis?

There is significant value in understanding Russian communication strategy through the lens of strategic narrative. On the one hand, it shows how events, quotes, individuals, and other newsworthy items are organized—and at times distorted—into unified narratives that support Russia's view of its role in the world. This usefully moves the discussion beyond fake news

Seeing Red. Sarah Oates and Gordon Neil Ramsay, Oxford University Press. © Oxford University Press 2024.
DOI: 10.1093/oso/9780197696422.003.0003

54 SEEING RED

or even classic ideas of propaganda because we're measuring the presence of certain narratives in the media ecosystem rather than arguing about whether they are true. In other words, we demonstrate that the value of a particular narrative lies in its resonance rather than its relationship to reality.

On the other hand, we can use knowledge of Russian strategic narratives to find and counter foreign propaganda much more effectively than engaging in a war of verification that amplifies rather than counters disinformation. We can even anticipate enemy action. As the *Fog of Falsehood* report from the Finnish Institute of International Affairs notes, Russian actions often can be traced directly to Putin's speeches, as when linguistic turns of phrase serve as signals of weapons being launched on Ukraine (Pynnöniemi and Rácz 2016, 60). If we can detect and monitor the linguistic signaling of an aggressive nation, this can serve as a critical element in national defense.

The Power of Narrative

All countries work at projecting their national status onto the global stage. While this is an acknowledged element of international relations, it is often addressed at a more abstract level by discussing national branding or how nations promote their sporting and cultural successes, for example. In this book, we operationalize the concept of strategic narrative so that we can measure it in texts ranging from Putin's speeches to RT to Fox News.

The concept of "soft power" was popularized by Joseph Nye (1990) and refers to using cooptation rather than coercion to get a desired outcome in international affairs. It has come to refer to elements of international relations linked to persuasion rather than military force. While a useful idea, soft power is a broad concept that is hard to operationalize. Strategic narratives, the rhetorical gist of national desires and goals, can be used as a critical way to understand how soft power plays out on the global stage. More importantly, narratives can be defined and measured in ways that can predict—and even counter—information warfare.

"Narrative" is a word used in a wide variety of ways. People can talk about the narrative in a film, a television series, or a novel to refer to a way of presenting collected events to tell a story. We generally recognize a narrative as having a beginning, middle, and end. Yet, narratives do more than tell stories: They also convey messages about characters, their motivations, their goals, their actions, and the outcome of all these factors. Narratives often deliver messages in ways that have powerful emotional resonance, which is a key reason we chose to look at news and propaganda through the lens of narrative for this book.

Traditionally scholars have discussed media framing far more than narrative. How does the well-developed concept of framing fit within the burgeoning idea of narrative analysis that would seem to better embrace Russian information strategy? Framing is a concept at the heart of political communication research; to engage in framing is to "select some aspects of a perceived reality and make them more salient in a communicating text, in such a way as to promote a particular problem definition, causal interpretation, moral evaluation, and/or treatment recommendation for the item described" (Entman 1993, 52). The key difference between the concepts of frame and narrative is that framing operates within an organized view of reality and generally accepted facts. A narrative is more about a story that may or may not be grounded in facts. While a frame highlights the organization of material, a narrative resonates with a way of looking at the world.

Framing illuminates a lot of patterns in news and propaganda. For example, U.S. media have traditionally framed homelessness around the failings of *individuals*, while some British media are more likely to frame it as a *society* failing its most vulnerable citizens. Frames play out implicitly and explicitly throughout media content. The concept of framing allows researchers to identify, code, analyze, track, and discuss how framing—of issues, individuals, social challenges, and so on—appears in different media content across time and space. Unsurprisingly, there is an enormous amount of political communication research that relies on measuring frames.

We operationalize a narrative as a concept broader than a frame, yet still detectable and measurable in news. While the concept of narrative is becoming of greater interest to political communication scholars, the field still lacks a shared definition of the term. Halverson et al. wrote that narratives are "powerful resources for defining cultures and framing actions, and it is particularly important to understand how they operate if we hope to understand and counter them" (2011, 1). A narrative is broader than a story, which Halverson et al. define as "a particular sequence of related events that are situated in the past and recounted for rhetorical/ideological purposes" (2011, 13), while a narrative is "a coherent system of interrelated and sequentially organized stories that share a common rhetorical desire to resolve a conflict by establishing audience expectations according to the known trajectories of its literary and rhetorical form" (2011, 14).

It can be argued that the power of a narrative often transcends language or logic; it becomes so resonant and embedded within societies, texts, and the minds of citizens that it can act as an inoculation against inconvenient truths. It allows people to navigate complex and often frightening realities. This can be positive; for instance, rallying a population to action to overcome a war or an epidemic through acts that operate against self-interests such as sending their sons to fight, rationing, accepting a new vaccine, and so forth. But it also can become a very powerful tool that challenges democracy because it can create a disconnect between information and governance, making it considerably more difficult for citizens to be reasonably informed.

For authoritarian leaders with little regard or interest in serving the citizens or the public good, a focus on propaganda narratives over news can turn elections into conduits for accumulating power rather than representing voters. In other words, while frames can lead (or mislead) citizens about policies, actions, individuals, and so on, narratives can become more powerful and persuasive agents of particular worldviews. Viewing the transmission of information through the lens of narratives can illuminate how specific stories fit into compelling and widely shared narratives. Thus, while scholars such as Starbird (2017) were initially justly puzzled by the prevalence of demonstrably false conspiracy theories having surprising popularity in the online sphere, the existence of "false flags" and "crisis actor" conspiracies make more sense within the *narrative* that the government and the media cannot be trusted. Conversely, as Yablokov and Chatterje-Doody (2021) note, conspiracy theories often have underlying narrative elements—particularly of powerful elites who crush the common people through trickery and deception—that imbue them with strong, if often irrational, appeal.

Miskimmon et al. (2017) offer a range of approaches on how to specifically define narratives by narrowing the concept of narrative into a specific category: "strategic" narrative used by countries for propaganda. According to this categorization, strategic narratives have the following components (Miskimmon et al. 2017, 7): character or actors, setting/environment, conflict/action, tools/behavior, and a resolution (either suggested, realized, or merely a goal). For example, a Russian strategic narrative that democracy is fatally flawed may include stories about media bias, examples of media corruption, or lack of fair coverage. Roselle et al. argue that narratives are "more important for ordering the chaos" in a world "with leaders who are ill-prepared for its complexities" in a more interdependent global community (2014, 74).

By establishing recurring stories about conflicts and consequences, states intend strategic narratives to shift audience expectations about certain actors and influence future audience perceptions. While states carry this out for both domestic and foreign audiences, this book focuses on Russian narratives aimed at the U.S. audience. In particular, we are interested in the intersection of U.S. political news with Russian strategic narratives.

Russia's strategic narratives form the foundation for its influence operations. State-directed media outlets for the international market (notably RT and Sputnik) mold news coverage to fit strategic narratives that push audiences toward Moscow's policies on given issues (Yablokov and Chatterje-Doody 2021). The goals for strategic narrative are both concrete and more ephemeral, as Szostek notes: "A state's struggle through strategic narrative to be recognised as a particular kind of self is driven simultaneously by the desire to achieve concrete political and economic objectives and the desire for more abstract rewards—pride and prestige" (2017, 576).

But where do these strategic narratives come from? In the case of democracies, they are often linked to long-term social issues and desires of the citizens, although they are also shaped by powerful leaders and institutions. In authoritarian regimes with controlled media systems, the narratives are constructed much more purposefully and disseminated from the top down. In the case of Russia, strategic narratives can be traced to public speeches and statements by Putin and other elite government officials. Narratives are relatively consistent, stable, and predictable in Russia, although they will adapt and change somewhat given the circumstances, such as when Russia decided to launch a full-scale invasion of Ukraine in 2022. However, four central strategic narratives in Russia have remained the same for years. This chapter will trace not only how these narratives arise from Russian and Soviet history, but also how they have shifted and adapted to events during Putin's regime.

The Past as Prologue: Tsarist Russia, the Soviet Union, and the Modern Russian State

Strategic narratives reflect national desires rooted in history, values, and beliefs. In other words, to understand where a nation wishes to go, you need to know where it's been. In the case of Russia, this means reflecting both on its Soviet and Tsarist history and the more recent path of the Russian nation.

58   SEEING RED

At the beginning of the 20th century, Russia was a largely agrarian nation with a relatively small aristocracy, middle class, and urban working class. Despite minor reforms in the early 20th century, Russia was ruled by an autocratic monarch, Nicholas II, and an ineffective and outmoded bureaucracy. Russian industrial, economic, and social development lagged behind other European nations; and Russia faced catastrophic losses during World War I. The dearth of effective leadership ushered in an era of chaos, in which the more radical wing of the Communist Party was able to take control of the country after a revolution and bloody civil war.

The Soviet regime, which lasted from the Russian Revolution of 1917 to 1991, created one of the most comprehensive reorganizations of society in history. While technically ruling in the service of the working class, the Communist Party of the Soviet Union controlled the population through strict laws and draconian punishment. Every aspect of life was coordinated by the state, although the scope of this control varied from draconian under Josef Stalin (1924–1953) to more tolerant under leaders such as Nikita Khrushchev (1953–1964). Private property was abolished; all industries and land were owned by the state. Strict censorship was enforced, and all media outlets were "organs" of state propaganda.

When considering the widespread repression in the Soviet Union, which included tens of millions of people sent to prison camps and the starvation of millions of Ukrainian peasants under Stalin, it is easy to lose sight of the elements that Russians celebrate in their Soviet history. First, life under Tsarist rule was difficult for most Russians, as there was little chance for most of the population to escape a life of poverty. Communist rule at least offered some redistribution of wealth and opportunity for classes that had lived in wretched conditions with few rights under the tsars. Many, if not most, Soviets took pride in their country and regime, particularly for their hard-fought victory in World War II after Germany reneged on the Molotov-Ribbentrop Pact and launched a surprise invasion in 1941.

The final Soviet leader, the relatively young and dynamic Mikhail Gorbachev who was appointed in 1985, saw the many flaws in the communist system and sought to renew the party through increased transparency (*glasnost*) and economic reform (*perestroika*). He introduced elected assemblies as well as some freedom of the press. Gorbachev's administration was soon plunged into fierce fighting between party traditionalists who opposed reforms and newly elected leaders, such as Boris Yeltsin, who pushed for much broader freedom. This created an opening for territories that had been forcibly annexed and occupied by the Soviets since World War II to fight for independence, ranging from East Germany to the Baltic States. The Soviets lost control of most of Eastern Europe after the fall of the Berlin Wall in 1989. The entire Soviet Union collapsed after a reactionary coup and counter-protest in 1991.

All fifteen of the former Soviet republics became independent countries. Yeltsin assumed the role of president of the new Russian Federation, which was the largest and most powerful successor state of the Soviet Union. While the transition from the Soviet Union to Russia was relatively bloodless, the early days of the Russian Federation were chaotic. Hyperinflation, shortage of goods, rampant corruption, and unemployment as state industries collapsed created widespread misery for the population. Yeltsin struggled to impose a vision of a market-based economy on a society that had enjoyed little autonomy but had strong social guarantees for the past several decades. Tensions reached a boiling point in 1993 when Yeltsin used tanks to shell his own parliament that continued to challenge his leadership.

While the West celebrated Yeltsin as a visionary democrat, most Russians saw him as at best ineffective and at worst a corrupt alcoholic who was manipulated by a band of thieves who surrounded him. Much national wealth was stripped off by opportunistic oligarchs, who amassed huge fortunes overnight by expropriating state assets. A series of elections did little to stabilize the country or inculcate democratic institutions: Parliamentary elections attracted dozens of parties that had little ability to govern, and Yeltsin had to resort to extensive media manipulation to fight off a communist challenger for the presidency in 1996.

Most Russians remember the Yeltsin era (1991 until late 1999, when Yeltsin resigned and Putin became acting president) as a terrible time of chaos, when pensions were wiped out by inflation and many people went hungry. Western-style capitalism had not, for many Russians, delivered anything except misery, fear, and the type of massive inequality not seen in the Soviet era. For Russians, the benefits of market-based democracy were outweighed by the abrupt end to the social safety net, guaranteed jobs, and economic stability.

While prices, the economy, and society had stabilized to a degree by the time Putin took over as president, the difficult times in the 1990s left their mark on the Russian public. Russians—and their leaders—were not interested in taking an inferior place in the international sphere. Fortunately for Russia, it has vast reserves of oil and other precious resources, not surprising

60 SEEING RED

given that it has the largest land mass of any country in the world and spans eleven time zones. While much of this wealth has been diverted to oligarchs who managed to secure ownership in oil and other state enterprises, natural resources have been a critical lifeline to the Russian state. Under Putin and until the 2022 invasion of Ukraine, the Russian economy had stabilized with a relatively secure ruble.

Authoritarian control by the Russian state also has grown significantly during Putin's long reign, particularly through a constitutional referendum in 2020 that allows Putin to essentially remain president for life. But while elections have become increasingly rigged over time in Russia, the Kremlin still must invest significant resources in maintaining its electoral autocracy (Smyth 2020). The pro-Kremlin United Russia political party, now essentially a political machine rather than a party, has become markedly more nationalistic and populist over the years.

But there is ample evidence that Putin doesn't need to antagonize the West to maintain his support. In the first place, Putin enjoys a relatively high popularity rating and has for the past two decades. Partly this is due to a lack of a viable alternative, but there is significant evidence that many Russians approve of Putin as a leader absent regional or global conflicts.

But if Putin does not need international conflict to shore up his domestic support, why does he seek conflict through small wars and eventually a huge invasion of Ukraine? As discussed throughout this book, a central strategic narrative for Russia is that of threat from the West. This echoes the Cold War, in which the avowed goal of the United States and the Soviet Union was the destruction of the other. This was manifested not only by espionage but also in proxy conflicts in places such as Vietnam and Afghanistan.

Before 2014, Russia was seen as a troublesome state that meddled in other countries but not as a serious world threat. In 2014, Russia staged a covert seizure of the Crimean Peninsula, rich in oil reserves and a strategic Black Sea port, from Ukraine as well as invaded Eastern Ukraine on the pretext of supporting Russian nationalists in the region. The invasion was carried out with a propaganda campaign designed to divert attention from the actions on the ground: Putin initially denied the seizure of Crimea by Russian troops. Russia continues to deny its missile launched in Eastern Ukraine shot down a civilian passenger jet, Malaysia Airlines Flight 17, killing all 298 aboard in July 2014.

The 2014 invasion of Ukraine marked a new era of more aggressive Russian foreign interference. The next major incident was Russian intrusion into the 2016 U.S. presidential elections. This took the form not only of fake social media accounts and attempts to widen divisions among U.S. citizens, but also a campaign against the Democratic Party via a phishing attack that yielded access to personal emails among its officials. It was this ability to divert the news agenda with these emails from Trump's crude sexism on the leaked *Access Hollywood* tape that may have undermined support for Clinton enough to tip the election to Trump (Jamieson 2018).

From Soviet Propaganda to Russian Strategic Narratives

Russia's history in the Cold War created a powerful legacy of information warfare with the West in general and the United States in particular. The avowed goal of the Soviet Union was to create a worldwide communist state run by and for the workers of the world. Both domestic and international propaganda narratives portrayed capitalism as the enemy of the people and the Soviet system as the champion of humanity.

Important elements of this narrative included the superiority of Soviet technology, the better life of Soviet workers, the evils of capitalism such as racism or class divides, and the military might of the Soviets. This was countered by U.S. strategic narratives, including through Russian-language outlets such as Radio Liberty and Voice of America, although both U.S. media norms and law prevent the presentation of propaganda as news. This is a contentious point, as foreign adversaries would argue that American news is biased toward the interests of the United States specifically as well as more generally toward a market-based economy that works in American interests.

Rid (2020) provides a rich history of Soviet disinformation tactics, or more specifically the "active measures" employed by the Soviets and their allies. A study of "Operation Infektion" shows how the Soviet government attempted to insert clandestine propaganda into the Western media. Operation Infektion started with an 'anonymous' letter that was published in 1983 in an English-language newspaper in India. The letter claimed that U.S. biological warfare scientists created the HIV/AIDS virus and were planning to continue research in laboratories in Pakistan (Boghardt 2009). The letter was planted by Soviet officials. Using that fake letter as an anchor, Soviet sources and others then amplified the story for it to gain credibility. This was a complex operation, and in an era before the internet and social media, it took years to gain traction.

62   SEEING RED

What is the contemporary parallel of the Operation Infektion campaign from more than forty years ago? The Infektion disinformation campaign amplified concerns about biological warfare already present in the U.S. and elsewhere. This attempt to exploit existing narratives—especially conspiracies—is echoed in contemporary Russian disinformation. It is a single example of an ongoing, broad-scale propaganda war with the West (Rid 2020). The modern media ecology allows a very useful global, immediate intensification of this type of plant-and-misinform activity as well as a range of other tactics. While Soviet officials struggled to implant messages in the mainstream Western media, now "Moscow can easily and steadily reach Western consumers, and thus deliver its propaganda and disinformation messages directly" (Pynnöniemi and Rácz 2016, 48).

Emergent and Resurgent Russia

In the chaotic period after the collapse of the Soviet Union in 1991, the young Russian state struggled with its identity in the world order. Under Putin, Russia has become progressively more antagonistic toward the West, particularly the North Atlantic Treaty Organization (NATO). Russia also has matched deeds to words in terms of anti-Western movements, including invading Georgia, seizing the Crimean Peninsula, invading Eastern Ukraine, and fighting against Western forces in Syria. Russian leaders were particularly threatened by the Euromaidan democratic revolution in Ukraine in 2013–2014, in which popular demand and demonstrations led to the ouster of the Russia-backed president. In 2022, Russia launched a full-scale invasion of Ukraine.

Russia regularly issues foreign policy "concepts" that outline basic principles, priorities, and goals for international relations (Ruiz-Gonzalez 2013, 2). As set out in its Foreign Policy Concept of 2013, Russia is committed to creating instruments for influencing how it is perceived in the world, developing its own effective means of information influence on public opinion abroad, as well as counteracting information threats to its sovereignty and security. Russian strategic narrative has been the subject of many studies, including Roselle et al. 2014; Szostek 2017; Hinck et al. 2020; Orttung and Nelson 2019; and Ramsay and Robertshaw 2019.

Two strong common threads in the study of Russian narratives, particularly in the English-language content (Orttung and Nelson 2019; Ramsay and

Robertshaw 2019), are the portrayal of NATO as the American-led enemy of the Russian state and the collapse of democratic institutions worldwide. While many studies have identified the Kremlin's propaganda campaigns around specific events and in particular countries, it is sometimes difficult to see the grand strategy at work. However, studies of Russian propaganda show the four consistent pro-Russia and anti-Western narratives outlined above that will be discussed in depth throughout the book.

While Russia has moved on from communism, its history of political communication matters. Giles (2016, 78) writes that "for all their innovative use of social media and the internet, current Russian methods have deep roots in long-standing Soviet practice." Indeed, modern Russian strategic narratives reflect elements of Soviet-era narrative strategies, but they have evolved with the development of the Russian state, communication technology, and globalization. Some analysts see more continuity than others, given that the Soviets also relentlessly stuck to narratives and used tactics such as denial and attack on those who were telling the truth. Others, such as Pynnöniemi and Rácz, see a fundamental difference in approach, highlighting how the Russians claim both that the West sponsors violence in Ukraine and that the West is turning a "blind eye" to what happens there (2016, 14):

> The fact that these claims are mutually contradictory is a characteristic feature of Russian strategic deception and something that makes it different from Soviet propaganda campaigns. Soviet propaganda was anchored in ideological truth claims, whereas the contemporary Russian variant can be compared to a kaleidoscope: a light piercing through it is instantly transformed into multiple versions of reality.

From at least about 2004, the "self-identity dominating the Russian state's strategic narrative has been that of a great power and a strong, autonomous state" (Szostek 2017, 576). Szostek notes a stronger "anti-Western flavour" in Russian strategic narratives after Putin was reelected in 2012 and in the wake of both the Arab Spring and significant domestic protests about election irregularities in Russia in 2011–2012.

While Russian strategic narratives may be less logical than their Soviet predecessors, they are still powerful. Strong strategic narratives need linguistic 'hooks,' words, or phrases that deeply resonate with the public and the core idea of the narrative. Gatov (2015) identifies this as a type of political metonymy, building on the linguistic concept of an element of an attribute

64   SEEING RED

substituting for the concept itself (such as "wall" instead of "national border between the United States and Mexico"). Aside from metonymy, Gatov found three other distinctive features of Russian political speech after 2012: self-questioning, proactive commentary, and "criminal" vocabulary that previously had not been a part of Russian formal speech.

The *Fog of Falsehood* report suggests that Russia's strategic narratives and its international propaganda campaign mirror how the state controls and uses Russian domestic media, following Vladimir Lenin's concept of the media as a megaphone for state messaging (Pynnöniemi and Rácz 2016, 312). However, while Russians can continue to use the same classic propaganda tactics of the "four Ds" (dismiss, distort, distract, dismay) defined by Nimmo (2015), they cannot control the supply chain of media outlets in the same way in foreign countries as they can in Russia. Indeed, the *Fog of Falsehood* report found that the influence of Russian "metanarratives" in the Ukraine 2014 invasion was "largely limited" in the European news media. However, propaganda can be relatively successful when it is pushing at an open door, as the presence of "already existing political affiliations" often dictated whether European media picked up Russian narratives (Pynnöniemi and Rácz 2016, 313).

Pynnöniemi and Rácz do note that "historical comparison should not be pushed too far" (2016, 15) because the world has moved on in so many ways since the early 20th century. For example, while social media can be used as a platform to disseminate propaganda, it also allows people to trace the origin of propaganda with far more precision. However, it's important to understand that Russians are using "a combination of tools perfected during the Soviet" era that have been "reactivated . . . first in the context of a domestic power struggle and later in that of Russian foreign and security politics" (Pynnöniemi and Rácz 2016, 16). When this disinformation strategy is combined with a physical invasion, it becomes hybrid warfare. According to Hoffman, hybrid warfare incorporates a "full range of different modes of warfare, including conventional capability, irregular tactics and formations, terrorist acts including indiscriminate violence and coercion, and criminal disorder" (2007, 8). Strategic narrative has become an integral part of current conflicts, such as in Ukraine, and will be a critical part of understanding state intentions and actions in future wars.

The *Fog of Falsehood* report uses the concept of "metanarrative," citing the definition by Holmstrom (2015, 119) that a metanarrative "describes the past, justifies the present and presents a vision of the future. It offers a

STRATEGIC NARRATIVES   65

framework for the plot in the setting of a story. It provides context for raw information and facts and helps to shape how we perceive ourselves in the world in which we live." The study of Russia's propaganda and disinformation in the 2014 Ukrainian invasion uses Entman's (1993) definition of framing to identify "metanarratives." This is a bottom-up approach of adding elements together to find patterns; this book uses a top-down tactic of finding content that fits four previously defined Russian strategic narratives.

As Pynnöniemi and Rácz (2016) note, narratives shape and are shaped by specific events. They trace this in their study of four events in 2014: the official Russian annexation of Crimea, the burning of the Trade Unions Building in Odesa, the attack on Malaysia Airlines Flight 17, and the fighting by Russian troops while the first Minsk peace agreement with Ukraine was signed. The study (2016, 58) analyzed how the framing of these events was formed by Russian officials and agencies (including the Russian Ministry of Foreign Affairs, the Kremlin, members of the Russian parliament, other government officials, as well as the Russian representative in the United Nations). Further analysis showed how these messages flowed into the mainstream media of target countries and local blogospheres. The report also notes that statements by Putin most often "signaled a new turn in Russian policy" in Ukraine in 2014 (Pynnöniemi and Rácz 2016, 60).

However, it should be noted that the details of information *production* are not critical to understanding the nature of the *messages* themselves. This framework explains the Russian narrative effort as a "coordinated campaign" rather than "an orchestrated operation" and better reflects the dynamic nature of contemporary Russian narrative construction (Vilmer et al. 2018, 21). In practice, this may present as Ministry of Foreign Affairs spokeswoman Maria Zakharova repeating a narrative from a Putin interview during her weekly press briefing or Russian Foreign Minister Sergey Lavrov quoting an RT story about Syria during a press conference.

Sometimes, however, quotes are not important. Many analysts believe a key issue in Russian disinformation is as much about attempting to deny reality as it is about shaping worldviews. This leaves a blank slate for the state to project its own version of reality. This idea forms the basis of Peter Pomerantsev's book about Russia, *Nothing Is True and Everything Is Possible*, as he argues that the point of contemporary Russian propaganda is not to persuade anyone but to keep the viewer hooked and distracted. He describes this as a "new type of Kremlin propaganda, less about arguing against the West with a counter-model as in the Cold War, more about slipping inside

66 SEEING RED

its language to play and taunt it from inside" (Pomerantsev 2014, 48). A U.S. Senate Committee on Foreign Relations (2018) report quotes the head of the BBC Board of Governors John Lansing as saying that Kremlin messaging is "really almost beyond a false narrative. It's more of a strategy to establish that there is no such thing as an empirical fact" (p. 39). This has echoes of Trump adviser Kellyanne Conway calling false statements from Trump "alternative facts" on a January 22, 2017, edition of NBC's *Meet the Press*.

Paul and Matthews characterize contemporary Russian propaganda as "the firehose of falsehood" because of two of its distinctive features: high numbers of channels and messages and a "shameless willingness to disseminate partial truths or outright fictions" (2016, 1). Rogers and Tyushka (2017) argue that Russian strategic narratives are destructive rather than constructive. This view of Russian disinformation connects specific disinformation campaigns from the shooting down of Malaysia Airlines Flight 17 to interference in the Western elections to illuminate a larger strategy: "For the Kremlin, the specific outcome of these operations does not necessarily matter: what matters is that the West's democratic institutions are gradually discredited and dislocated, ultimately depriving it of its claim to normative superiority" (Rogers and Tyushka 2017, 37). Kivimäki (2014) describes propaganda strategies being developed at different levels of the Russian government, but other times arising from a direct response to a "provocation or incident" such as the downing of Malaysia Airlines Flight 17.

While there is evidence of Russian propaganda sowing chaos, there are also clear recurring themes and messages. Kolga (2019, 15) writes that the Kremlin's "tactics and objectives remain fundamentally the same today as they were in the 1940s" and sees three general goals of Russian propaganda: "generate support for Kremlin positions; discredit critics and opponents using all means available; and sow confusion and turn societies against each other in the West." While Kolga does not seek well-organized or proactive strategic narratives from Russia, he cites Galeotti (2017, 2) as claiming there is "a broad strategy of weakening the European Union and NATO, distancing Europe and the United States from each other, and generally creating a political and cultural environment more conducive for Moscow and its interests." Kolga also mentions a constellation of Russian state media and pro-regime propaganda media platforms, including "conspiracy theory websites, proxy organizations, and agents of influence" who "reinforce, support, and relay narratives" (2019, 15).

The January 2018 Senate Committee on Foreign Relations report also states that "Putin's regime and most of the Russian people view the history of the late 20th century and early 21st century in a starkly different light than most of the West does" (2018, 13). The report found the popular historical narrative in Russia "paints this period as one of repeated attempts by the West to undermine and humiliate Russia," which supports a "Fortress Russia" concept from Putin that glosses over any domestic issues and allows him to paint himself the "leader of a wartime nation" (2018, 13). Elements of the Fortress Russia concept include the core theme of "enemy encirclement, conspiracy, and struggle, and portrays the United States, NATO, and Europe as conspiring to encircle Russia and make it subservient to the West" (2018, 13). Yet, the report also mentions how the Kremlin attempts to broadcast a picture of a strong Russia, such as in the Russian involvement in the Syrian conflict in 2015: It was "a carefully constructed narrative of Putin as the responsible and humanitarian actor who was intervening to stop U.S.-generated chaos in the Middle East" (2018, 29). The Russian state media clung to this narrative of a successful fight against ISIS, although "facts on the ground indicated the Russian bombs were in fact targeting the Syrian opposition to Bashar al Assad" (2018, 29).

The Senate report also focused on the Russian goal of exploiting "discontent and grievances" in its foreign propaganda:

> The Kremlin's disinformation operations do not necessarily try to convince foreign audiences that the Russian point of view is the correct one. Rather, they seek to confuse and distort events that threaten Russia's image (including historical events), undercut international consensus on Russia's behavior at home and abroad, and present Russia as a responsible and indispensable global power. (U.S. Senate Committee on Foreign Relations 2018, 39)

The committee identified both RT and Sputnik as important Russian disinformation platforms. However, while there is ample evidence of the tactics outlined above, Russia does also broadcast its affirmative wishes for world order: Russia as a resurgent great power and the protector of the Russian people worldwide.

Szostek has noted several paradoxes within Russian strategic narrative. In a study of official speeches and political news on Russia's state-run Channel 1, she found that Russian official sources tried to attack the United States

68   SEEING RED

while using "mega-projects," such as the 2014 Sochi Olympics, to brand Russia as a welcoming place for innovation and business. This showed a significant disconnect between domestic and international strategic narrative formation: Domestic narratives focused on attacking the West, while international branding emphasized the concept of "Russia—Great, New, Open"! (*Rossiya—Velikaya, Novaya, Otkrytaya!*) for the Sochi Olympics. The point that connects the domestic and foreign narratives is Russia's desire to be seen as a world power, but the domestic media was markedly more negative about the West (Szostek 2017).

Szostek suggests that the hypocrisy of Russian narratives goes beyond the disconnect between domestic and foreign messaging. On the one hand, Russia wishes to be an influential part of the world order and resents the way it believes it has been sidelined by the West in general and the United States and NATO in particular. On the other hand, as Russia complains about a lack of international respect, it carries out actions, such as invading Ukraine, that put it outside the bounds of international law and demonstrate a lack of respect for sovereign states. Russia simultaneously wishes to be a part of the world order but also to subvert it. From the Russian perspective, Russia can only gain strength if it takes power away from other states, or as Szostek puts it, "the Russian public and elite experience greater affirmation of their desired international status by defying Western criticism than by pursuing Western approval on Western terms" (2017, 572).

Of course, Russia is not the first state to engage in hypocritical or covert military activity, but that does not mean it is acceptable or even effective behavior. Szostek notes that "heavy-handed attacks on the identities of other states boost collective self-esteem among Russian citizens, but they fail to produce—and arguably obstruct—desired responses among foreign audiences" (2017, 571). The research by Szostek and others cited above ultimately illuminates a theme at the core of Russian information strategy: Russia wishes to tear down a Western-dominated world order in which it has failed to gain dominance and create an imperial Russia that is a global power in a world dominated by authoritarian ideals. To do so, it must first destroy the old order and project an image of the new articulated through its strategic narratives.

If these narratives are "strategic" in a war of global influence, how effective are they as rhetorical weapons? Research by Ramsay and Robertshaw (2019) shows how distinctive phrases and text from Russian sites such as RT and Sputnik filtered into British tabloid news and apparently were designed to do so. We know, therefore, that elements of Russian-led narrative do appear in Western news in the form of disinformation disguised as newsworthy content. In the struggle for international political capital, it is still hard to say that aggressive Russian strategic narratives are 'winning' any particular war. The most compelling case that Russian strategic narrative is linked to actual warfare is in Ukraine, where the effort to counter Russian disinformation both within and about Ukraine has been a significant challenge for the Ukrainian state. Chapter 6 will discuss how Russian propaganda about Ukraine is echoed in the West, mostly notably by putting discussions about alleged NATO overreach onto the U.S. news agenda. But arguably Russian actions and Ukrainian counter-narratives have done more for building a strong and positive image of the Ukrainian nation than anything else.

This discussion of Russian strategic narratives cannot offer evidence regarding the audience's reception of these messages. While we can observe the nature of Russian strategic narrative and trace its flow through the media ecosystem via keywords and even computational linguistics (Oates et al. 2018), we need audience studies to determine the degree to which these narratives have any effect on citizens in the West. For example, Eady et al. (2023, 1) demonstrate that exposure to Russian messaging in the U.S. 2016 election was limited to a small handful of social media users and found "no evidence of a meaningful relationship between exposure to the Russian foreign influence campaign and changes in attitudes, polarization, or voting behavior." But while it is important to consider the influence of traditional and social media, this book takes a much broader approach showing how the Russian government and media outlets attempt to shape events, crises, and individuals into its desired view of the world through strategic narratives as they circulate in the media sphere. While Ramsay and Robertshaw (2019) identified a small, yet significant amount of Russian propaganda recycled directly into British news, this study seeks to analyze this issue more comprehensively.

Four Key Russian Strategic Narratives

This section discusses the genesis and development of four key Russian strategic narratives. Over time, the Kremlin has directed Russian television and other central media outlets to develop dominant narratives, including Russia as a resurgent great nation; the West and NATO are out to destroy Russia; Russia protects Russians no matter where they live; and Western democracy

70 SEEING RED

is flawed and failing (Oates and Steiner 2018; Steiner and Oates 2019). These definitions of central Russian strategic narratives arise partly from a wide range of studies, many of which are discussed above, but also from our observations and analysis of Russian propaganda over the past decades.

While these themes wax and wane, especially as world events unfold that challenge narratives, the Kremlin reliably returns to these core ideas. As noted below, these narratives overlap and support each other. When facts or even general reality do not support these narratives—as they often do not—Russians use disinformation, including unsourced or falsified claims; non-credible claims with sources; claims based on earlier unsourced or non-credible claims; and conspiracy theories (Yablokov and Chatterje-Doody 2021).

Russia is a resurgent great power

The brief history of the Russian state outlined above underscores the core grievance of a once-powerful nation that suffered economic, political, and military collapse within the lifetime of most of its current leaders and many of its citizens. Just as powerful American traditions were forged in an 18th-century revolution, the twin convictions of past humiliation and desire for a return to world dominance are authoritative elements in Russian political life. Much of this is oriented toward Russia's role in World War II, which is often called the Great Patriotic War (*velikaya patriaticheskaya voina*) in Russia. It is logical to try to restore and build pride in national identity, although Putin's emphasis on the Russian role in World War II glosses over the fact that the Soviet Union initially allied with the Nazis.

Thus, the aspirational construction of an emergent identity that recalls this proud past and—even better—restores this affirmation to the Russian people is a very attractive narrative. While part of this narrative asserts the positive aspects of the Russian state, including innovation, creativity, and international events such as the 2014 Olympics (Szostek 2017) and hosting the 2018 Football World Cup, a greater part of it now rests on military aggression. While some of this narrative need was satisfied through limited military interventions as in Syria (Pynnöniemi and Rácz 2016, 29) and other places, the invasions of Ukraine are the most powerful way to showcase this narrative. While these narratives have generally found little traction in the United States, they are still important in understanding what messages Russia wishes to project.

Russia protects Russians no matter where they live

The natural extension of the resurgent Russia narrative outlined above is the protection of the Russian people whether they live within the borders of the Russian Federation, in the former Soviet territories, or farther abroad in Europe. Russian nationalism and identity are defined as primordial rather than instrumental (Smith 1998): Being Russian is linked to bloodlines rather than either self-definition or a location. This is in opposition to the historic view of the "melting pot" of American identity, which suggests national identity comes from a range of ethnic backgrounds. While White nationalism is resurgent in the United States, Americans, in general, are far less primordial in their understanding of ethnicity than Russians or Europeans.

As such, the Russian state would consider those of Russian genetic descent to be fully Russian (while not considering those who live in Russia, speak Russian as their native language, but who are a different ethnicity such as Tatar or Georgian to be Russian). While there were attempts to eliminate ethnic boundaries in the Soviet Union and in the earlier days of the Russian Federation, this was never successful in changing the essential view of primordial identity.

This strong sense of primordial ethnic identity—as well as the shared Soviet experience of Russians—encourages the Russian state to project its power onto ethnic Russians who live in other countries. One of the most prominent examples of this was the fabricated story by "Lisa F.," a thirteen-year-old ethnic Russian teen who was living in Germany and claimed to be raped by strangers after disappearing from her home for a day in 2016. The case prompted demonstrations of ethnic Russians living in Germany, although German police quickly proved that the teen had fabricated the story (Deutsche Welle 2016; Meister 2016). Russian media covered the story extensively with claims that Lisa F. had been raped and German officials were trying to cover up the story. This is evidence of how easy it is to ignite feelings of ill-treatment and abuse among Russians living abroad, although it should be noted that there was a significant engineered propaganda campaign to exploit the story (Meister 2016).

Other tensions over the Russian diaspora are much more enduring and complex. During the Soviet period, ethnic Russians were often used to colonize areas that had concentrated non-Russian ethnic populations (including Latvia, Lithuania, and Estonia). The Soviet Union suppressed non-Russian ethnic identities and imposed Russian as the official language. Those who

72 SEEING RED

were not Russian in ethnicity often faced discrimination and suppression of their own ethnic language and identity.

When the Soviet Union collapsed, many countries phased out Russian as an official language and promoted their own ethnic identities and languages after decades of suppression. In the Baltic States, this has led to significant tensions with the Russian populations there. In other post-Soviet countries, including Ukraine, meaningful efforts were made to include the Russian language and Russian identity in the new political order. However, as with other strategic narratives, the reality of how ethnic Russians are treated abroad is often irrelevant: It is too easy to play on fears and emotions about prejudice. As with other narratives, this is both unfair and ironic given how the Soviet Union suppressed non-Russian ethnic identities and gave preference to the Russian language.

This narrative is mostly relevant to Russia's invasion of Ukraine in the analysis for this book. Much of the justification for the war on Ukraine is both a defense against perceived Western and NATO aggression (discussed below), but a good deal of it also plays on the emotive theme of alleged poor treatment of the large Russian-speaking population in Ukraine. As will be discussed in Chapter 6, Putin stretched this idea much further by claiming that Ukrainians actually *are* Russians and hence must be "saved." Eastern Ukraine is dominated by both ethnic Russians and the Russian language, although there were no significant ethnic tensions in Ukraine before the 2014 Russian invasion. At that time, Ukraine still had Russian as an official language, and 30 percent of the country spoke Russian as their first language (Translators Without Borders n.d.) with no significant issues in terms of education or employment. The 2014 Russian invasion spurred a change in this policy in Ukraine, with an increasing emphasis on Ukrainian language and customs. In this way, the "protect Russians" narrative became a self-fulling prophecy.

The West, especially the United States and NATO, is out to destroy Russia

This narrative resonates with the resurgent Russia theme outlined above. Yablokov (2018) identifies "Fortress Russia" as a core concept for the Kremlin's identity of the country. Hemmed in by its (increasingly Western) enemies, Russia must tap into its traditions of military strength and fight for its very survival. This narrative brings together historical fears of invasion, mostly rooted in World War II, with the reality of conflict with its former republics that do not wish to be ruled by Moscow's interests. Former Soviet countries that have broken openly with Russian dominance in the region have faced threats from Russia, ranging from constant warnings of intervention in the Baltic states, to military attacks in a brief war in Georgia, to the full-scale invasion of Ukraine.

Russia has been aggrieved about NATO expansion since the collapse of the Soviet Union, but particularly since the 1999 war in Yugoslavia in which NATO conducted bombing raids without seeking Russian approval. The war in Kosovo had a complex range of actors, but Russia traditionally allied with the Serbians, who were deemed the aggressors by NATO. The war was in an area traditionally under Soviet and Russian influence, yet Russia felt excluded from critical decisions and negotiations in the war. Indeed, the NATO bombings of Yugoslavia were still routinely discussed in Russian English-language propaganda almost 20 years after the war, although the issue received little coverage in the mainstream U.S. media.

A constant theme in Russian discussions of NATO is reference to alleged promises by the United States that NATO, founded after World War II as an alliance to keep Soviet power in check, would not expand its membership after the inclusion of Eastern Germany when it reunified with West Germany in 1990. Russia attempts to frame this as a broken promise or even a treaty violation. However, as discussed in more depth in Chapter 6, there was never a formal agreement that NATO would not accept new members after the breakup of the Soviet Union. In addition, any promises made before 1991 would have been with the now-defunct Soviet government, and this grievance ignores the rights of nations to self-determination. However, the "broken promise" on NATO expansion complaint is a dominant part of this Russian strategic narrative.

Russia's expanded invasion of Ukraine in 2022 brought discussion of the role of NATO and the European Union in international defense onto the Western news agenda. Ukraine already had reached the status of candidate for accession to the European Union by June 2022, a process that was greatly accelerated by the Russian invasion. In terms of NATO, Russia has demanded that Ukraine never be allowed to join because it threatens the Russian border and national interest. Ironically, Russia's claims that its invasion of Ukraine was motivated by fears of NATO expansion have brought

74 SEEING RED

about NATO expansion as Finland has joined and in 2023 Sweden planned to follow suit. As noted above, strategic narratives are not necessarily logical.

While Russia has voiced grievances relating to NATO and U.S. influence in countries around the world, it can be difficult to sustain the notion of being a victim of international aggression when Russia itself has launched a massive, unprovoked attack on a neighboring country. To a degree, the "West is out to get Russia" reflects narratives such as the "War on Terror" frame constructed by the White House in 2001 (Entman 2003): It aggregates and focuses legitimate security fears on the wrong actor or actors. In the case of the War on Terror, this led to a re-invasion of Iraq and Afghanistan, although U.S. ally Saudi Arabia was deemed by elite journalists to be a more relevant target to counter terrorism. In the case of Russia, the "West is out to get us" is used as a justification for the invasion of a neighboring democracy.

Democracy is flawed and failing

Even though the narrative above embraces fear of Western states as powerful aggressors, the democracy is flawed and failing strategic narrative claims that these countries—especially the United States—are on the brink of collapsing into chaos. This narrative emphasizes the inequities found in democratic systems and seizes on any evidence that democratic institutions, particularly elections or the exercise of deliberative democracy, are flawed. Any violence or conflict in the system is amplified, with an emphasis on street demonstrations. For example, there is persistent demonization of Black Lives Matter protests as well reports warning about Antifa (especially during demonstrations in Portland, Oregon, in 2020).

Events in the United States from 2016 onward lent enormous support to this narrative (Hinck et al. 2020). Congressional inquiries and other reports identified Russian interference in the 2016 election, in part on social media and through a leak of Democratic National Committee emails just before the election. Although a report by U.S. Justice Department Special Counsel Robert Mueller (2019) found that while there was "sweeping and systematic" Russian interference in the 2016 U.S. elections (p. 1), the Trump campaign did not conspire or coordinate with the Russian government in these efforts. While the House went on to impeach and convict Trump for abuse of power and obstruction of Congress for attempts to manipulate Ukrainian officials into attacking Joe Biden, the Senate did not convict him on the charges.

There is little evidence that the Russian ads in the 2016 campaign influenced voters (Eady et al. 2023). However, outrage over Russian interference was a huge gift to Russian propagandists. Not only did it showcase the power of the Russian state—echoing the first narrative above—but it also demonstrated vulnerabilities in the U.S. campaign system. In 2020, Trump's decision to refuse to accept the election results amid his allegations of a stolen election that led directly to the Capitol insurrection also provided compelling evidence to weave into a narrative about the flaws of American democracy. This narrative forms the basis for the studies in Chapter 4 (on the Election 2020 campaign) and Chapter 5 (the "Stop the Steal" conspiracy and the Capitol insurrection).

Attempts to highlight the problems of a democratic society in the COVID epidemic—in particular tensions over vaccine mandates, wearing masks, and reopening society—are not a part of this study. Russia, while initially denying the spread of COVID, also struggled with controlling the outbreak. Although there were attempts to use the COVID pandemic to attack the United States and the West, particularly by raising questions about Western vaccines and possible "lab leaks," this book will not address this propaganda as we are more interested in Russian disinformation explicitly aimed at political issues.

The 2022 Invasion of Ukraine and Russian Strategic Narratives

Until Russia launched a full-scale invasion of Ukraine in 2022, the "flawed-and-failing democracy" narrative was most relevant to this study. But as discussed in more depth in Chapter 6, the demands of a full-scale war called for augmented narratives. Russian propaganda also consistently claims that there is extensive U.S. influence in Ukraine and that the overthrow of a Russian-backed president in 2014 was engineered by the United States. There is little evidence for this, although Ukraine had become increasingly interested in Western engagement.

Although Russia cites NATO encroachment and Western influence on Ukraine, the evidence suggests that Russia mostly fears the example of self-governance and democracy in its own backyard. Anti-Western strategic narratives have an inherent paradox when taken together with attacks on democracy: If democracy is flawed and failing, why does it pose an existential

76 SEEING RED

threat to Russia? The paradox extends even further when considering Russian actions. While complaining that NATO is threatening Russian security, it was Russia who invaded a peaceful neighboring country—first in a limited conflict in 2014, then with a full-scale invasion in 2022. This has then triggered a more urgent role for NATO, causing countries in the region to petition to join the alliance. While Russia complains that the United States meddles in Ukrainian affairs, the Russian army kills thousands of Ukrainians, and the Russian government even pledges annihilation of the Ukrainian nation.

The four key Russian strategic narratives come together to justify the 2022 invasion of Ukraine, although Putin added the dimension of needing to "de-Nazify" Ukraine by purging its leaders and denies the existence of a Ukrainian nation. The war reflects the fruition of anti-Western sentiment, justified by claiming the United States and NATO had infiltrated Ukraine, as well as the resurgent Russia that protects all Russians no matter where they live. None of this reflects the facts on the ground: Ethnic Russians in Ukraine had few grievances, and the United States was not controlling the Ukrainian government. Yet, Ukraine served as a theater in which Putin and the Russian government could play out their fictional narratives.

When Putin vowed to "de-Nazify" Ukraine, one can see historical elements at play that would resonate with Russian and Soviet history. Ukraine was the second-largest republic and a powerful part of the Soviet Union. Ukraine, whose name literally means "borderlands" in Russian, was considered a colony of Tsarist Russia. In Soviet times, Ukraine was particularly resistant to the Soviet takeover, resulting in a manufactured famine by Stalin in which millions of Ukrainians starved to death in 1932 and 1933. Parts of Ukraine were occupied by Nazi forces in World War II, and some Ukrainians collaborated with the invading forces, leading to a Soviet conviction that Ukrainians were politically suspect. Ukrainians, for their part, point to a distinctive language, history, and culture that has been oppressed by Russians and Soviets alike (e.g., see Plokhy 2017).

Thus, the notion that there are "Nazis" in Ukraine would find resonance among the Russian population, particularly given the well-known history of World War II. But it's also surprising that Putin chose that specific narrative as a fundamental justification for the invasion. All the other four strategic narratives, which were well developed over a long period, could be used to justify the invasion. While they are not necessarily logical, they are at least defensible at a certain level. The myth about neo-Nazi leaders in Ukraine—particularly given that Ukrainian President Volodymyr Zelenskyy is Jewish—transcends the realm of strategic narrative and fits into the sphere of conspiracy theories.

The way Putin shifted narratives for the war in Ukraine demonstrates how strategic messaging will adapt and morph over time. Notably, strategic narratives shift to signal events (such as the attack on Ukraine in 2022), or they adapt to, react to, or even take advantage of world events (such as the Capitol insurrection as a deep crisis of American democracy). It's important to acknowledge that we have chosen these four main strategic narratives based on a review of Russian messaging, a knowledge of Soviet and Russian politics, and a review of other studies, as well as seeking narratives that have relevance in terms of understanding Russian propaganda. They are not meant to embrace the full range of Russian strategic messaging, but they allow us to carry out our work of operationalizing narratives and testing Russian influence on U.S. news.

Do Strategic Narratives Work?

The concept of strategic narratives allows us to think about the fusion of propaganda, media, and international relations. But do they work in terms of meeting the international goals of a country? While it's useful to think of these communicative strategies and tactics within the notion of "soft power" or "hybrid war," it's much harder to benchmark the success of propaganda than it is to follow success or defeat on actual battlefields.

If it is a question of capturing the hearts and minds of foreign citizens measured through public opinion polls, the overwhelming evidence suggests that Russian propaganda doesn't work on the U.S. audience. For example, a Pew Research survey found that 92 percent of Americans held an unfavorable view of Russia in the spring of 2022 (Wike et al. 2022). Yet, if the measure is how much Russia can insert its desired worldview into the media ecosystems of other countries, there is more evidence of success. Until 2016, there was almost no coverage of Russia in the U.S. media and very little knowledge or concern about Russian affairs. More U.S. college students study Latin than Russian (Looney and Lusin 2018, 13). In general, Russia was vilified or ignored, so there was little coverage to measure whether Russian strategic narratives were reflected in U.S. news.

Szostek notes that the impact of Russian propaganda sources, such as RT and Sputnik, is limited by "their own profile and market share relative

78 SEEING RED

to outlets carrying alternative and incompatible narratives about Russia" (2017, 589). Indeed, the relative share of the market and public attention for RT and Sputnik are low in the United States, and RT closed its American operations in 2022. However, as this book demonstrates, it is not the spread of the individual stories that is of concern in terms of propaganda seeping into the U.S. media system: It is how strategic narratives of foreign states such as Russia are amplified by factors in the U.S. media system itself.

For Western-targeted narratives, beyond RT and Sputnik, there is a constellation of Russian state news outlets, websites, and individuals who amplify Russian messages in the West. Rogers and Tyuskha (2017, 51–52) discuss how the Kremlin carries out this campaign

> through the loose but powerful network of local proxy spoilers ... and 'useful idiots' as well as more pragmatic actors involved in what has been called 'reputation laundering.' These more pragmatic actors include Western lobbying firms, Public Relations agencies, and other 'reputation launderers' (including individual representatives of Western political elites) that have been hired by the Kremlin in a semi-clandestine manner.

However, it is not those in a "semi-clandestine" relationship with Russia who have the most influence. Much praise for Russia and Putin comes directly from U.S. political actors, notably Trump. An analysis by CNN showed that Trump praised Putin on Twitter eighty times from June 2013 to February 2017 (Kaczynski et al. 2017). Trump's admiration for Russia also served as a counterpoint to Mueller's investigation into how Russia helped Trump's campaign, which Trump and his Republican allies derisively dubbed Russiagate. Trump's praise of Russia, often packaged as attacks on Democrats, was echoed by Fox News throughout his administration.

In a study of Sputnik News and strategic narrative in Sweden from 2014 to 2018, Wagnsson and Barzanje (2021) analyzed Russian propaganda aimed at a democratic state through the lens of "antagonistic" narratives that they labeled as "suppression," "destruction," and "direction" (p. 239). They observed a major change in the field of propaganda studies since new information technologies and media consumption patterns enable "aggressive practices that are qualitatively different from old-style propaganda. . . . Actors no longer rely on secrecy, but can openly make use of social media and media outlets in foreign languages to destabilize other states and societies from within" (p. 239).

By using a detailed analysis of narrative, Wagnsson and Barzanje (2021) noted that it is less about the sheer volume of propaganda and more about how the stories told through propaganda can embed themselves in a national media conversation: "What is lacking is detailed narrative analysis that asks not what is said, nor how much is said, but rather how the story is told and what harm this can inflict" (p. 240). An analysis of Sputnik stories about Sweden revealed a narrative of a "once orderly, powerful Sweden that has lost capabilities and capacity. The political leaders are no longer the heroes in control but have turned into fools, the villains are uncontrollable, the victims are beyond salvation and the heroes are impeded from saving the country" (p. 246).

Even a relatively cursory examination of RT content will show a distinctive anti-Western slant. As much as Russian officials may have tried to argue that RT is merely an "alternative" news source, the central purpose of the outlet is to promote the Russian worldview. Attracting an audience with relatable content brings them into RT's sphere and then exposes the users to Russia's political messages. Measuring the reach of RT's political content is difficult, but Moscow's consistent narrative projection through the outlet demonstrates a degree of faith in its potential. In particular, much of the content is designed to criticize other countries—particularly the United States—rather than inform the audience about Russian affairs.

Regardless of the reach of outlets such as RT and Sputnik, their political coverage presents a compelling way to assess Russia's intentions. Russia's foreign-targeted media provide specific and useful insights into Russian foreign policy ambitions and actions. While decoding policy from messages in these sources requires a robust understanding of Russian narratives and contexts, they signal Russia's desired outcomes on the world stage. Recognizing them as foreign policy instruments that broadcast Russian global intentions is useful for gaining a more detailed and timely understanding of the Kremlin's ambitions and future actions.

Strategic Narratives in a Changing World

Strategic narratives provide a useful and compelling way to define how countries wish to articulate their national interests on the world stage. In the case of Russia, there are some parallels between international communication tactics in the Soviet era to the present day. Yet, while traces of former information operations remain, the game has shifted significantly. Unlike the Soviet Union, Russia has a different story to tell the world. Rather than the ultimate triumph of communism and workers' rights, Russia seeks to dominate in a world where Russia is a resurgent great nation while democracy and the West are defeated. The strategic narratives focus on both attacking the enemy and attempting to create a global vision in which an authoritarian state will dominate. While some of the disinformation tactics are familiar, the message is different.

Four Russian strategic narratives, from attacks on democracy to the promotion of Mother Russia, are relatively stable throughout Russian information operations. However, these narratives interact and resonate with events in U.S. and world politics in different ways. In the following chapters, we will present how Russian strategic narratives were echoed in the U.S. media in the 2020 U.S. presidential elections, the Stop the Steal conspiracy, and the Capitol insurrection. In addition, we will consider how Russia's full-scale invasion of Ukraine relied on these long-standing narratives but also called into play newer and more fantastical visions of Russia's role in the world.

4

U.S. 2020 Presidential Campaign Narratives and Russian Propaganda

Trying to make sense of U.S. presidential campaigns from 2016 onwards is confusing for citizens and scholars alike. Our historic understanding of how media are supposed to function in a democracy is challenged. In large part, this is because Donald Trump broke so many rules about political communication and still won an election against an established Democratic opponent. At the same time, compelling evidence of foreign interference in the 2016 election by Russian operatives illuminated the vulnerability of democratic media ecosystems to malign influence. In a bewildering environment that came to feature constant attacks on the free press and other democratic institutions from the White House itself, by the time of the 2020 election it became very difficult to discern the boundaries between domestic and foreign disinformation.

In this chapter, we compare campaign news in the 2020 U.S. presidential election in Russian English-language sources such as RT and Sputnik and in key U.S. news outlets. While we characterize and compare the nature of campaign coverage in differing outlets, we're particularly interested in analyzing the campaign news through the lens of narratives that presented the acrimonious election in ways that promoted a particular view of the world. How did Russian outlets characterize the U.S. 2020 presidential campaign for its English-speaking audience? How did this converge with—or diverge from—how *The New York Times*, *The Wall Street Journal*, *USA Today*, *The Washington Post*, CNN, and Fox News presented the key campaign issues and their implications for the American audience?

Although we found significant differences between the Russian and U.S. campaign narratives, Fox News was often both closer to the Russian narratives and stood apart from other U.S. news outlets, particularly on coverage of "Russophobia." This narrative that Russia is unfairly attacked by the U.S. media and politicians was also reflected in the Hunter Biden laptop story. In addition, we found that both Russian propaganda and Fox News

Seeing Red. Sarah Oates and Gordon Neil Ramsay, Oxford University Press. © Oxford University Press 2024.
DOI: 10.1093/oso/9780197696422.003.0004

framed Black Live Matter protests and the amorphous Antifa movement as plunging U.S. cities into chaotic violence, a narrative promoted by Trump. It would appear that the lines separating political convictions, conspiracy theories, and campaign narratives were relatively thin for RT, Sputnik, and Fox. Yet, in each case, the shape of the coverage is determined not only by a particular editorial approach but also by the broader historical context of narratives.

As discussed in Chapter 2, the U.S. news ecosystem was sharply divided by the 2020 elections, with Trump supporters particularly loyal to Fox and other news outlets that reflected Trump's rhetoric. We were interested in how much the actual content of the news reflected these divisions in terms of these narratives. As a result, we chose to approach the study of U.S. campaign news in 2020 not through the analysis of specific outlets or partisan labels but rather through the study of specific campaign narratives.

Given that narratives reflect a way of seeing the world and striving for outcomes—which can range from open borders to banning all migrants—this allowed us to avoid the slippery notion of tagging coverage as negative or positive. As life in 2020 America showed, what was negative to one voter was often positive to another. For example, an issue such as banning immigrants might seem negative to many Biden voters but would seem quite positive to many Trump voters. Given that the U.S. 2020 election was very much about two different views of the past, present, and future of America, analyzing narratives best reflected critical information flow in the election.

We found times when Russian propaganda and Fox News converged, and both were defensive about negative comments about Russia. However, the Russian outlets were less enthusiastic about Trump than Fox. While Fox showed support for Trump and attacked the Democrats, the Russian outlets supported Russia, attacked democracy more than the Democrats, and were critical of both U.S. presidential candidates. Russian outlets, however, were happy to quote Trump when he attacked the idea of Russophobia. In addition, both Russian sources and Fox attacked the U.S. media system.

In other words, while Russian sources and Fox were amplifying Trump's messaging for different reasons, their content often looked very similar. Our analysis revealed a persistent pattern that can be defined this way: RT and Sputnik amplified Trump and his messages because they attacked democracy in ways that resonated with Russian propaganda. Fox News also amplified Trump's messages because Fox supported Trump over Biden, but in doing so, it also boosted Trump's antidemocratic rhetoric. Other U.S. news outlets avoided relaying Trump's anti-democratic messages and, as a result, were less likely to resonate with pro-Russian messaging.

This chapter presents our analysis of campaign narratives using text analytics from MarvelousAI and Provalis deployed on 3,039 articles from Russian sources and 10,588 articles across six U.S. sources. The analysis covers the final weeks of the 2020 campaign in a country torn by strident political divisions, widespread protest against police killings of Black citizens, and an anxious wait for a vaccine after months of lockdowns in the COVID pandemic. While COVID precautions limited much of the traditional rituals in U.S. elections, such as party conventions, we chose to analyze the campaign coverage from the date of the stripped-down party conventions in mid-August through Election Day eve on November 2, 2020.

The campaign season also was marked by an unprecedented number of absentee ballots given fears of infection and a much broader promotion of advance, absentee, and mail-in voting directed at the American public. While many viewed this as a positive development that offered alternatives to crowded voting precincts during a pandemic and lengthened the window for voting from a single day, Trump interpreted the pivot to mail-in and other forms of advance or absentee balloting as a threat. He did not base this attack on any credible evidence of fraud or tampering but rather on a mix of innuendo and disinformation. This resonates with data that shows Trump increasingly relied more on disinformation and propaganda than facts as his presidency progressed (Kessler et al. 2021).

This chapter explores coverage of Russophobia, including how the Hunter Biden laptop story fits into that narrative. We also analyze the coverage of protest and the alleged strength of the nebulous Antifa movement in destabilizing America. These issues are not only dominant in Russian propaganda, but they also were closely allied with Trump's view of the world: the Russia "hoax," the unsafe streets of America, and alleged corruption in the Biden clan. Russian media performance in the aftermath of the election and the narrative of a stolen election propagated by Trump and his allies, culminating in the Capitol insurrection in January 2021, is covered in Chapter 5.

Given previous studies (such as Patterson 1993, 2016), we expected much of the election news to focus on the "horse race" aspect for candidates: Who was behind, who was ahead, who was rising or falling in the polls. There was also a great deal of concern about the accuracy of survey results in a close election, especially given that polls had overwhelmingly and inaccurately

84   SEEING RED

predicted victory for Hillary Clinton in 2016. While reporting on poll results can show bias (Groeling 2008), we weren't particularly interested in analyzing the coverage of surveys in 2020. Rather than focusing on how outlets reported on survey results, we were interested in how news outlets portrayed the nature of American politics and society in the context of the 2020 election. We were concerned specifically with whether this dovetailed with how Russian international outlets made these characterizations.

As discussed in Chapter 3, Russia has a strategy of promoting its interests by exploiting the open media system in the United States. We designed this study to identify Russian communication goals and look for evidence of messaging around these goals in U.S. media content. This builds on earlier work (Oates and Gray 2019; Oates et al. 2020; Oates and Steiner 2018; Steiner and Oates 2019) to operationalize Russian propaganda narratives so they can be tagged and tracked in U.S. media content. This chapter echoes that approach by illuminating how specific stories fit into compelling and widely shared narratives. Just as Miskimmon et al. (2017) selected an area of focus for strategic narratives, so did we by choosing to analyze campaign narratives surrounding the 2020 U.S. election. Given the power of conspiracy narratives (Starbird 2017), we were particularly interested in messaging that resonated with a conspiratorial view of the world, such as the idea that the U.S. is out to destroy Russia or that all Democrats are corrupt.

Moscow on the Potomac: Russian Coverage of the 2020 Presidential Election

How was the 2020 election covered by Russia for the American audience? International outlet RT, formerly Russia Today, markets itself as an "alternative" media outlet but is funded by the Russian government and promotes Kremlin messaging. Sputnik is also a Russian government-funded outlet launched in 2014, which generates a large amount of content in languages other than Russian. Both RT and Sputnik were registered as foreign agents with the U.S. Department of Justice during the 2020 election. Other work has explored the links between these news outlets and Russian government messaging (for an overview of the studies of Russian state-funded broadcasters, see Crilley et al. 2022).

As we've noted in earlier chapters, both RT and Sputnik generally have the look and feel of news, but threaded among the stories are pro-Russian and anti-American propaganda and conspiracy theories. Yablokov and Chatterje-Doody (2021) analyze the content and nature of RT, concluding that it "presents a curious case of an international media organisation that has instrumentalised conspiracy theories and turned them into a tool of international politics" (p. 1). They note that RT's "brand identity is . . . built on its capacity to raise questions, rather than providing any detail or credible answers" (p. 13).

Research Approach

Our initial approach to finding Russian narratives about the U.S. campaign was inductive. While we were aware of Russian propaganda strategy aimed at the United States as outlined in Chapter 3, the four main Russian strategic narratives that we had identified in previous work—democracy is flawed, the West is out to destroy Russia, Russia protects Russians no matter where they live, Russia is a resurgent great nation—were not all directly relevant to the 2020 U.S. election and its aftermath. We observed that the first narrative on flawed democracy was the most relevant for study, but we needed a much more specific approach. Like nesting dolls, which U.S. campaign narratives could be found within the main narratives that Russia projects to the world? Or would the campaign narratives take a different direction?

This chapter first employs content analysis that uses human annotation of content paired with a machine-learning system developed by a company called MarvelousAI (https://marvelous.ai/).[1] We used RT and Sputnik election news as examples of Russian English-language content. MarvelousAI's StoryArc platform provided tools for collecting publicly available news or social media stories, annotating text, and building machine-learning models using those annotations. For this project, the data pipeline involved the following steps:

- Continuously collected news mentions for keywords (such as "Trump" and "Biden") using Google alerts for specific news websites.
- Scraped the full text of relevant articles.
- Applied heuristics to extract paragraph-sized snippets centered on the keyword matches.

[1] One author (Oates) is an advisor to the company.

86 SEEING RED

- Allowed users to label the snippets with one or more predefined narrative tags or as explicitly not fitting a narrative. We began with roughly 100 positive examples for each narrative.
- Built supervised binary classifiers for each narrative using the annotations. In this process, snippets were first converted into vector representations using an adaptation of the BERT pre-trained language model (Reimers and Gurevych 2019). We then used principal component analysis to reduce the number of dimensions in the training set and fit a support vector machine (Cortes and Vapnik 1995) model to discriminate between positive and negative examples.
- Used the resulting models to classify all snippets in a particular time period and surface the results to the user, including samples of snippets that the model classified as belonging to a narrative and not belonging to a narrative. The user could then correct the model's mistakes, thus creating more training data that was targeted at the less confident parts of the model.
- Retrained models using the larger training sets.

The MarvelousAI system scraped stories on RT.com and Sputniknews. com that mentioned "Trump" or "Biden" for several months in 2020. Human coders then read the coverage from August 14, 2020, which was three days before the 2020 Democratic National Convention through election eve on November 2. The project identified a range of promising campaign narratives, nine of which we used to label text excerpts in the Russian English-language corpus (see Table 4.1). As news coverage on Election Day (November 3, 2020) was both huge in volume and almost completely focused on the horse race aspect, we did not include that in our analysis. We also observed that by the night before the 2020 election, it was becoming increasingly clear that Trump had lost, and the news coverage became overwhelmed by Trump's refusal to accept the election results.

The most dominant campaign narrative on RT and Sputnik was that Biden was bad for America. This included accusations that Biden and his son, Hunter Biden, were corrupt. An example of this is the Sputnik story on October 30 headlined "More Voters Believe Joe Biden Was Engaged in Corruption as Situation Heats Up Before Election" (Gorbachev 2020). The story refers both to the *New York Post* article on October 14, 2020, that claimed a laptop belonging to Hunter Biden with incriminating evidence about him had been discovered and to a survey in which 45 percent of the respondents

Table 4.1 Russian English-language propaganda narratives on RT and Sputnik, August 14, 2020–November 2, 2020

RT/Sputnik narratives	Political slant	Snippets (documents)*
Biden is bad for America	Republican	260 (83)
The liberal media lies	Republican	251 (47)
Russophobia	Republican	188 (45)
Trump is incompetent	Democrat	127 (25)
Trump is better for America	Republican	117 (24)
Trump hates China	Republican	43 (15)
Trump and the Republicans bring disorder	Democrat	27 (11)
Biden is better for America	Democrat	27 (7)
Attacks on Trump supporters	Republican	2 (2)
Total		1,042 (259)

*Snippets identified by human coders. Snippets defined by content adjacent to the keyword and could range in size from a sentence to a paragraph.

Source: Author's research

believed that the two Bidens had broken the law. Sputnik provides no link to the poll, which was reported in the right-leaning *Washington Examiner* on October 21 (Antle 2020). Biden was also mocked for gaffes, suggesting that he was senile. Sputnik carried a story on November 2, 2020, entitled "Joe Biden Misses Obama's Call to Take the Stage Three Times at Michigan Rally" and said that Biden had another "senior moment" by missing his cue (Tweedie 2020a).

Although the results produced by MarvelousAI found that attacks on Biden were more prevalent, RT and Sputnik did criticize Trump as well. While the three most dominant narratives on RT and Sputnik were pro-Republican—Biden is bad for America, the liberal media lies, and Russophobia—there was also discussion of how Trump was an incompetent leader. While there was a focus on the 'chaos' in America (discussed below), the Russian content suggested that both Trump and the Republicans as well as Biden and the Democrats were disorderly forces in America.

Thus, this initial analysis showed that U.S. campaign narratives on RT and Sputnik were not one-sided but were overwhelmingly negative. While the qualitative review found a greater tendency for the Russian outlets to

88 SEEING RED

mock Biden and the Democrats rather than attack Trump, it also showed deep skepticism toward both. Overall, the Russian content suggested there were no good choices in the 2020 election, which demonstrated the failure of the American political system specifically and democracy in general. In keeping with studies of U.S. media content in elections (such as Patterson 1993, 2016), there was a significant focus on personalities and the horse race of who was ahead or behind rather than a deeper discussion of issues or ideology. Threaded throughout the campaign coverage were complaints about Russophobia that were often fueled by Trump's promotion of that narrative.

A Deeper Dive into Russian and U.S. Campaign News

Our first qualitative review was based on a sample of 259 Russian stories, but we wanted more content for a larger study.[2] So we then used a much larger group of stories to further explore both Russian and U.S. campaign coverage with text analytics. Using an application programming interface (API, a computer application that allows users to access data from a website or other online archive), we scraped the RT and Sputnik websites for reports containing both the words "Biden" and "Trump" from August 15 to November 2, 2020. We also found and downloaded 200 reports from TASS (the Soviet era telegraph agency, Telegrafnoe Agenstvo Sovetskovo Soyuza, now an official newswire of the Russian government) and twenty-four reports from Russia-aligned commentary websites (strategic-culture.org with fourteen articles and global.resarch.ca with ten articles). This analysis focuses on RT and Sputnik.

One issue that was apparent in the Russian English-language content is that while some of it had the format and tone of Western news, pieces that were labeled as analysis or opinion tended to contain much more obvious anti-Western messaging. This is unsurprising and led to the consideration of whether we should attempt to separate news from opinion or analytical pieces. Given that our unit of analysis was mentions of Biden or Trump and not entire articles, we decided to code all the material together. We also note that American audience members are unlikely to distinguish between news

---

[2] The MarvelousAI tool was trialed on U.S. news content for automated analysis, but at the time the system could not ingest and reliably parse the news articles into coding segments (typically paragraphs). However, we did find resonance in discussions of 'Russophobia' in the Russian content and some U.S. sources (Oates et al. 2020).

and opinion, even when it is labeled by the outlet (Mitchell et al. 2018). We also included analytical pieces on news websites for our U.S. content, although we did not include any broadcast political discussion shows such as Tucker Carlson on Fox or Anderson Cooper on CNN.

We used the commercial analytics software Provalis QDA Miner to analyze 13,627 stories across eight sources from Russia and the United States. While the broader study with Provalis echoed the Russia findings from the MarvelousAI analysis on some points, we could widen and deepen our study when we focused on U.S. news. We chose to examine online stories from four major U.S. newspapers that span different political orientations yet are regarded as agenda-setting outlets: *The Washington Post*, *The New York Times*, *USA Today*, and *The Wall Street Journal*. We also included the news websites for CNN and Fox News, as Fox was particularly important in the promotion of Trump (Yang and Bennett 2021).

In the review of Russian narratives using MarvelousAI shown in Table 4.1, there was an emphasis that Biden was bad for America and that the liberal media lies to Americans (two narratives that also were part of Trump's rhetoric). But other campaign narratives were quite mixed in terms of support for Trump or Biden, including the narrative that Trump was incompetent. Instead of looking for all the major narratives in the U.S. election news, we looked for overlap. We did this through human-in-the-loop analysis.

Starting with each campaign narrative from the MarvelousAI study, we used keywords to initially identify content that would relate to the topic in Russian and U.S. election news. Here there is an element of linguistic chance, in that some narratives lend themselves to a specific set of keywords while others are more verbally diffuse. In addition, it rapidly became apparent that we would need to find storylines that served as "hooks" for particular strategic narratives. For example, one of our central case studies of Russophobia represents the broader Russian strategic narrative that the West is out to destroy Russia. By the same token, mentions of Antifa generally relate to the conviction that the U.S. streets are overrun with violent rioters, while mentions of Hunter Biden's laptop suggest that Democrats are corrupt. But some narratives that the news audience could easily absorb from U.S. election news—that Biden was senile and unfit to be president or that Trump was incompetent and unfit to be president—were not linguistically distinctive enough to be measured through automated or even semi-automated content analysis.

90   SEEING RED

We found that Russophobia was a particularly robust, measurable campaign narrative that threaded through both Russian and U.S. content. In addition, Antifa/unsafe streets and Hunter Biden's laptop were distinctive elements of broader narratives. This allowed us to both characterize and compare how these three campaign narratives were represented between Russian and U.S. content, as well as among the six U.S. sources. While this is only a partial representation of the election coverage, this is a deliberate focus on the elements that can be compared between Russian and U.S. campaign coverage. Indeed, this is not surprising as it would be unlikely for a foreign country to cover U.S. campaigns in the same way as domestic sources.

Russophobia in Russian Propaganda and U.S. News

Through this analysis, we found that Russophobia was a dominant narrative in the final months of the U.S. 2020 presidential campaign in both Russian propaganda and on Fox News. The *Collins English Dictionary* defines Russophobia as "an intense and often irrational hatred for Russia, or especially the former Soviet Union, its political system etc."[3] For this project, we defined Russophobia as the idea that the *U.S. unfairly hates and punishes Russia, attempting to denigrate and deny the country its fair place in the world order.*

The Russophobia narrative has roots that go back more than a century, as Chapter 3 notes in its discussion of the history of the U.S.-Russia relationship. But in contemporary U.S. politics, Russophobia is linked to Trump and his campaign connections with Russia. As detailed by Jamieson (2018), there was clear evidence of Russian interference in the 2016 election in favor of Trump. This was done through disguised disinformation such as planted posts as well as paid campaign ads on social media for both candidates, although overt pro-Trump messaging originating from Russia found far more resonance on social media. More significantly, the leak of Democratic Party emails that drove negative coverage of Hillary Clinton in the closing days of the 2016 campaign was linked to a Russian intelligence operation.

While scholars and analysts debated whether Russia provided the tipping point for Trump to be elected in 2016, Trump was enraged that his legitimacy was undermined by continual coverage of Russian interference. His strategy

---

[3] https://www.collinsdictionary.com/dictionary/english/russophobia, accessed April 30, 2023.

of constant denial and obfuscation made any rational discussion of the issue very difficult—either for the White House staff or the reporters who covered the story. It was this 'fog of falsehood' emanating from Trump himself that allowed the uncertainty around Russian interference in U.S. elections to flourish.

During Election 2020, the Russophobia narrative was used by Republicans to mock Democrats. The Republicans claimed that Democrats were using Russophobia to assert that Russia propelled Trump into office and that Trump was a Russian "puppet" (Radnitz 2021, 182). While this narrative started as a response to reports of Russian interference in the 2016 election, it gained traction during the later investigations into the interference and because it was so often amplified by Trump and right-wing pundits. Trump and his supporters then extended the Russophobia narrative to suggest that the "Russia hoax" was a ploy by Democrats to cover up their own malfeasance that was supported by the "liberal media."

There were several key investigations and events that were affiliated with "Russiagate" from 2016 through 2020. In response, Trump complained that the news was "Russia, Russia, Russia" (Nussbaum, 2018). While the fallout from Russian interference in 2016 lasted throughout Trump's presidency, Trump reignited Russiagate and triggered his first impeachment with attempts to blackmail Ukraine into both investigating Biden and defending Russia from accusations of planned election interference for 2020.

In April 2019, the U.S. Department of Justice released a report by Special Counsel Robert Mueller into Russian interference in the 2016 election, links between associates of Trump and Russian officials, and possible obstruction of justice by Trump and his associates (Mueller 2019). The Mueller investigation, carried out from May 2017 to March 2019, found that although the Trump campaign welcomed Russian interference, there was insufficient evidence of criminal conspiracy to charge Trump. The investigation did result in charges against thirty-four people and three companies, eight guilty pleas, and the conviction of Trump campaign chairman Paul Manafort of conspiracy against the United States as well as conspiracy to obstruct justice. Manafort, who was shown to have ties with the Russians, was sentenced to more than seven years in prison, but he was pardoned by Trump in December 2020 after serving two years.

The first impeachment trial for Trump (he was subsequently impeached for his role in the Capitol insurrection) began in December 2019. The Democrat-majority House of Representatives adopted articles of impeachment against

92 SEEING RED

Trump for abuse of power and obstruction of Congress. The inquiry found that Trump withheld military aid to Ukraine in order to influence Ukrainian President Volodymyr Zelenskyy. Trump wanted Zelenskyy to announce an investigation into Biden's alleged meddling in Ukrainian affairs to help his son Hunter and to promote the disinformation that Ukraine, not Russia, had interfered in the 2016 election. The Republican-majority Senate acquitted Trump of the charges. The U.S. Senate Intelligence Committee released its final report spanning almost 1,000 pages on November 10, 2020, detailing its bipartisan investigation into Russian interference in the 2016 election, finding significant connections between the Trump campaign and Russian operatives (U.S. Senate Select Committee on Intelligence. 2020).

Coding for Russophobia

We searched for mentions of Russophobia by starting with the keywords "Russophobia" and "Russiagate" in the Russian English-language articles. There were only eight mentions of Russophobia in the Russian collection of 3,039 articles, but there were 131 mentions of Russiagate, the label attached to charges that Russia was involved in Trump's campaign. Human coding found that all eight of the Russophobia mentions—unsurprisingly—fit the Russophobia narrative as defined above. Russiagate also was a good fit: Human content analysis by one author (Oates) found that 108 of the mentions of Russiagate also fit the Russophobia narrative. Twenty-three mentions were either brief labels that didn't indicate negative issues with Russia or the word "Russiagate" was merely part of a list of other news stories with no actual coverage of the topic. Those mentions were eliminated because they would have skewed the automated classifier by introducing unrelated words into the model.

Here is an example of a direct Russophobia mention in Sputnik the week before the U.S. 2020 election: "The Cold War was the next phase of US-led Western antagonism against Moscow. For nearly five decades, the world lived under the shadow of nuclear annihilation as American politicians and media constantly spewed Russophobia" (Cunningham 2020a). Another Sputnik story published on September 2, 2020 (Clark 2020), criticized the Democrats as being "obsessed" with Russophobia:

To defeat Trump you have to do a little bit more than falsely accuse him of being a 'Russian agent.' You have to try and outdo him in the populist stakes. You have to reconnect with the Rust Belt. You have to talk the language of Main Street. But today's Democrats are too Wall Street, too Hollywood for that. They have largely abandoned the blue-collar working-class voters who were once the bedrock of their support for elitist 'liberals,' obsessed with Russophobia, excessive political correctness, extreme wokeness and ID politics.

Using the 116 paragraphs that were originally coded by humans with the Russophobia narrative, we directed the machine classifier in Provalis QDA Miner to match this content to any additional content it identified as part of the Russophobia narrative. We found 626 mentions of the Russophobia narrative in the Russian content. We coded sets of 200 paragraphs identified by the classifier until it began to return either repeats or irrelevant paragraphs. This human-in-the-loop approach relies on the judgment of both the text classifier and the human coder. It is not possible to say that the classifier finds every example of a desired narrative such as Russophobia. However, human coders also miss examples and are subject to variations and errors in judgment in coding. Given that the method is the same on all content coded for this chapter, it is reasonable to assume that it generates a measurement that is valid across varying narratives and content.

Most of the matching Russophobia content from Russia focused on the U.S. 2016 election controversy over Russian interference, with a general tone of dismissal or sarcasm. There were several mentions that it was Hillary Clinton who masterminded Russiagate, which is not a mainstream idea featured in the U.S. coverage aside from Fox News (discussed below). There were some mentions of other issues, including using Russophobia as a reason for claiming that Russian operatives had attempted to assassinate Kremlin critic Alexei Navalny with the Soviet era poison Novichok in August 2020.

Here are two examples of Russophobia in 2020, the first from RT on November 2 and the second from TASS on October 1:

A special place here belongs to the media, who first told everyone the 2016 election was supposed to be Jeb versus Hillary, then that Clinton would win convincingly, and later that 'Russiagate' was real. Rather than apologize and try to repair their credibility, they seemingly set out to prove Trump right about being "fake news" and "enemies of the people," openly embracing

94 SEEING RED

> Biden and the Democrats and launching a gaslighting effort unprecedented in size and scope. (Malic 2020)

> Kremlin critic and opposition figure Alexei Navalny, recovered from his apparent poisoning, has given his first public interview since his coma. He blames the Russian government and President Putin for the crime, despite the dearth of real evidence. The Kremlin has flatly denied all allegations. Russian FM [Foreign Minister] Sergei Lavrov slammed western "arrogance," pointing out that the quick thinking and professionalism of Russian pilots, doctors and investigators were crucial in saving Navalny's life. (TASS 2020)

Note that the second example does not have any of the original keywords; it was identified by the machine classifier once it was trained on the original content selected by human coders. In this way, the system automatically finds content that is on a specific narrative, such as Russophobia, but can't be found automatically through keywords.

Overall, the discussion around Russophobia in the Russian content promoted the idea that Democrats unfairly amplified fear of Russia as a way to attack Trump and that Russia was unfairly accused of interfering in U.S. politics. Coders found no meaningful coverage of the extensive investigations by the U.S. government, Congress, journalists, and researchers that have provided compelling evidence of Russian interference in the U.S. election on the behalf of Trump and Trump's first impeachment. Instead, the focus is on a supposed hysterical dislike of Russia, rooted in fear and the desire to crush Russia on the world stage. Stripped of facts and context, the U.S. discussion around Russiagate and Trump can be used as evidence for anti-Russia hysteria.

The discussion of Russophobia in the Russian content serves two important purposes for Russian propaganda. On the one hand, it is useful to suggest that America regards Russia with prejudice and criticizes the country unfairly. This supports the fundamental Russian strategic narrative that the West is out to destroy the Russian nation. At the same time, Russophobia demonstrates that Russia can intimidate the powerful Americans as well as project a fearsome force in world affairs, a kind of wink-wink-nudge-nudge idea that perhaps Russia really *is* capable of undermining U.S. elections. This adds to the core strategic narrative that Russia is resurgent as a great nation as well as to the narrative that democracy is flawed and failing. Having not one, but two Russian strategic narratives interwoven in a U.S. presidential campaign gave significant political capital to Putin's authoritarian regime. Arguably, this was a critical way to empower Russia to invade Ukraine in 2022, which will be discussed in Chapter 6.

The coverage in the Russian articles dovetailed with Trump's protestations about Russiagate, which he frequently referred to as the "Russia hoax." For example, here is a typical way that Trump would be quoted about the Russia hoax in Russian content from a story on August 28, 2020, on RT titled "Trump and Dems Take Turns Playing 'Russian Card'—Which Only Proves It's the Joker": "On that score, Trump was no doubt correct in calling out 'Russiagate' as a 'big hoax.' No evidence has ever been produced to substantiate those claims, which have largely relied on innuendo and feverish conspiratorial speculation" (Cunningham 2020b). The words "Russia" and "hoax" appear together in seventy-eight paragraphs of the U.S. news coverage—most prominently in Fox News, with twenty-seven mentions (35 percent), more than double the ratio of the other U.S. news content analyzed (16 percent).

In Trump's view, there were three compelling reasons for his claims of Russophobia: He often expressed anger that his victory was attributed to foreign help, and he believed that the Democrats used Russophobia as a way to criticize his legitimacy as an elected leader. There also was the element of deliberately provoking liberals—a frequent tactic with Trump—by professing to side with Russia against the interests of the Democratic Party or rejecting liberal ideals in general. In addition, the well-documented links of his campaign staffers with Russian operatives were further inducement for Trump to deny any Russian wrongdoing in the elections or otherwise. This led to the ahistorical convergence between Republicans and Russians, in which both framed themselves as victims of Democratic smear campaigns.

Comparing Russian and U.S. Election News

If Russian outlets and Trump embraced Russophobia, how did this narrative play out in the U.S. 2020 election news? We deployed the linguistic pattern that had been identified in Russian content (via human coding and machine learning by the QDA Miner software) to analyze how this narrative appeared in U.S. campaign news more broadly. One of the most striking findings was how well the linguistic pattern worked in identifying paragraphs within U.S. news stories that mentioned Russophobia. In a way, this is not surprising because the keywords associated with the narrative are distinctive (Russophobia, Russiagate, Russia, Manafort, etc.). However, again it was particularly useful that the linguistic classifier worked at finding related words that did not match known keywords that would have been missed by human coders.

We identified 963 paragraphs as being in the Russophobia narrative in the U.S. news content. Overall, "Russophobia" appears in 399 news stories (about 4 percent of all U.S. news stories analyzed). That's a modest proportion compared with the presence of "Russophobia" in the Russian content, where it appears in 267 (about 9 percent) of the articles. However, it is not surprising that a Russian source would more prominently feature a narrative relevant to their country and not unexpected that RT and Sputnik would promote a narrative that corresponds to Russian state propaganda.

We examined the most common words in the Russophobia content across both the Russian sources and the U.S. news sources (see Figure 4.1). There were some striking differences in word frequencies among the Russian sources, Fox only, and the U.S. sources without Fox. Fox was much more likely to mention Biden in its Russophobia coverage, while other U.S. news

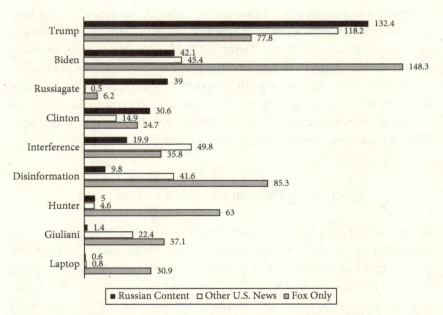

Figure 4.1 Mentions As Percentage of 10,000 Words In "Russophobia" Content

sources and the Russian sources were more likely to mention Trump. While it is difficult to extrapolate in-depth meaning from word frequencies, this does suggest Fox was more likely to connect Russophobia to either Joe or Hunter Biden. In addition, it is clear from the word frequencies that Fox was much more likely to cover the Hunter Biden laptop story in the Russophobia content, while this is virtually not mentioned in either the other U.S. news or the Russian content. Fox also features more mentions of Rudy Giuliani, who widely broadcast the claims relating to Hunter Biden's laptop having criminal evidence. Fox mentions disinformation much more frequently than the other sources. However, the term "Russiagate" only appears with any frequency in the Russian content, with a faint echo on Fox with a total of seven mentions. The term Russiagate is found only twice in all the other U.S. Russophobia news that did not include Fox.

How is the Russophobia narrative distributed among the U.S. news sources? Due to the different volume of the news sources, the number of stories from each of the six U.S. news outlets differs significantly. As Figure 4.1 shows, once the content is adjusted for volume, Fox News was more than twice as likely to mention Russophobia as the other five news sources in the election coverage (adjusted to show it as a percent of mentions by paragraph).

There were more similarities than differences across the remaining five U.S. news sources other than Fox. While acknowledging that investigations had never revealed a direct link between Trump personally and Russia, the coverage of the Mueller report and the Senate investigation highlighted evidence of connections between those in Trump's circle with Russian operatives. This was against the background of discussions of documented Russian information operations in the 2016 U.S. campaign—both in terms of social media ads and the leak of the Democratic National Committee emails—as well as suspected ongoing Russian interference in U.S. elections in 2020.

These five media outlets consistently called out Trump for his disinformation campaign around Russiagate, as seen in this excerpt from CNN:

Trump, with the help of outlets like Fox News, has been pushing a dishonest narrative in touting intelligence documents that his administration declassified last month on the eve of the first presidential debate. They claimed the information was a supposed smoking gun proving that Hillary Clinton and the Obama administration sought to frame Trump with a Russian collusion scandal. (Cohen et al. 2020)

Media narratives tend to coalesce around particular events. While the Russian content unsurprisingly dismissed accusations that the Hunter Biden laptop story was Russian disinformation, these five U.S. outlets consistently pointed out both the characters involved (particularly Giuliani) and the strange provenance of the story (a laptop suddenly discovered at a repair shop) as having the classic earmarks of a Russian disinformation campaign. There were overt parallels drawn between the Russian "hack and dump" operation to discredit Clinton in 2016 (which was enthusiastically approved of by the Trump campaign team) and the attempts to claim Hunter Biden was morally and financially corrupt based on the material on the laptop. The laptop also allegedly linked Joe Biden to Ukrainian (not Russian) interference in the 2016 election.

These five U.S. media outlets not only report that Trump is promoting the "hoax" idea, but they also discuss and debunk Trump's attempts to prove that emails allegedly found on Hunter Biden's laptop are evidence of corruption or collusion with a foreign government. The U.S. news reports aside from Fox also highlight the credibility issues surrounding those promoting the Hunter Biden corruption narrative. In considering the Russophobia narrative, it's also striking how often CNN rebuts reports by Fox News or even the "conservative media." Overall, there is regular mention of other news outlets (see Figure 4.2). The most common media citation was Fox News referencing CNN (in 17.2 percent of its stories in this study) and MSNBC (7.4 percent of its stories). This was more often done in a critical manner. *The New York*

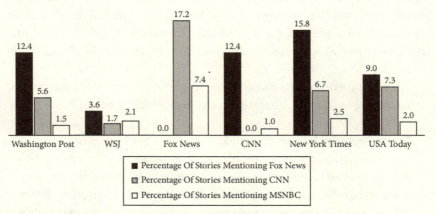

Figure 4.2 Referencing Other Media Sources

Times, The Washington Post, and CNN also mentioned Fox News in 15.8 percent, in 12.4 percent, and again in 12.4 percent of their coverage respectively. *The Wall Street Journal* rarely referenced Fox News in its election coverage.

As expected, given the variation in approaches to political news in the United States (Groeling 2008), there are some differences in coverage even among outlets that would be tagged as "left" (*The New York Times, The Washington Post,* CNN) or "centrist" (*The Wall Street Journal, USA Today*). For example, in keeping with the reputation of *The New York Times* as the newspaper of historic record in U.S. politics, the outlet ran several stories documenting the 2016 Russian interference and discussing its links with the Trump campaign. In particular, the *Times* provided detailed information and interpretation of the lengthy Senate Select Committee on Intelligence report on Russian interference and the 2016 Trump campaign. As expected of a prominent national newspaper, the *Times* provided significantly more in-depth discussion of political affairs, which meant the coverage tended to take a different form than cable news outlets.

However, despite the difference in approach and format (*Times* and *Post* articles typically are several paragraphs longer than cable news items, as Table 4.2 shows), the rejection of Russophobia as a "hoax" is the same. This framing suggests there is compelling evidence of Russian contact with the Trump campaign in 2016, that Russia was involved with the leak of damaging information for the Democrats at a critical point in the 2016 campaign,

Table 4.2 Russophobia in U.S. news

Source	Number of articles	Number of paragraphs	Russophobia mentions in paragraphs	Average number of paragraphs per article	Mentions of Russophobia by paragraph, %
Washington Post	1,331	70,518	142	53	0.2
Wall Street Journal	534	13,888	42	26	0.19
Fox News	2,239	60,780	332	27	0.55
CNN	1,910	70,518	131	37	0.19
New York Times	3,540	149,339	349	42	0.23
USA Today	409	14,976	15	37	0.10

Source: Author's research

and that the Hunter Biden laptop scandal story involved the same actors and types of evidence as in the 2016 Russian disinformation campaign aimed at U.S. voters. When Giuliani is named as a source, he is often described as discredited and allied with Russians, as in this CNN opinion piece written by Democratic Senator Chris Murphy (2020):

> The strange tale of a purported Biden family laptop's data ending up in the hands of Rudy Giuliani is a likely sign that Russia's campaign to plant fictional, anti-Biden propaganda into the US political debate may just be ramping up. Though DNI Ratcliffe [Director of National Intelligence John Ratcliffe] claims there isn't intelligence to support Russian interference, a recent letter from 50 former intelligence officials disagreed, arguing that the operation had all the hallmarks of a Russian operation.

Both the *Times* and the *Post* focused more on attempts by Trump to limit the investigation of Russian interference in U.S. elections, with the *Times* reporting on September 3:

> The Trump administration has long faced accusations of underplaying the threat of Russian election interference, especially when it is geared toward helping the president. Mr. Wolf has said the department is focused on disinformation campaigns and election interference. But President Trump has made clear that he expects the agency to emphasize immigration enforcement and border issues over its other missions, such as cybersecurity or information-sharing, former Homeland Security officials have said. (Kanno-Youngs 2020)

There was less coverage of Russophobia in *USA Today* and *The Wall Street Journal* even given that there were fewer articles from these outlets analyzed in this research. *USA Today* had just twenty-three mentions of Russophobia, for the lowest percentage in the sample at just 0.1 percent of its election coverage. This is about half the frequency of mentions in *The Washington Post, The Wall Street Journal, The New York Times*, and CNN and five times less than Fox News (see Table 4.2). The tone of the Russophobia coverage at *USA Today* came closer to the character of coverage in the *Times*, albeit without the depth of reporting or political nuance. For example, in covering the Senate Intelligence Report on Russian interference in the U.S. 2016 election, *USA Today* quoted Republican Senator and Trump ally Marcio Rubio as exonerating Trump while validating the evidence of Russian interference:

> "We can say, without any hesitation, that the Committee found absolutely no evidence that then-candidate Donald Trump or his campaign colluded with the Russian government to meddle in the 2016 election," said Sen. Marco Rubio, R-Fla., the committee's acting chairman. "What the Committee did find, however, is very troubling. We found irrefutable evidence of Russian meddling." (Phillips and Johnson 2020)

It's interesting to note that the article could have used just the first part of the quote to exonerate Trump—or the last part of the quote to frame the issue of Russian interference in a different way. The inclusion of the full quote is important for balance. In the same article, *USA Today* also included a quote from a Democrat: "The committee's vice chairman, Sen. Mark Warner, D-Va., said the 'breathtaking level of contacts between Trump officials and Russian government operatives' is a 'very real counterintelligence threat to our elections'" (Phillips and Johnson 2020).

The Washington Post reported extensively on the 'inside baseball' of the national government, particularly the tensions between the White House and federal agencies as Trump attempted to limit any investigation of Russia. The discussion in the *Post* takes the perspective that Trump's dismissal of reports on Russian interference and attempts to steer federal officials away from investigating Russia are more problematic than the actual Russian election interference itself.

Fox and Russophobia: A Different Narrative

The discussion around Russophobia on Fox News is distinctive from the coverage on the other U.S. sources in this study, which is expected given the difference in the keywords discussed above and displayed in Figure 4.1 as well as taking into account Fox's support for Trump. Fox highlighted what Trump dubbed the Russian "hoax," the assertion that the Democrats used fake stories of Russian collusion to smear Trump.

102　SEEING RED

While Fox News does report on the findings that the 2016 Trump campaign had links with Russia, this is downplayed and dismissed. The storyline was that the evidence in the Mueller and Senate Intelligence reports misleads the public by not focusing on the alleged malfeasance of the Clinton campaign in creating the hoax that Russia was involved in the 2016 Trump campaign.

For example, Fox News published this on October 1:

> And second, even if there were concerns that allegations of a Clinton-approved scheme to smear the Trump campaign was Russian disinformation, why was this allegation omitted from the thousands of pages of five declassified reports released by the Intelligence Committee on Russian meddling in the 2016 election? This is a significant piece of information that the committee should have informed the American people about and let us judge for ourselves. (Fleitz 2020)

This is a fascinating bit of misdirection: Evidence from a range of sources, including federal investigations and criminal convictions, traced the link between Trump campaign staffers and Russian operatives. In standard news practice, one could *question* this evidence, but Fox goes a step further by not only dismissing the evidence but also inventing a new conspiracy out of the events. For example, here is the type of statement that readers would encounter in Fox News coverage in this article on October 7, 2020:

> These are remarkable revelations when you consider that [Obama CIA Director John] Brennan continued calling the duly elected president of the United States a Russian asset for years, despite appearing to know the allegations were just Clinton-inspired political sabotage. Furthermore, it begs the question of why the CIA was involving itself in domestic affairs. (Flood 2020)

Other Fox News reports whitewash events, such as the statement that "Mueller's investigation yielded no evidence of criminal conspiracy or coordination between the Trump campaign and Russian officials during the 2016 election" (Singman 2020a). The Mueller report, however, does state that the Trump campaign not only failed to report this interference but also welcomed it.

Hunter Biden's Laptop

There was extensive criticism and discussion of the Bidens in both Russian and U.S. election coverage, with Fox News particularly focused on the alleged corruption of Biden and his son Hunter. Stories about Hunter Biden's business dealings in Ukraine and China, among other places, have been a feature of coverage of Biden for many years. However, a story that there was incriminating evidence about Hunter Biden's business dealings and his character on a laptop that was abandoned at a repair shop broke in the final weeks of the campaign in October 2020. The main publicist for the alleged scoop was Giuliani, then serving as Trump's personal lawyer.

To understand the coverage of the laptop story, one should put it in the context of the history and nature of the Russian and U.S. media systems. In the 2016 campaign, U.S. media outlets devoted heavy coverage to the leak of Democratic Party emails that were later shown to have been provided by a Russian spying operation. The U.S. media, which was covering the Trump campaign more as a spectacle than as a serious bid for power in 2016, extensively reported on the emails, although they failed to put even the mild allegations in context with the general practice of officials merging their personal and official emails (Patterson 2016, 17). After Trump's surprise victory and the revelation of Russian involvement in the leak, many elite U.S. media outlets were forced to reflect on whether they had best served the public in their approach to 2016 election coverage (O'Hare 2020).

The laptop story had many markers of a Russian propaganda operation. Unsurprisingly, it was covered extensively on RT and Sputnik, with Hunter Biden mentioned 496 times and specific mentions of Hunter Biden's laptop 117 times. In fact, Hunter Biden figured in almost 6 percent of Russian election stories, and it would be difficult to find a positive mention. But the divergence in coverage in the U.S. sources studied for this book is stark: Fox gave the laptop story enormous play, while other U.S. outlets essentially ignored it. Overall, the phrase "Hunter Biden laptop" is mentioned 117 times in eighty-three stories in the Russian content. It is mentioned 172 times in the U.S. coverage in 117 stories. But 143 of these mentions (83 percent) are on Fox News (see Table 4.3 and Figure 4.3).

Understanding why the coverage differed means exploring the broader forces at work in the U.S. media in Election 2020. While right-wing pundits were quick to claim there was censorship in the mainstream and social media—particularly when Twitter banned links to the Hunter Biden report

Table 4.3 Mentions of Hunter Biden's laptop

Source	Number of articles	Number of paragraphs	Hunter Biden laptop mentions in paragraphs	Average number of paragraphs per article	Mentions of Hunter Biden laptop by paragraph, %
Washington Post	1,331	70,518	6	53	0.01
Wall Street Journal	534	13,888	4	26	0.03
Fox News	2,239	60,780	143	27	0.24
CNN	1,910	70,518	6	37	0.01
New York Times	3,540	149,339	11	42	0.01
USA Today	409	14,976	2	37	0.01
Russian content	3,036	37,451	117	12	0.31

Source: Author's research

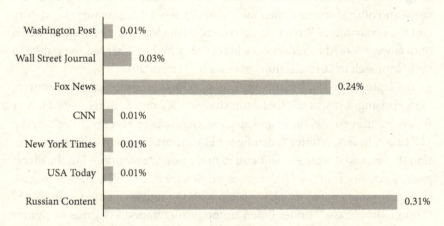

Figure 4.3 Percentage of Paragraphs Mentioning Hunter Biden Laptop

in the *New York Post* as disinformation (Paul 2020)—the explanation is more complex. Mainstream media outlets did not hesitate to cover Joe Biden and his family, but given the way the U.S. media had fallen for a Russian propaganda campaign over the Democratic Party emails in 2016, they were particularly keen to avoid the same mistake.

Although the story later became more ambiguous and details emerged that suggested that parts of the information on the laptop might be legitimate, at the time there was very little evidence that the laptop had belonged to Hunter Biden. Giuliani, as a Trump spokesperson, clearly had an agenda in promoting Biden disinformation, and he had been identified as a target for Russian influence operations (Harris et al. 2020). In 2016, the mainstream media would have covered the story, even with significant doubts. In 2020, with a president undermining the news media and attacking the concept of a free press, the mainstream media were operating under significant caution against amplifying any disinformation from the White House and its allies.

Fox News, however, went in the opposite direction on the Hunter Biden story, covering it extensively and echoing both Russian and Trump accusations about the Biden family. It's not surprising that there is variation in the U.S. campaign coverage, as there is always some variation among different media outlets. But the coverage on Fox of the laptop deviates from that on other mainstream U.S. news outlets and looks far more like propaganda than news. An example of the typical framing of the laptop story can be seen in this excerpt from a Fox story from September 19: "Democratic presidential nominee Joe Biden has remained mum on questions about his knowledge of his son Hunter's overseas business dealings, which were discussed in a series of emails purportedly found on a laptop belonging to his son" (Singman 2020b).

We initially considered the coverage around Hunter Biden's laptop as a separate narrative, but we found that the coverage was dictated by one of three narratives tied to different outlets. The Russian coverage mostly dismissed the labeling of the laptop as a Russian disinformation operation with contempt, claiming it was just another example of Russophobia. Within this was a somewhat smug message that this was simply more of an example of the chaos in the U.S. elections, media system, and party politics, with a hint that the Russians were indeed crafty enough to carry out yet another disinformation campaign against the American electorate if they so chose.

The coverage in most of the U.S. media is dismissive: It firmly placed the laptop story in the zone of "deviance" (Carlson 2016; O'Hare 2020),

106   SEEING RED

not investigating the allegations and labeling Giuliani as not only unreliable but also likely working with Russia. On Fox, the laptop story serves as a way of reinforcing different conspiracy narratives. First, the 'evidence' on the laptop—which has never had a reliable provenance—supported the idea of Biden family corruption. Aside from promoting salacious stories about Hunter Biden, the laptop story supported the Biden-Ukraine conspiracy theory, which alleged that when Biden was vice president he used his influence to protect his son from a corruption investigation in Ukraine. The much more compelling use for the laptop story was to highlight that the mainstream U.S. media was anti-Trump (as well as Russophobic) and was hiding evidence of Democratic malfeasance. Fox leaned into the Russophobia narrative by claiming that the Democrats were manufacturing claims of Russian interference to demonstrate not only their hatred of Russia but also to cover their tracks.

Antifa/Unsafe Streets

If you were to read the articles on RT and Sputnik about Black Lives Matter protests during the 2020 U.S. election campaign, you would come away with the impression that citizens were no longer safe on any American streets. The coverage had a significant focus on isolated violence rather than the widespread peaceful protests, with an emphasis on the unrest in Portland, Oregon. The national wave of protests was a culmination of a movement in the wake of a series of videos that revealed the killings of Black citizens by police, culminating with the murder of George Floyd in Minneapolis in May 2020. Anger over Trump's overt racism and policies also fueled the protests, although the core demands were for changes in policing and justice for those who were killed.

While the sample of 259 Sputnik and RT articles in our preliminary research did find mention of anti-Biden and anti-media narratives, the larger corpus contained wider mention of the disintegration of U.S. society into chaos due to street protests and violence. This was easy to find as linked to the keyword "Antifa," which was presented as a widespread and violent group of far-left agitators on RT and Sputnik. In fact, Antifa (short for "anti-fascist") is a largely decentralized and nebulous label that is sometimes adopted by protestors and even more rarely used by violent agitators. However, mentions of Antifa in the Russian articles suggested that the movement was a highly organized, widespread group of armed militants who were destroying U.S. society. It was linked with Black Lives Matter, which was also labeled as destroying U.S. society through violence. All of this contributed to the Russian strategic narrative that democracy is flawed and failing. A typical mention of Antifa in the Russian content would be this quote from RT on October 1, 2020:

> Now, the narrative has shifted at warp speed. It's no longer about Russian collusion. The new narratives that matter are virtue signalling, identity politics, critical race theory, record hypocrisy and a dual justice system where murder, looting and arson are justified because those on the right are all Nazis and the radicalized left's enforcers, Antifa and BLM thugs, are only "peaceful protestors." (Feierstein 2020)

What is missing from the Russian coverage is either the reporting that widespread protests against the police killing of Black citizens were largely political rather than violent in nature and that protest is a normal part of a democratic society. That's not surprising, since one would not expect a nuanced discussion of democratic practices from a Russian state propaganda outlet. Nor would that acknowledgment serve their propaganda purposes. The violence is linked to Democrats in the Russian coverage, although there is some acknowledgment of violence from Trump supporters as well.

The word "Antifa" appears 151 times in 101 articles out of the 3,039 Russian articles in the analysis (3.3 percent of the case). Protest in general gets far more coverage (784 mentions in 14.7 percent of the articles) while riot is mentioned forty-seven times (in 1.1 percent of the articles). Black Lives Matter is mentioned 278 times (in 197 articles or 6.5 percent of the articles). The phrase "defund the police"—which was generally used by Republicans to falsely claim that Biden and Democrats wished to stop paying police forces in America—appeared thirty-four times in twenty-six articles.

While Russophobia is clearly a reflection of a Russian strategic narrative, matching a discussion of unsafe streets in Russian English-language content and U.S. news should be more challenging. We would expect more nuance and contextualization in the U.S. news. As news tends to dramatize and emphasize violence over more routine protest events, we would expect some stories that highlight violence (and there was violence that led to murder in Portland). However, particularly from legacy news outlets such as those in our U.S. sample, we would also expect stories to explain the political frame of the protest. In the Russian content, you were often left with the impression that the mobs were just unruly thugs running amok for no reason.

The way that Fox promoted Antifa as a significant force, even a "terrorist" group, more closely paralleled Russian coverage than other U.S. coverage. At the same time, Fox closely echoed how President Trump characterized the protests. In examining this narrative in the U.S. news, we found a difference between Fox News and other outlets in the lens through which Antifa was portrayed (see Table 4.4 and Figure 4.4). We were aware, as noted above, that

Table 4.4 Mentions of Antifa in U.S. news

Source	Number of articles	Number of paragraphs	Antifa mentions in paragraphs	Mentions of Antifa by paragraph, %
Washington Post	1,331	70,518	83	0.12
Wall Street Journal	534	13,888	20	0.14
Fox News	2,239	60,780	195	0.32
CNN	1,910	70,518	23	0.03
New York Times	3,540	149,339	165	0.11
USA Today	409	14,976	9	0.06

Source: Author's research

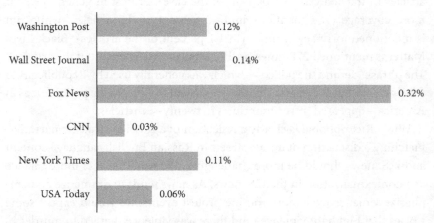

Figure 4.4 Percentage of Paragraphs Mentioning Antifa

the highest number of the mentions of Antifa were in the Fox articles. But it's not enough to note that Fox talked about Antifa more than other U.S. news outlets, although it does seem extraordinary. What is even more important to consider is *how* Fox talked about Antifa. Did its characterization dovetail with the Russian presentation of Antifa? Did the coverage of Antifa by Fox differ from how other U.S. news sources talked about it? A qualitative review of the paragraphs that mentioned Antifa in both Fox and other U.S. sources shows a significant difference in the framing of the group.

For example, a typical mention of Antifa on Fox News would link it with anarchy and violence, such as this article on September 30, 2020:

> Disingenuously, Biden now says he supports the police, but after the statements and actions this summer of both he and his running mate— Sen. Kamala Harris, D-Calif.—can't be trusted. When pressed by President Trump, Biden failed to name one single police organization that supports his candidacy and refused to condemn Antifa anarchists by name. (Bossie 2020)

Other U.S. news outlets are more careful to note that Antifa was a label, rather than an organization, and called out Trump for claiming that Antifa was a large, organized group of domestic terrorists as in this October 14, 2020, article on CNN:

> The problem for Trump is that knowing he has a problem in the suburbs and fixing it are two very different things. Trump, as his quote on Tuesday night makes clear, has tried to scare women in the suburbs into voting for him; if Joe Biden wins, he claims with little subtlety, roving gangs of Antifa supporters will invade your suburban paradise. (Cillizza 2020)

We modeled the unsafe streets narrative in the Russian content by starting with all segments that mentioned Antifa. We then asked the QDA Miner classifier to return matching paragraphs. We found several hundred, eventually identifying 484 mentions of unsafe streets (in 269 articles or about 9 percent of the coverage). This meant a substantial portion of election coverage in the Russian content promoted the idea that the streets in the United States were chaotic and violent, resonating with the larger idea of the collapse of democracy in general.

110   SEEING RED

Table 4.5 Mentions of unsafe streets in U.S. news

Source	Number of articles	Number of paragraphs	Unsafe streets mentions in paragraphs	Mentions of unsafe streets by paragraph, %
Washington Post	1,331	70,518	50	0.07
Wall Street Journal	534	13,888	34	0.24
Fox News	2,239	60,780	153	0.25
CNN	1,910	70,518	6	0.01
New York Times	3,540	149,339	293	0.20
USA Today	409	14,976	11	0.07

Source: Author's research

We identified 547 paragraphs in the U.S. news reports that matched the unsafe streets narrative from the classifier trained on the English-language Russian content. However, a qualitative review showed a difference in tone that was significant. The U.S. news outlets, aside from Fox, were careful to explain that the protests were political and generally peaceful, although they reported when protests turned violent or even deadly. They did report on Trump's concerns about Antifa, although often contextualizing it by pointing out that Black Live Matter and Antifa were not linked and right-wing groups such as the Proud Boys were far more highly centralized and organized. However, Fox echoed Trump's narrative about Antifa much more closely. Unlike the focus on Antifa that was clear on Fox, the mention of unsafe streets was prominent not only on Fox but also in *The Wall Street Journal* and *The New York Times* (see Table 4.5 and Figure 4.5). As noted above, however, the tone was different.

Conclusions

Measuring a propaganda narrative in U.S. news represents a significant and vital challenge for content analysis scholars. As a democratic society, we should be able to distinguish relatively easily between domestic free speech and foreign propaganda. Given that the United States has few legal limits on speech, it is easy for foreign actors to pose as angry citizens or even distribute

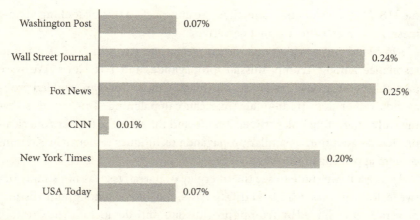

Figure 4.5 Percentage of Paragraphs Mentioning Unsafe Streets

their propaganda claiming to be news. What we quickly discovered in our study, however, is that it was often difficult to tell the difference between messages from the Russians and those from the Trump campaign, a synergy also noted by Jamieson (2018). Because Fox echoed Trump, the U.S. network also echoed Russian narratives. As Yablokov and Chatterje-Doody note about RT, its "coverage of the allegations of Russian meddling in the US Presidential elections often amplified conspiratorial allegations that had come out of the Trump administration itself" (2021, 62).

While we started this research with the idea of analyzing how Russian strategic narratives penetrated U.S. news, we found that the landscape of campaign narratives was more interconnected because of the way Trump's campaign narratives dovetailed with Russian strategic narratives. As Trump was attacking core elements of both democracy and U.S. society while defending Russia, it became very hard to tell at times where Trump's messaging ended and Russian propaganda began. And as Fox worked to amplify Trump's messaging, it became very difficult to tell when they were supporting Trump and when they were supporting Russian propaganda goals. In the end, Trump, Fox, and Russia were all supporting each other.

We are not attempting to study whether there was active cooperation among Trump, the White House, and the Russian government or to imply that this may have been the case. Rather, we are interested in how Trump's messages dovetailed with Russian propaganda during the final months of the U.S. 2020 presidential campaign. We approached this by looking at how messages coalesce into distinct narratives.

After studying a wide range of campaign narratives in 2020, we found resonance among Trump, Russian propaganda, and Fox News. We were particularly struck by how Trump's messaging more closely resembled propaganda rather than traditional American campaigning. This suggests that the truly interesting link between Trump and Russia is the former American president's adoption of similar propaganda techniques rather than Kremlin content appearing in U.S. news.

As a result, we came to see the interplay of narratives was not simply between Russian propaganda and U.S. news, but rather among four distinct players who are linked by Trump's pro-Russian, anti-democratic rhetoric (see Table 4.6). Using campaign narratives—Russophobia, Hunter Biden's laptop, Antifa, unsafe streets—we found the strongest convergence was between Fox and Trump messaging, given that RT and Sputnik were less pro-Trump than Fox. This overlap between Fox and Trump has been documented, especially by Yang and Bennett (2021). However, the convergence of Fox and the Russian coverage is striking and was measurably different from that of five other mainstream U.S. media outlets we studied (see Table 4.6).

As discussed in Chapter 2, we would expect U.S. news to follow what Siebert et al. (1956) defined as a libertarian model with some elements of social responsibility. Instead, what we witnessed from Trump and Fox was often closer to Siebert et al.'s authoritarian model, in which the media are coopted to work in the interests of the elite rather than for the public. Hence, our detection of a very similar Russophobia narrative in both Russian English-language propaganda and Fox News suggests that part of the U.S. media functioned during the 2020 campaign more as an authoritarian echo chamber than as a traditional libertarian media outlet, shifting to a role that favored propagandizing subjects over enlightening citizens.

We have identified challenges in the work of tagging and tracking narratives automatically. First, we found that while we can perceive some narratives as humans, many narratives lack specific linguistic features that allow them to be recognized by machine classifiers. In our initial study with MarvelousAI, we also struggled with establishing a clear unit of analysis for campaign news. We found the human must stay 'in the loop' for longer than anticipated, as the output of each iteration of training a machine classifier needs to be checked by humans until the classifier is reliable. We also noted that the specific vocabulary around a narrative, including Russophobia, will

2020 PRESIDENTIAL CAMPAIGN NARRATIVES 113

Table 4.6 Narrative interplay between Russian propaganda and U.S. news in the 2020 election

Narrative	Russian content	U.S. except Fox	Fox	Trump campaign
In-depth coverage of Russiagate that tells both sides of the story	No	Yes, although some variations	No	No
Russophobia is conspiracy that unfairly denigrates Russia	Yes	No	Yes, with a focus on Democrats	Yes, with a focus on Democrats
Dems are using Russophobia to attack Trump	Somewhat	No	Yes	Yes
Criticizes Trump	Yes	Yes	No	No
Criticizes Clinton/ Dems	Yes	Somewhat	Yes	Yes
Attacks the free media system	Yes	No	Yes, frames it as complaints about "liberal" media	Yes
Antifa is significant threat to America	Yes	No	Yes	Yes
Hunter Biden laptop proves Democratic corruption	Yes, but more that the whole system is corrupt	No	Yes	Yes
Unsafe streets/America in chaos	Yes	No	Yes	Yes

Source: Author's research

shift over time as events unfold and new actors enter the sphere. Thus, we recommend retraining a classifier at regular intervals, particularly when a major news story on the narrative emerges. Still, this system allows coders to identify the presence of narratives in thousands of news stories far more efficiently and accurately than with either human coding or AI alone.

Although we had considered how to study a certain period that chimed with pivotal election events, this project underlines that narratives will rise and fall very quickly with events. For example, there was some evidence of an election malfeasance narrative prior to Election Day on November 3, as Trump hedged his bets by attacking the integrity of mail-in ballots (which

114   SEEING RED

were likely to favor Democrats). Trump's rhetoric resonated with Russia's strategic narrative about flawed democracy and the coding team did see some mentions of issues with mail-in voting as well as criticism of the decentralized nature of U.S. elections.

But the Stop the Steal narrative changed and solidified from the evening of November 3, 2020, as Trump realized that the mail-in ballots would likely cost him the election. Thus, just as a human needs to be in the loop to authenticate a narrative for machine classifiers, humans need to track and consider world events shaping online content. The next chapter analyzes how Trump's Stop the Steal messaging and the subsequent Capitol insurrection became an important part of Russian propaganda.

Finally, what do these findings say about how Russian propaganda may flow in U.S. news or that an American president and significant elements of his party see the U.S. media as a vehicle for propaganda rather than a pillar of democracy? The presence of the Russophobia narrative, pushed by Trump and echoed by Fox, could be considered a legitimate use of the media to voice dissent from the Democrat-led effort to investigate Russian collusion with the Trump campaign. Yet, the similarity of campaign narratives from Russia and Fox News suggests that Fox, with its promotion of Trump, played a greater role in propaganda promotion than news dissemination.

5

Curating Chaos

Election Fraud Claims and the Capitol Insurrection

On April 18, 2023, Fox News and its parent company Fox Corp. agreed to pay $787.5 million in a legal settlement to Dominion Voting Systems, a company that supplies voting machines and software used in U.S. elections. The lawsuit was one of several faced by Fox and other right-wing news networks following their broadcasting of claims that voting machines were part of a conspiracy to steal the 2020 election. This conspiracy theory came to define the aftermath of the election and was catalyzed by President Trump, who refused to accept defeat and acted—alongside a series of allies—to originate, repeat, and amplify a vast array of assertions of electoral fraud. Sustained coverage of the conspiracy theory ultimately played a significant part in the violent attempt by Trump supporters on January 6, 2021, to overturn the election.

The role of the right-wing U.S. media ecosystem in these events—with Fox News and other broadcasters such as Newsmax in the vanguard—is substantial and raises serious questions about the erosion of traditional journalistic values within a democracy. Meanwhile, watching from the wings were Russian media presented with a gift that provided copious source material for the strategic narrative that democracy is flawed and failing.

The Russian outlets did not let this opportunity pass them by. As the research presented in this chapter shows, RT and Sputnik devoted extensive attention to the aftermath of the election, particularly to the idea of electoral fraud in one form or another. The continual publication of articles by Russian media making claims of electoral fraud shifted dramatically after the events of January 6, 2021. After the Capitol insurrection, RT and Sputnik provided high volumes of coverage of the violence, its consequences, and the recriminations and conflicts that it sparked. For Russian media, as well as U.S. media, the convoluted conspiracy theory of a stolen election was built around the statements and behavior of elite actors led by the president. However, RT and Sputnik had access to an additional resource when it

Seeing Red. Sarah Oates and Gordon Neil Ramsay, Oxford University Press. © Oxford University Press 2024.
DOI: 10.1093/oso/9780197696422.003.0005

came to building their coverage: the output of Fox News and other U.S. news sources aligned with the right.

The coverage by Russian and U.S. right-wing news media during this critical moment in American democracy indicates three worrying trends. First, while the motivations and intentions of Russian and American media may have been different, U.S. outlets such as Fox applied little or no scrutiny to false statements by political figures with a clear interest in projecting a misleading picture of the election. Second, Russian media have a track record of publishing content to denigrate and delegitimize U.S. democratic institutions. The fact that they could draw on certain U.S. media to transmit this narrative is significant, and we even found a few instances in which Russian content was directly republished by U.S. media to push the stolen-election narrative. Third, while the Dominion case shows there was some accountability for U.S. media that published false claims of electoral fraud, there is no such accountability for hostile foreign media that publish those same claims and construct narratives that are then pushed on the American audience.

Elite Messaging, News Values, and the Building Blocks of the Fraud Narrative

In terms of getting news coverage, the high-volume campaign by Trump, his close political affiliates, and sympathetic media voices to assert endemic electoral fraud during the 2020 election ticked all the boxes. As the campaign against the official results of the election morphed from a combination of the absurd and the desperate—the daily repetition of unsupported claims from the losing side of the election, then the filing of speculative and ultimately unsuccessful lawsuits—into violence and tragedy on January 6, 2021, it was monitored closely by media.

Whether the claims of fraud were viewed with sympathy, derision, or as worthy of further investigation, they could not be ignored under any iteration of media logic. The spectacle included a cast of elite sources making claims and counterclaims. There was the elevation of partisan conflict to questions of the peaceful transition of power and the survival of the state with daily—often hourly—dramatic twists. Finally, there was the spectacle of the U. S. Capitol overrun by a violent mob seeking the reversal of a democratic election.

While these events were clearly newsworthy, they also provided fodder for outlets with more propagandistic aims: raw material in the form of quotes, claims, narratives, and imagery that could be used to support the premise that the election had been stolen. For hyper-partisan media supportive of Trump, news agendas could be filled with familiar and trusted sources confidently stating some of the most serious allegations that can be leveled at a democratic system. As conspiracy theories reverse-engineer new information to fit predetermined conclusions, the flood of material generated by disparate statements on social media, media coverage, and disinformation could all be used to craft a self-sustaining interpretation of reality.

For outlets with a remit to present democracies as flawed and failing, it is difficult to envisage a more welcome set of events than those that unfolded at the top levels of American politics in the sixty-five days between Election Day 2020 and January 6. As this chapter demonstrates, during that period and in the immediate aftermath of the Capitol insurrection, RT and Sputnik published more than 1,200 articles containing allegations of electoral fraud. While in many cases the allegations were inserted by the article author, most the coverage of fraud was based on social media statements by U.S. political figures or lifted from other media sources. When discussing electoral fraud, the content of these Russian state-linked outlets for English-speaking audiences echoed that of partisan right-wing media in the United States.

The research presented in this chapter investigates the extent of alignment in the news agendas, explanatory narratives, and content appropriation from American to Russian news sites during the post-election period and in the aftermath of January 6, 2021. We contrast the agendas of RT and Sputnik, as well as how they incorporated and represented claims and allegations of electoral fraud into their reporting, with coverage by Fox News and Newsmax. In this way, we investigate both similarities and divergences of narratives interpreting the events of the election and its aftermath in Russian and U.S. right-wing news.

Fraud Allegations and the Road to the Capitol Insurrection

Tracing a causal pathway from the 2020 election campaign to the outbreak of violence at the U.S. Capitol on January 6, 2021, is of course beyond the scope of this book. However, there are certain events and actions that attracted high-intensity news coverage and dominated news agendas. Many in-depth useful journalistic accounts exist of events before (such as Kessler and Rizzo 2020) and after (such as Rosenberg and Rutenberg 2021) the election that relate to allegations of electoral fraud and to the efforts to overturn or delay the certification of the election results. Academic studies conducted in the aftermath of the attack have identified the framing of the events in news media (Zulli et al. 2022) and the link between claims of electoral fraud and citizen beliefs of illegitimate results (Justwan and Williamson 2022), but a more complete picture of the different threads of rhetoric and action will emerge in the coming years. What follows here is a summary of the statements and actions that featured prominently in coverage by the news sources analyzed for this chapter to provide a guide to key events.

Trump had been making claims about the likelihood of electoral fraud for several months before the election, including assertions in April 2020 that mail-in ballots were "dangerous" and "fraudulent," allegations that would be repeated by Trump and some associates sporadically throughout the summer (Inskeep 2021). The language used was an early indication of a trend that would be prolific in later rhetoric and is documented in the analysis in this chapter—vague statements that insinuate impropriety, without providing details or explanations of how fraud worked in practice.

Public reactions to the COVID pandemic, which had yet to reach its peak, had a significant effect on the administration of the election, which took place at a time when new infections were trending at approximately 100,000 per day (Centers for Disease Control and Prevention n.d.). This contributed to a substantial rise in votes being delivered by mail or at drop-off locations. Crucially, partisan affiliation affected the tendency of voters to decide not to vote in person, with Republican voters less likely to perceive risks associated with going to polling places and more likely to view mail-in ballots with suspicion, in part due to the elite-level messaging on this subject over the preceding months (Atkeson et al. 2022). As the pandemic had become an anchor point for conspiracy theories (Romer and Jamieson 2020), so the effects of the pandemic on procedural aspects of the election also attracted conspiratorial thinking.

The rise in mail-in voting, therefore, presented a series of opportunities to those who would seek to cast doubt on the legitimacy of an unfavorable result. Delays in counting mail-in ballots—particularly those postmarked before polling day but arrived after November 3—as well as the patchwork of different rules and regulations on ballot counting and validity in different states created procedural uncertainty. In addition, it caused a delay in the determination of the final results, a period of several days in which narratives of fraud and a stolen election could be amplified.

The partisan element played into this as well. Since mail-in ballots were more likely to have been submitted by Democratic voters, there was a high likelihood that in states with a large proportion of mail-in voting early results would favor Republican candidates but would gradually trend toward Democrats. A simplistic narrative of Republican wins being erased by fraudulent mail-in ballot results, with the added dramatic element of the "inevitable" fraud playing out gradually and consistently in real time, was there to be exploited.

After polls began closing on November 3, Trump immediately started to make statements that fed off—and into—this uncertainty, announcing his own victory and accusing others of stealing the election (Nagourney and Rutenberg 2020). These statements were augmented by claims of election fraud by close associates, including Trump's family members and legal advisors (Karni and Haberman 2020), and then by a growing cast of elected officials and public figures affiliated with the Trump administration (Edmondson et al. 2020).

This linkage with pro-Trump sources—some of the most powerful and recognizable political actors in the country—ensured visibility, virality, and newsworthiness of the claims. The frequency of claims ensured that there was no shortage of material to work with for news outlets looking for content. For building narratives, real events—such as isolated incidents of possible fraudulent voting or over-zealous local officials preventing access to polling sites—were reinterpreted as indicators of systematic electoral fraud. The research discussed below shows that RT and Sputnik drew heavily on elite claims and the long list of different articulations of fraud, which they then repeated consistently in the subsequent months.

Some voting fraud claims were specific, such as accusations of rigged voting machines, which could then lead to legal jeopardy as Fox News would learn with its reporting on Dominion and Smartmatic. Other fraud claims were vague, such as Trump's accusations that only rarely attributed responsibility for fraud or details about actual voting behavior. Elected officials frequently used formulations of words that strongly alleged rather than claimed fraud, such as the need to ensure that "only legal votes" are counted (Cochrane 2020). These statements often cited or accompanied a flurry of lawsuits filed in November and December 2020 in various states by multiple plaintiffs, which were largely attempts to prevent the counting of late-arriving votes or to delay or overturn the certification of election results. Of sixty-two lawsuits filed by the president, his campaign, lawyers, and affiliates in the aftermath of the election, sixty-one failed, with many dismissed for lack of standing (Cummings et al. 2021). Yet the lawsuits provided sustenance for continuing claims of a stolen election.

Other events provided opportunities for increased coverage and the amplification of fraud allegations. These events included the December 14 confirmation of results by members of the Electoral College and a December 27 lawsuit arguing that Vice President Mike Pence had discretionary power to select "alternate" electors. This lawsuit was dismissed for lack of standing but provided fuel for a narrative that Pence was engaged in a betrayal of both Trump and the voters. In addition, there were two runoff elections in Georgia on January 5, triggered by no candidate receiving a majority of votes in either Senate election. While allegations of fraud were continually made and amplified between November 3, 2020, and January 6, 2021, spikes in coverage and the emergence of new narratives occurred at these news events.

By January 6, there had been two full months of repeated and strongly amplified claims of electoral fraud. For anyone seeking validation of the idea that their vote had not counted or their shared victory had been stolen, there was ubiquitous "evidence" in the form of thousands of statements by elite sources and reports about them. These inherently newsworthy data points—claims of the subversion of a democratic election by figures in positions of authority—were also source material for the construction of narratives of democratic betrayal, dysfunction, and decline.

Though it will never be completely possible to determine to what extent certain political actors fully believed that the electoral fraud they were insinuating at the time had actually occurred, it is possible to analyze how this was presented in news coverage. This can be done through an examination of the content, quotes, and claims that were repeated and amplified during this period. In particular, it is important to consider which sources were given space to articulate unchallenged allegations of a stolen election. Through this research, we can see the extent to which Russian and some U.S. news sources constructed narratives that supported claims of fraud, attributed blame, and then interpreted the cause and significance of the events of January 6, 2021.

Sampling and Analyzing News Coverage of Fraud Allegations and Political Violence

The research included in this chapter is based on mixed-methods content analysis, combining automated online article collection and tagging with manual analysis by human researchers applying a coding framework. The open-source computational content analysis toolkit Steno (www.stenoproject .org) was used to study online news articles collected by a series of custom scrapers configured to collect and store content from all URLs published on a list of news sites between November 1, 2020, and January 31, 2021.

The Steno toolkit is made up of two main components. The first enables the collection and storage of news content from sites targeted by configured scrapers. These scrapers are deployed to scan sites at intervals of three hours and log every new URL published in that interval. Duplicate URLs are ignored, new pages are scraped, and selected metadata is stored. The system collects information including the article text, headline, text in embedded social media posts, date, and time of publication.

The second component is a user interface where researchers can pull articles from the collection according to a specified date range, and then use a search bar and tagging functions to perform semi-automated or manual content analysis on the resulting set of articles. Tagging and deletion scripts can be used to partially automate some basic analytical functions and to facilitate the cleaning of data sets.

Four news sites were selected for in-depth analysis. RT.com and Sputniknews.com represented Russian English-language news media, while Foxnews.com and Newsmax.com represented right-affiliated U.S. news sites associated with claims of electoral fraud and partisan alignment with the Trump administration and the Republican Party. While a wider range of sources was analyzed in Chapter 4, the research found that Fox News more closely echoed Russian narratives. As a result, we decided to focus on Fox News when studying the critical intersection between U.S. news and Russian propaganda for this period. We also analyzed Newsmax, as the right-wing outlet gained a significant segment of Trump supporters after the 2020 election (Flint 2023).

We examined the months of November 2020, December 2020, and January 2021. Scripts were used to tag all articles published on the domains www.rt.com, www.sputniknews.com (changed to sputnikglobe.com after the 2022 invasion of Ukraine), www.foxnews.com, and www.newsmax.

com. The resulting lists of articles were then checked to identify and remove those that were not suitable for textual analysis, including photo galleries, embedded videos with little or no accompanying text, promotions, and consumer reviews, as well as lists of links.

Short text files containing pre-set logical commands were then applied to automatically tag articles with a high likelihood of relating to the U.S. election, allegations of electoral fraud, or the Capitol insurrection. The exact search terms (outlined below for different analyses) were designed to be inclusive to minimize the probability of eligible articles being missed. Researchers then manually checked each article to verify whether the articles were correctly tagged and excluded those that were not. Omitted content included articles about foreign elections or allegations of fraud unrelated to the election.

The selected news sites differ significantly in the style, volume, and format of content that they publish. Sputnik and Newsmax published high volumes of online text-based articles daily during the sample period (approximately 100 articles per day), RT somewhat fewer (approximately sixty to seventy articles per day) and Fox News considerably fewer (ten to twenty per day, once video-based articles were removed from the sample). The analysis was conducted on the full list of eligible articles published by each outlet during the selected timeframe.

Election and Fraud Allegations on RT and Sputnik

Existing research on the online output of RT and Sputnik has identified a strong and consistent focus on political dysfunction in democratic societies. In particular, Russian propaganda deploys this narrative on countries that Russia identifies as adversaries, with narratives of decline and institutional or societal failure then projected to international audiences (Ramsay and Robertshaw 2019; Wagnsson 2023). Such research also shows the extent to which RT and Sputnik engage in the curation of information to support these narratives. At the same time, these outlets publish multiple inconsistent and competing explanations of events, with the evident aim of sowing confusion or uncertainty among audiences.

The 2020 U.S. election, the "Stop the Steal" conspiracy, and the Capitol insurrection are perfect sources of material for Russian media with a track record of amplifying themes of democratic decay. The subject matter on its own is relevant, as it relates to a dispute over the legitimacy of the central component of a democratic system. The destabilizing effect of disputed elections both within the host country and in the international community is another incentive to amplify a story for strategic purposes. In addition, the sheer amount of material—quotes, tweets, a cast list of newsworthy actors—means that a news space can quite easily be filled with stories about shocking, funny, serious, or tragic incidents that have wide audience appeal.

To assess how RT and Sputnik chose to represent the election and the theme of electoral fraud, Steno was used to collect all articles published on rt.com and sputniknews.com between November 1, 2020, and January 31, 2021. After collection, tagging scripts were used in Steno to identify all articles with a very high likelihood of mentioning the election and—if present—claims of electoral fraud. The scripts used general keywords such as, in the case of elections: "election," "vote," "president," "trump," "biden," and so on. The search and tagging function in Steno is designed to identify different cases of words, so for example, "voting," "voted," and "voter" were also automatically tagged. These were broad terms that intentionally generated many false positives as a cost of minimizing the chance of false negatives.

Researchers then checked headlines and article content to determine whether the designation was correct or incorrect and removed tags as needed. Articles were determined to mention the election if at any point in the headline or the article text the election was referenced, either as an ongoing process or as a past event with relevance to the subject of the story. An article was tagged as "fraud" if at any point in the article an assertion or refutation of the existence of electoral fraud was included. For instance, the November 25, 2020, article by RT headlined " 'Why wouldn't they overturn an election?' Trump claims huge step of nullifying Biden's victory justified by Dems' alleged 'fraud' " (RT.com 2020a) was tagged as both "election" and "fraud" due to the assertions made by Trump within the body of text and repeated in the headline.

Conversely, a Sputnik article dated December 15, 2020, on Putin's congratulatory message to President Biden following the electoral college vote of the previous day was also designated as mentioning electoral fraud due to the presence of the passage "however, the incumbent president Donald Trump has challenged the results of the vote, citing claims of ballot tampering and illegal vote counting" (Serebriakova 2020). The claims differ in terms of direct quotation versus indirect attribution and in their centrality to the story, but in each case the issue of electoral fraud is present. The difference between direct and indirect attribution is discussed later in this section.

124   SEEING RED

Table 5.1 lists the number of articles published online by RT and Sputnik during the three-month sample period, as well as the number of those articles designated as mentioning the election and those that also mentioned electoral fraud. The results show that RT and Sputnik devoted a significant portion of their overall output to the U.S. election, often through the lens of electoral fraud.

Unsurprisingly, the intensity of coverage was highest in November 2020, with almost a quarter of all articles published on both RT and Sputnik mentioning the election in that month. RT published an average of sixteen articles per day on the election and Sputnik was even more prolific, with twenty-six articles each day. This rate decreased in December before rising again in January 2021 as the Georgia runoff elections were quickly followed by the events of January 6 and the ensuing fallout. Overall, across the three months, RT published 896 online articles mentioning the election, approximately 15 percent of all output on the site. Sputnik was slightly higher proportionally, with 1,630 articles representing around 17 percent of all articles. Overall, the U.S. election was a big story for the Russian outlets.

The main theme of this coverage was electoral fraud. Table 5.1 shows that a large proportion of articles mentioning the election also contained one or more references to electoral fraud. There were 768 articles published on

Table 5.1 RT.com and Sputniknews.com coverage of the 2020 U.S. elections

Outlet	Coverage type	November 2020	December 2020	January 2021	Total
RT.com	All articles	1,981	2,107	1,889	5,977
	Mentions election	478 (24.1%)	143 (6.8%)	275 (14.6%)	896 (14.9%)
	Mentions electoral fraud	183 (9.2%)	82 (3.9%)	78 (4.1%)	343 (5.7%)
Sputniknews.com	All articles	3,237	3,310	3,285	9,832
	Mentions election	769 (23.8%)	290 (8.8%)	571 (17.4%)	1,630 (16.6%)
	Mentions electoral fraud	329 (10.2%)	201 (6.1%)	238 (7.2%)	768 (7.8%)

Source: Author's research

Sputnik that mentioned electoral fraud—an average of 8.5 articles each day representing 47 percent of articles that referenced the election in any way.

While the number of election articles dropped significantly from November to December 2020, the 201 fraud articles published by Sputnik in December represented 69 percent of all articles about the election. The trends on RT were similar, but the number of fraud articles was lower both in absolute numbers and as a proportion of all election articles. However, fraud was still a prevalent theme in RT's U.S. election coverage, accounting for 38 percent of the 896 articles that mentioned the election.

It should be noted that mentions of electoral fraud could also include repudiations of the fraud or even a defense of the electoral system. A secondary analysis assessed all articles tagged as containing one or more mentions of electoral fraud and allocated them to three categories. The first category contained all articles in which the claim of fraud was presented without challenge. The second category consisted of all articles in which the claim of fraud appeared with an explicit rebuttal of the fraud or a statement of skepticism that fraud had taken place. An example of this second category is a November 27, 2020, article on RT.com titled "Trump says Biden can only move into White House if he 'PROVES' his votes weren't 'illegally obtained'" (RT.com 2020b). The article devotes several paragraphs to parsing a tweet and a separate statement by Trump, listing multiple claims of voter fraud. The claims are balanced by two final paragraphs listing the multiple failures of the challenges brought by Trump's legal team to claim fraud. This included a typically irreverent editorial statement that is emblematic of Russian media's mocking tone when covering U.S. politics, that the Trump campaign's "litigious efforts keep swinging and missing."

A third category covered articles that contained only a denunciation or rebuttal of the idea that fraud had occurred. For example, a Sputnik article on November 6 cross-promoted an interview on Sputnik's radio arm, summarizing the comments of a guest who was strongly critical of the merits of the early legal challenges by the Trump campaign (Sputnik International 2020a). In addition, cases where a claim of fraud was mentioned only to contextualize a source's rebuttal of the idea within the same passage of text were recorded as a rebuttal only. An example of this could be found in a December 2, 2020, article on RT.com where Trump's position on the presence of electoral fraud was cited by the article as a lead-in to a statement by former National Security Advisor Susan Rice stating that there was "no proof, nor even credible evidence" of electoral fraud or irregularities (RT.com 2020c).

126   SEEING RED

Table 5.2 Claims and denial of electoral fraud in RT.com and Sputniknews.com coverage

Outlet	Content Type	November 2020 (articles)	December 2020 (articles)	January 2021 (articles)	Total
RT.com	Articles referencing fraud	183	82	78	343
	Fraud claim(s) unchallenged	113	52	58	223 (65.0%)
	Claim and rebuttal	51	24	17	92 (26.8%)
	Denial of fraud only	19	6	3	28 (8.2%)
Sputniknews.com	Articles referencing fraud	329	201	238	768
	Fraud claim(s) unchallenged	245	126	166	537 (70.0%)
	Claim and rebuttal	73	66	51	190 (24.7%)
	Denial of fraud only	11	9	21	41 (5.3%)

Source: Author's research

Table 5.2 shows the balance of these three categories of fraud-tagged articles published online by RT and Sputnik. Articles containing unchallenged claims of fraud were far more prevalent than the other categories across all three months. Almost two-thirds of all articles mentioning electoral fraud on RT presented the claim without any contesting viewpoint. Articles in which both an assertion that electoral fraud had taken place and a counterargument were included made up slightly over one-quarter of coverage, and less than one-tenth contained only the view that no electoral fraud had taken place. On Sputnik, the ratio was even more strongly in favor of unchallenged claims of fraud. Seven out of every ten articles mentioning fraud contained an uncontested assertion, while only around one in twenty contained an unchallenged denial of the presence of electoral fraud.

Not all assertions of fraud were of equal prominence, however, and it should be mentioned that both RT and Sputnik tended to present assertions of fraud indirectly in the final paragraphs of articles in which the legality of the election was not the central topic of the piece. A typical example of this can be found in the final paragraph of a December 15 Sputnik story about U.S. Senate Majority Leader Republican Mitch McConnell congratulating Biden on winning the election: "Trump has repeatedly claimed he won the election, but the victory was stolen from him via massive election and voter fraud and acts of impropriety. His team has initiated recounts in several states as well as filed lawsuits in state and federal courts to seek relief" (Chegodaeva 2020).

This insertion of a conspiracy narrative at the end of various articles is not new. This has been observed as a trait of RT and Sputnik in previous studies, that is, the consistent repetition of claims within editorial content when covering a broad range of often-unrelated topics (Ramsay and Robertshaw 2019).

Of course, *how* fraud claims were featured is also important. To test this, we measured the identity of the source; whether the claim came from a direct quote or was indirectly attributed to a source; whether any quotes were from Twitter posts; and whether the claim included an attribution of blame for the fraudulent activity. Sources were recorded once per article even if they featured multiple times in that article (so articles containing multiple assertions of fraud by Trump, for example, would only register one instance of a source asserting fraud). When recording whether the source attributed fraudulent activity to different actors, a catch-all category of "multiple" was used to indicate that more than one specific allegation of fraud had been made.

The main finding of this analysis, shown in Table 5.3, was the ubiquity of Trump as an instigator of the majority of fraud claims featured on RT and Sputnik. On RT, there were 411 instances of sources making an assertion that electoral fraud had taken place, and Trump accounted for slightly over half of these. In 209 articles Trump featured as the originator of a claim of electoral fraud. Of these, slightly more than half were indirect attributions, such as statements pointing out Trump's claims of fraud.

In other words, Trump's direct quotes were a rich source of material on RT, but his past statements of fraud also were routinely inserted into articles about the election. A similar practice also was detected on Sputnik, where Trump accounted for 62 percent of all sources of fraud claims featured in news articles about the election. Indirect attribution was very common, occurring in 335 articles from November to January. In addition, Trump's

128 SEEING RED

Table 5.3 Trump as a source of electoral fraud claims on RT.com and Sputniknews.com

Content type	Outlet	
	RT.com	Sputniknews.com
Distinct claims of electoral fraud	411	920
All claims by Trump	209 (50.9%)	579 (62.9%)
Directly quoted claims by Trump	99 (24.1%)	244 (26.5%)
Indirect attribution of claims to Trump	110 (26.8%)	335 (36.4%)
Trump quotes derived from Twitter posts	58 (14.1%)	138 (15.0%)

Source: Author's research

use of Twitter to circulate claims of fraud was prominent in coverage on both RT and Sputnik.

This raises two significant points. The first is that Trump was a vital source of electoral fraud claims for RT and Sputnik. From the perspective of traditional news values (Harcup and O'Neill 2017), this is unsurprising because this was part of an ongoing story with sources from the power elite stoking political conflict and making surprising or shocking claims about a key component of civil society. However, both RT and Sputnik continued to attribute claims of fraud to Trump regardless of whether he was featured in the article. His claims could be, and were, inserted consistently into articles in which Trump himself was not quoted.

There are additional implications here that shed light on editorial processes in Russian news sources. First, the ubiquity of Trump as a source of fraud claims was not due to the credibility or specificity of his claims. Of 209 RT articles in which Trump was a source of one or more claims of electoral fraud, 162 (about 78 percent) did not include any attribution of responsibility. Repetition of vague claims such as his November 7 tweet "I WON THIS ELECTION, BY A LOT" was common.

A similar proportion of Sputnik articles in which Trump was a source of fraud claims also contained no detailed attribution of responsibility by the president (466 out of 579). Where Trump did attribute blame, it was most often leveled at "Democrats" (eleven articles on RT; twenty-nine on Sputnik) or at a range of actors (fifteen articles on RT and thirty-six articles on Sputnik saw the president blame multiple actors). An example of this scattergun attribution of blame can be seen in articles where multiple tweets by Trump are summarized, such as in a November 15 Sputnik article that cited his claims that Democrats had altered votes, local officials had covered up vote manipulation or counted ineligible votes, and that voting machines were responsible for manipulating results (Geydarova 2020). Lists of accusations like this frequently formed the spine of a story, without interrogation of the claims or acknowledgment of their lack of detail.

No other single sources came close to Trump's prominence on both RT and Sputnik, although various groups made up the remainder of claims of fraud. Members of Trump's campaign or his associates were frequently cited as claiming electoral fraud. Often these claims were anonymous or attributed generally to the campaign or "team" around the president. When associates were quoted directly or had claims attributed to them, former New York mayor and Trump advisor Rudy Giuliani (sixteen RT articles, thirty-seven Sputnik articles) appeared most frequently, followed by one-time Trump lawyer Sidney Powell. Powell appeared in thirty-two articles across both sources, where she made direct claims about electoral fraud due to voting machines in twenty-five articles.

Elected officials were less common as sources, making claims of fraud in twenty-three RT articles and thirty-nine Sputnik articles. Ken Paxton, the Texas attorney general who filed legal challenges against election results in multiple states, appeared most often (in fifteen articles), with Republican Senators Josh Hawley (six articles) and Lindsey Graham (three articles) among the few who appeared more than once. In general, Republican members of Congress were frequent sources in Russian articles that mentioned election fraud, but a qualitative review showed that language often stopped short of making specific or direct claims that fraud had taken place.

Beyond elected officials, a long tail of other sources of fraud claims was featured: seventy-seven separate claims in RT articles (unnamed U.S. Postal Service workers appeared six times, followed by Alex Jones of Infowars and James O'Keefe of Project Veritas three times each). On Sputnik, eighty-six claims were made by sources in this "undefined" category, with former U.S. National Security Advisor Michael Flynn appearing four times and the anonymous U.S. Postal Service workers seven times. Sputnik articles were more likely to attribute fraud claims to groups, with variations of "Trump supporters" having claims of electoral fraud attributed to them on eighteen occasions.

130   SEEING RED

These findings demonstrate that the frequent and high-profile assertion of electoral fraud by Trump and affiliated voices presented an opportunity that was not passed up by Russian news sources. The election was a prominent part of the news agendas of both outlets, and a very large proportion of electoral coverage carried allegations of electoral fraud. The allegations were only rarely challenged or rebutted and often enjoyed a long "half-life," with indirect attributions of assertions of fraud included in hundreds of articles.

Building Fraud Narratives from U.S. Media Content

The tendency of Russian media to lift content to build news agendas that focused heavily on electoral fraud was not limited to the statements of Trump and other sources in American politics. RT and Sputnik also drew upon U.S. news content, particularly Fox News. The lawsuit filed by Dominion against Fox News provides a useful timeline of the primetime or weekend broadcast shows on the network in which claims that Dominion hardware and software had been used to perpetrate electoral fraud were aired (*New York Times* 2023, 21–43).

An analysis of RT and Sputnik coverage in this period demonstrates that the Russian outlets were monitoring and reporting on Fox programming, at least in the immediate aftermath of election day. As well as the programs cited by Dominion in its lawsuit, other Fox output was regularly cited by RT and Sputnik when repeating claims that voting machines were involved in electoral fraud. Fox was also a go-to source for Russian media for other claims of fraud.

According to the Dominion lawsuit, the first show on which a fraudulent claim by lawyer Sidney Powell was made alleging the involvement of voting machines in electoral fraud was *Lou Dobbs Tonight*, which aired on November 6, 2020, three days after the election. On this show, Powell did not explicitly name Dominion but instead alleged the U.S. Central Intelligence Agency was involved in using computers to change votes. Neither this show nor the claim appears in RT or Sputnik content analyzed for this project. Two days later, however, Powell again appeared on Fox, where she claimed on *Sunday Morning Futures* that the company had an "algorithm" that was used to "steal the election"—a claim derived from an email sent to Powell and various Fox News hosts that made a series of bizarre claims (*New York Times* 2023, 24–25). Powell's appearance was reported in depth later that day on RT,

ELECTION FRAUD CLAIMS 131

in the article "Trump attorneys will expose Biden's 'abject fraud,' says lawyer on president's team" (RT.com 2020d).

On November 13, Powell appeared again on *Lou Dobbs Tonight* to repeat allegations that voting machines had been used to subvert the election. This appearance attracted two reaction articles on the Russian outlets: "'I'm going to RELEASE THE KRAKEN': Michael Flynn's attorney vows to expose Dem collusion behind prominent voting machine firm" (RT.com 2020e); and "'Trump Won This Election in a Landslide': Flynn Lawyer Vows to Prove Mass Vote Fraud Plot Soon" (Tsukanov 2020). Later in November, an RT article revisited the appearance: "'Kraken on Steroids': Sidney Powell says she 'understands' Trump's lawyers distancing themselves from her, vows to fight on" (RT.com 2020f). Powell represented Flynn when he was charged with making false statements to the FBI.

As Fox continued to feature people making allegations about the role of voting machines in the theft of the election, Russian sources continued to report on these claims. An appearance by Giuliani and Powell on *Sunday Morning Futures* on November 15 yielded three Sputnik articles: "President of Soros-Linked Voting Software Firm on Biden Transition Team - Trump Lawyers" (Tweedie 2020b); "CIA Head Gina Haspel 'Should Be Fired' Over Election Software 'Glitches,' Trump Lawyer Says" (Burunov 2020); and the explainer article "What's Really Behind Trump's Legal Team's Strategy & Do His Lawyers Believe in Victory?" (Blinova 2020). RT covered the fallout of a dispute between Fox host Tucker Carlson and Powell that played out between November 18 and November 20 (RT.com 2020g; RT.com 2020h), but the Russian outlets did not cover subsequent programs that Dominion later accused of containing defamatory claims.

Overall, Fox News was being steadily mined for content around which Russian outlets could build articles containing allegations that voting machines were involved in electoral fraud. Eight more articles on RT and Sputnik were identified in which information sourced from Fox carried claims of voting machine fraud:

- "Trump Lawyer Wants Recount in 28 States With 'Glitch' That Flipped 6,000 Votes to Biden" (Sputniknews.com, November 7, 2020)
- "Fox News Host Hannity Slams 'Media Mob' For Failing to Question 'Error-Prone' Vote-Tallying System" (Sputniknews.com, November 13, 2020)

132   SEEING RED

- "Doubling down: Tucker claims other Trump legal team members yet to see evidence on rigged election software from Sidney Powell" (RT.com, November 21, 2020)
- "Trump Says DoJ, FBI May Have Been In On Large-scale Voter Fraud" (Sputniknews.com, November 29, 2020)
- "My Pillow guy says Trump will '100% be PRESIDENT' for next four years after speaking with lawyers" (RT.com, December 4, 2020)
- "Flynn Says Obama's Plan of 'Spying on Trump' Has Fallen Apart, Claims He Scared the Ex-President" (Sputniknews.com, December 6, 2020)
- "Military Campaign & 'Law-Abiding' Union: Trump Supporters Urge to Act Over SCOTUS Move on Texas Suit" (Sputniknews.com, December 12, 2020)

Fox News was also a frequent source of other allegations of fraud beyond voting machines republished by RT and Sputnik. Four additional articles by RT and seventeen by Sputnik drew on Fox content with examples such as a Trump interview with Fox in which he made vague allegations that the election had been stolen (Ekimenko 2020) and claims by an anonymous source in an interview with Fox host Laura Ingraham that they had witnessed voting fraud at a polling location (Sputnik International 2020b).

The fact that an array of different allegations was skimmed from Fox highlights two key points. First, it shows that U.S. right-wing media were involved in a process of agenda-building that appropriated information of dubious credibility to feed the narrative that the election had been stolen. At the time, it demonstrates that RT and Sputnik exercised weak or nonexistent filters on the quality of information they were prepared to republish. This two-step process of surfacing any available suspicion of impropriety in the election goes some way to explaining convergence in political news agendas across certain U.S. and Russian media and why the narrative of a stolen election continued to be amplified up to January 6, 2021, and beyond.

Russian Coverage of the Capitol Insurrection

The events of January 6, 2021, represented a momentous and unexpected event that again provided material to support consistent claims on Russian media of electoral dysfunction in a democratic adversary. The insurrection indeed indicated a profound series of failings on the part of the American

ELECTION FRAUD CLAIMS   133

Table 5.4 Attributions of responsibility for Capitol insurrection, RT.com and Sputniknews.com

Articles covering Capitol insurrection	Number of articles	
	RT.com	Sputniknews.com
All articles	272	542
Responsibility attributed to Trump	96	273
Responsibility attributed to protestors	89	215
Responsibility attributed to other actor	22	21
No mention of responsibility	68	51
Violence linked to claims of electoral fraud	19	168

Source: Author's research

body politic and provided a wealth of material to advance Russian narratives of the dysfunction of democratic societies and the hypocrisy of states that claim the superiority of democratic institutions internationally.

The extent to which the repeated claims of fraud were a primary driver of the violence at the U.S. Capitol on January 6 will continue to be a point of contention. The protestors who participated in the demonstration were brought together in part under a banner literally called "Stop the Steal" and prior to the outbreak of violence had been spectators at a speech by Trump where they were exhorted by him to "fight like hell." As the dust settled on the events of the day, Trump claimed that he had attempted to placate the crowd and that from a legal standpoint his speech was free expression protected under the First Amendment.

Since RT and Sputnik had taken the topic of fraud and used it prolifically, their coverage was assessed to see how they represented this violent event linked to a conspiracy theory that the election had been stolen. Table 5.4 shows that, like electoral fraud, coverage of the Capitol insurrection was a very prominent issue on the Russian sites. Between January 6 and the end of the month, RT published 272 articles referencing the events, while Sputnik published 542—over twenty articles per day on average.

While a small proportion of articles mentioned the events without attributing blame, the largest number of articles attributed responsibility to Trump, either due to his allegations of fraud in the preceding weeks or his actions on the day of the insurrection. There was blame attributed to the protestors themselves, particularly on Sputnik. Articles also were checked to

134   SEEING RED

see if there was an assertion that allegations of electoral fraud had played a role in causing the violence. On RT, there was relatively little mention of the violence as linked to claims of electoral fraud, but this was a major theme on Sputnik.

Comparisons of Russian Content with Fox News and Newsmax

Our analysis has shown a strong resonance between Russian sites and Fox, as both Sputnik and RT used Fox content to bolster their narrative of a failing U.S. democracy. This section examines the links among coverage of the January 6 insurrection on Russian sources, Fox, and the more right-wing Newsmax.

Table 5.5 shows the volume of total election coverage and election fraud coverage on the websites of Fox News and Newsmax from November 1, 2020, to January 31, 2021, with comparable data from RT and Sputnik reproduced from Table 5.1. There is a significant difference in the volume of coverage on the U.S. sites. Foxnews.com published less content overall than the other sources studied in this chapter. In total 1,495 articles on Foxnews.com were identified over the three months, while 6,969 articles were published on Newsmax, an amount bolstered by the latter's use of wire copy (253 of the 2,191 articles published by Newsmax in November 2020 included the phrase "associated press" and 194 included the phrase "thomson reuters").

Newsmax had the highest percentage of election coverage (27.7 percent of all articles) and the highest percentage of total articles that contained claims of electoral fraud (14.0 percent) of all four sources studied for this chapter. Although Fox was to become embroiled in a high-profile libel lawsuit over its election coverage on its cable TV talk shows, the Fox News website was the least likely to include election fraud claims of all the sources studied. While 19.2 percent of all the stories collected from Foxnews.com during the sample period mentioned the election, only seventy-three articles (4.9 percent) mentioned electoral fraud.

Table 5.5 also includes Russian media performance on the same measures. RT (14.9 percent of articles) and Sputnik (16.6 percent) devoted slightly less of their coverage to the election than Fox and considerably less than Newsmax. The proportion of all articles published by RT and Sputnik in the sample period that contained claims of electoral fraud was 5.7 percent and

Table 5.5 Coverage of the 2020 U.S. elections—Fox News, Newsmax, RT, and Sputnik

Outlet	Coverage type	November 2020	December 2020	January 2021	Total
Foxnews.com	All articles	374	573	548	1,495
	Mentions election	112 (29.9%)	49 (8.6%)	126 (23.0%)	287 (19.2%)
	Mentions electoral fraud	24 (6.4%)	17 (3.0%)	32 (5.8%)	73 (4.9%)
Newsmax.com	All articles	2,191	2,407	2,371	6,969
	Mentions election	829 (37.8%)	487 (20.2%)	617 (26.0%)	1,933 (27.7%)
	Mentions electoral fraud	440 (20.1%)	362 (15.0%)	172 (7.3%)	974 (14.0%)
RT.com	All articles	1,981	2,107	1,889	5,977
	Mentions election	478 (24.1%)	143 (6.8%)	275 (14.6%)	896 (14.9%)
	Mentions electoral fraud	183 (9.2%)	82 (3.9%)	78 (4.1%)	343 (5.7%)
	Mentions election	769 (23.8%)	290 (8.8%)	571 (17.4%)	1,630 (16.6%)
	Mentions electoral fraud	329 (10.2%)	201 (6.1%)	238 (7.2%)	768 (7.8%)

Source: Author's research

7.8 percent respectively. This was a slightly higher proportion than Fox News but significantly lower than Newsmax.

The extent to which each outlet depicted the election in terms of the fraud narrative is shown in Table 5.6. Perhaps the most significant finding is that just over half (50.4 percent) of all Newsmax articles about the election contained claims about electoral fraud in some form. This was more than Sputnik (47.1 percent) and RT (38.3 percent), which were two sites covering the election in support of the strategic narratives of a hostile state. The proportion of Fox News election coverage that referenced fraud was 25.4 percent, the lowest of all four outlets but still a significant amount.

136 SEEING RED

Table 5.6 Fraud narrative in election news, U.S. and Russian media

Outlet	Election articles	Fraud articles	Fraud proportion
Newsmax	1,933	974	50.4%
Sputnik	1,630	768	47.1%
RT	896	343	38.3%
Fox News	287	73	25.4%

Source: Author's research

Proportions of output, however, are a relatively blunt measure of the importance of the fraud narrative in the political content of Russian and U.S. partisan media. Table 5.7 analyzes whether RT, Sputnik, Fox, and Newsmax applied journalistic principles of balance to the allegations of electoral fraud to which they chose to devote coverage. This research was carried out through qualitative analysis.

The results indicate that the Russian sources were the most likely to include unchallenged claims of electoral fraud and were considerably less likely to publish articles where the only mention of fraud allegations was by sources denying or doubting that fraud had taken place. On RT, fewer than one in ten articles were built around countering the claim that the election had been stolen and on Sputnik this proportion was fewer than one in twenty.

We found Newsmax most closely echoed the patterns of the Russian sites. Newsmax also built its election news around unchallenged claims of fraud and was the least likely of all four sites to include views on both sides of the topic. This demonstrates that Newsmax had even less adherence to traditional U.S. news values than the Russian sites. The Fox News website, conversely, is on this relatively simple measure the most balanced. This suggests that the more partisan and opinion-based editorial approach on its primetime broadcasting does not apply equally across its different channels of output.

Conclusions: Diverging Motives, Common Themes

The conspiracy theory about electoral fraud woven by Trump and his associates in the aftermath of the 2020 election presented different opportunities to the news outlets analyzed in this chapter. We know from the

ELECTION FRAUD CLAIMS   137

Table 5.7 Presentation of electoral fraud claims, Russian and U.S. news sites

Content type	Proportion of articles mentioning electoral fraud, by outlet			
	RT	Sputnik	Fox	Newsmax
Fraud claim(s) unchallenged	65.0%	70.0%	37.0%	64.6%
Claim and rebuttal	26.8%	24.7%	34.2%	18.2%
Denial of fraud only	8.2%	5.3%	28.8%	17.2%

Source: Author's research

findings in the Dominion lawsuit that for Fox News it became a straitjacket, an article of faith to audiences that couldn't be ignored or underplayed. For Newsmax, it was a recruiting tool—signifying to their audience that they were prepared to go to any lengths to support their "truth." This was an important part of growing their audience. For RT and Sputnik, it was a gift, a pure distillation of the strategic narrative that U.S. democracy, like all democracies, is broken, corrupt, and rigged against the people.

However, the coverage of the issue of electoral fraud by Fox and Newsmax also shows how the erosion of traditional journalistic standards among U.S. right-wing media, as discussed in Chapter 2, can lead to the provision of content that is in some ways indistinguishable from hostile propaganda. Indeed, the U.S. right-wing media can even fuel the content needs of foreign adversaries in information warfare. The revelations of the Dominion lawsuit against Fox News help clarify how news content can devolve into propaganda when the principles of objectivity or the commitment to verification are discarded in favor of commercial or partisan interests.

Russian media focus on fraud shows a dedication to the core Russian strategic narrative that democracy is flawed and failing. They published extensively about electoral fraud and rarely included rebuttals or skepticism. They republished fraud claims for weeks after they were first made. Russian outlets harvested content from U.S. media to fill their agendas, and they continued to include claims of fraud when switching to blanket coverage of January 6, 2021, in the weeks following the Capitol insurrection.

The lawsuits filed by Dominion against Fox News in February 2023 made public the panicked decision-making behind the news network's airing of

138   SEEING RED

accusations that the voting machine company had participated in systematic electoral interference. This unmasked the subordination of the principles and fundamental norms of journalism to commercial concerns at Fox News. The evidence could furnish an almost perfect case study of the many ways that the hypercompetitive digital information environment can incentivize the corruption of basic journalistic standards.

The private communication between Fox News' owners, executives, producers, journalists, and hosts tells a different story from the bombast and apparently unshakable conviction of the on-screen political commentary on the network's flagship discussion shows in the aftermath of the 2020 election. The company's management was consumed by a dilemma: How to compete with upstart rival right-wing news organizations such as Newsmax that were poaching the Fox audience by giving airtime to intricate conspiracy theories about nationwide theft of the election, including the manipulation of voting machines and software.

As Fox management weighed the pros and cons of airing some of the most serious accusations that can be leveled in a democracy—charges that they privately believed not to be true—one statement by an executive of Primetime Programming and Analytics stands out: "This type of conspiratorial reporting [on Newsmax] might be exactly what the disgruntled FNC [Fox News channel] viewer is looking for" (*New York Times* 2023, 35).

Moments of clarity like this—when the processes by which news is made and journalistic standards are weighed against commercial and political interests are thrust into the spotlight—are exceptionally rare, and correspondingly valuable. The U.K.'s Leveson Inquiry (2011–2012) into phone hacking at Rupert Murdoch's *News of the World* and the collapse of self-regulation among British newspapers produced insights into the subversion of core journalistic standards and the influence of proprietors and political figures over editorial content that scholars had investigated in depth with limited success (Department of Digital, Culture, Media and Sport 2012).

The private communications between employees of another of Murdoch's media assets in the aftermath of Trump's loss in November 2020 likewise shows how the collapse of journalistic standards can result in serious democratic harm. More than that, they also indicate how the structures of the online media environment can reward bad-faith actors in the sphere of journalism and favor practices of narrative-building more akin to propaganda campaigns than to the provision of information on important civic matters.

First, Fox employees were concerned about the commercial implication of increased competition for their core audience. News sites and broadcasters who sought to outflank Fox on the right proliferated in the years even preceding the Trump presidency. Newsmax launched a broadcast venture in 2014, following the emergence of One America News Network (OANN) the previous year. While Fox's allegiance to the Republican Party has been well documented, these new competitors eschewed even the pretense of journalistic detachment during Trump's time in office in favor of hyper-partisanship and a willingness to provide airtime to conspiracies and convoluted narratives in support of Trump (Baragona 2020).

Fox News found itself faced with this supposedly existential threat after calling the election result of Arizona in Biden's favor (a call that was ultimately correct) on election night. This action was viewed as treasonous by Trump and a large portion of his supporters, who began to switch over to rivals such as Newsmax. The internal discussions over the response to this, which fatefully led to the airing of conspiracy theories about Dominion and other companies who supply voting machines, were framed almost exclusively as a commercial strategy to reverse the loss of audience—a "war footing" with Newsmax, who "have a strategy across all shows to try to steal and target our viewers" (*New York Times* 2023, 28).

Of course, the more detailed narratives of electoral fraud were not spontaneously generated. Nor were they—as the private communications of Fox executives attest—cooked up by right-wing media in conjunction with each other or with the Trump administration. While some fraud claims coalesced into self-sustaining theories that were universally reported across the right-wing U.S. media ecology, they generally originated with claims by elite sources who were then given a platform to repeat and develop them, often without challenge.

The frequency of the claims and the variety of allegations of fraud that were made provided ample source material for news organizations that sought the continued engagement of an audience receptive to the idea of a stolen election. The claim that voting machines were used to manipulate vote results was just a fraction of coverage that alleged fraud, as this chapter has shown.

140 SEEING RED

RT and Sputnik made use of the same building blocks of conspiracy and presented similarly distorted realities to their audiences. Information that supported the conspiracy was harvested from all available sources—political figures or U.S. news content—while information that contradicted the conspiracy was simply omitted. This convergence of U.S. right-wing and Russian media content demonstrates how the abandonment of democratic journalistic norms can contribute to the undermining of democratic institutions. In the case of Fox News, as the Dominion evidence shows, the commercial imperative in a competitive news environment meant that false claims of fraud were aired despite the private objections of professional journalists. In the case of Newsmax, although the internal decision-making has not been publicized in the way that those at Fox have been, a lack of adherence to a discipline of verification appears to be central to their 2020 election coverage (Roose 2020).

RT and Sputnik lack this commercial incentive, except to the extent that they represent an effective investment of Russian state funding. They are also not interested in the same journalistic norms despite their use of the presentational forms of journalism to produce content that mixes reportage with information that carries propagandistic messaging (Crilley et al. 2022; Tolz et al. 2020; Wright et al. 2020, Yablokov and Chatterje-Doody 2021). Rather, RT and Sputnik exist to promote the narrative of the Russian state. In this way, RT and Sputnik have an incentive to publish content that will attract the audience in the target countries. Thus, promoting the Trump conspiracy theories was a win-win for the Russian English-language outlets: It supported the key Russian narrative about flawed democracy and provided popular content attractive to Americans who were Trump supporters.

As well as commercial accountability, the decision by Fox News to settle the Dominion lawsuit is likely to have been influenced by legal considerations. Fox tried to argue that the fraud claims were being made by prominent figures and were therefore newsworthy even though known to be false and not questioned on air (Rizzo 2023). But in pre-trial hearings, the judge rejected the defense that newsworthiness trumped journalistic responsibility. As well as knocking down a line of defense in the courtroom, this also undermined the idea that spectacle beats truth when it comes to presenting information under a journalistic brand.

Of course, this is a form of accountability that doesn't apply to RT and Sputnik. When pushing propaganda in service of the strategic narratives of a hostile state, spectacle is important and truth irrelevant as well as often inconvenient. The similarity in content between Russian state-linked media and U.S. partisan right-wing media, although the motives for producing it may have been entirely different, is still a worrying indicator that journalism stripped of traditional professional values of objectivity, truth-seeking, independence, and verification looks a whole lot like propaganda.

6

Russian Strategic Narratives and the War in Ukraine

From Neo-Nazis to NATO

This chapter assesses the success of Russian strategic narratives in influencing the U.S. media coverage of the invasion of Ukraine in 2022 in three key ways. First, we consider the nature and meaning of the shift of Russian strategic narratives by Putin from long-standing grievances to more mythic anti-Ukrainian conspiracies on the eve of the 2022 invasion. This demonstrates that tracking narratives can provide useful signals in understanding planned military actions from Russia. In particular, we note that the long-standing Russian complaint that NATO threatens Russian sovereignty found significant traction and discussion in the West through a qualitative review of *The New York Times*, *The Washington Post*, and *The Wall Street Journal*. While our analysis shows that the mention of Russian conspiracy claims about neo-Nazism in Ukraine in the U.S. mainstream media increased dramatically around the 2022 invasion, there appeared to be little serious debate about whether actual neo-Nazis were in power in Ukraine.

This chapter allows us to demonstrate with more precision which Russian propaganda is more likely to resonate with U.S. news. The war in Ukraine does not echo partisan politics with nearly the same strength of Trump, Stop the Steal, and the Capitol insurrection. As a result, Russian narratives about Ukraine face a more difficult battle in gaining attention in the U.S. news. However, our analysis shows that while Putin's more fantastical notions about neo-Nazis in Ukraine were repeated in the mainstream U.S. news, his grievances about NATO were highlighted in what appears to be a void of knowledge about foreign affairs in the United States. As a result, significant questions about blaming NATO, the West, and the United States—as opposed to the actual invading Russian army—for the war were raised in three elite U.S. media sources.

Seeing Red. Sarah Oates and Gordon Neil Ramsay, Oxford University Press. © Oxford University Press 2024.
DOI: 10.1093/oso/9780197696422.003.0006

In this chapter, we move from a consideration of Russian propaganda that attempts to undermine U.S. democracy to Russian propaganda in the justification of an unprovoked attack on its neighbor. It is fairly straightforward to measure who is winning a war on land, at sea, or in the air as the metrics are relatively unambiguous. There are so many soldiers lost, so many civilians killed, so many aircraft downed, so much territory gained or lost—even if the final resolution may take years or even decades. It is much harder to understand who is winning the propaganda war that parallels military movements because the battle for hearts and minds is not visible on a map or tracked in figures. Rather, information warfare consists of a complex array of message production, dissemination, consumption, and response by the targeted audiences.

As a result, although analysts understand the critical importance of information warfare, much of the conversation about it lacks precision and clarity. Tracking strategic narratives allows us to more effectively understand and hence counter the more successful narratives, as well as interpret information signals that predict the next moves on the kinetic battlefield. As will be discussed in this chapter, the wide-scale invasion of Ukraine that significantly expanded the war from the Donbas region was preceded by a measurable change in Putin's rhetoric. At the same time, while U.S. media outlets became more careful about reporting on domestic disinformation by the end of Trump's presidency, they remain relatively susceptible to Russian propaganda on foreign affairs on which they have less historical knowledge or context.

Justifying War

The axiom that truth is the first casualty of war is particularly apt in describing how Russia attempts to justify the invasion of Ukraine. While the Kremlin uses many of the same strategic narratives it has long deployed into Western media ecosystems, there are unique elements to Russian propaganda about the invasion. In particular, Putin has chosen to augment Russia's long-term strategic narratives that emphasize Russia's role as both victim of Western aggression and a resurgent great nation by emphasizing conspiratorial elements about neo-Nazism. References to Nazism are not new in Soviet or Russian discourse, as the Soviet victory over Hitler's army remains one of the most important cultural memories in Russia (Laruelle 2021). Yet, while

Nazism has been part of Russian domestic dialogue, it has not been intrinsic to Russian international strategic narratives. So it is important to consider why Putin pushed a narrative that Ukraine is awash in neo-Nazis just prior to the 2022 invasion.

Russia first invaded Ukraine in 2014, with a covert seizure of the Crimean Peninsula and military intervention in the Donbas region in Eastern Ukraine. Initially portrayed by the Russians as an internal coup in the Donbas, Russia invaded the country and seized Ukrainian territory. Thus, Ukraine has been at war with Russia, which was occupying much of the Donbas by late 2023, since 2014. Russia maintains jurisdiction over the oil-rich Crimean Peninsula.

Analysts connect Russia's invasions of Ukraine, to a large degree, to Putin's concerns over the 2013–2014 Euromaidan revolution in Ukraine, which included massive protests against Russia-backed Ukrainian President Viktor Yanukovych. Despite popular and parliamentary support for moving closer to Europe, Yanukovych backed out of a cooperation agreement with the European Union in 2013. Protestors demonstrated, massing on the Maidan Square in Kyiv and eventually drawing fire from Ukrainian security services loyal to Yanukovych. After violent skirmishes, the protestors took control of government buildings. Yanukovych fled the country, and a new president was elected.

Russia consistently promotes the disinformation that the Euromaidan was a U.S.-backed coup, although there is no reliable evidence for this. Rather, the evidence shows it was a domestic protest movement that coalesced into a political revolt in large part in response to the violence by security services (Lokot 2021). The success of the Euromaidan movement in demonstrating the will of the people, much like the protests in the Arab Spring, stands as a tangible threat to authoritarian regimes such as Russia, particularly in how citizens self-organized via online platforms and mobile phones (Lokot 2021).

Russia deployed its familiar strategic narratives about Western threats, the protection of ethnic Russians, the corruption of democracy, and Russia as a resurgent great power to justify the 2014 invasion of Crimea and the Donbas in Ukraine. But what decisions did Russia make to justify the much broader 2022 invasion of Ukraine? Which narratives—old or new—are deployed in the invasion? Which appear to have worked, and which appear to have failed?

STRATEGIC NARRATIVES AND THE WAR IN UKRAINE   145

Finding a Frame for War

Robert Entman (2003) defined the system through which leaders could establish compelling, albeit sometimes untruthful, strategic messaging for war as "cascading activation." Using the example of the War on Terror, Entman demonstrated how President George W. Bush and the White House were able to create a powerful frame to respond to the 9/11 attacks with invasions of Iraq and Afghanistan. Although influential journalists tried to shift the focus to Saudi Arabia, America did not choose to launch military operations in an allied country. Entman argues that like a cascading waterfall, influential messaging from the top levels of government that do not encounter meaningful opposition or contestation can compel even a free media system to stay "on message" despite the underlying lack of logic in that message. In the immediate aftermath of the 9/11 attacks, no influential voices in the U.S. government were arguing against the invasions, although later reflection caused many in the United States to question the rationale for the second Gulf War.

Putin successfully implements "cascading activation" into Russia's controlled media sphere but faces much more opposition to his messaging on the global stage. The significant escalation of Russia's ongoing war in Ukraine is a manifestation of all four of the long-term strategic narratives discussed in this book: Russia is a resurgent great nation; Russia protects Russians no matter where they live; the West is out to destroy Russia; and democracy is flawed and failing. Yet, the Ukrainian war messaging from Russia also exhibits some new rhetorical characteristics that suggest the rise of conspiracy theories. As a review of Putin's speeches and other public statements in this chapter will show, Putin has broadcast his conviction that the Ukrainian people are part of historic Russia and not a separate nation. In addition, he has highlighted the idea that the innocent Ukrainian people are being cynically manipulated by Western governments to both separate them from their Russian family and force them to serve as a puppet state for NATO to threaten Russia.

While the territorial ambitions in the war on Ukraine amplify the desire to be a resurgent world power, Russia also has consistently claimed that Ukraine denies rights to the many ethnic Russians living there. These assertions are false, particularly given that Russian was widely accepted as a national language in Ukraine until Russia's initial invasion in 2014. Finally, Russians point to any democratic movements in Ukraine as dangerous, given that Western democracy is corrupt and failing.

146   SEEING RED

These narratives are not broadcast into a void. In addition to the four long-stranding Russian strategic narratives, Russia engages in constant, reciprocal signaling of desires and intentions with the United States and other countries. In a study of media and events listed on GDELT, an open-source system that collects data worldwide, Stulberg and Murphy (2022) found that Russia and the United States spoke differing languages in terms of international threat and coercion in 2021. By analyzing the content of millions of websites with computational linguistics, Stulberg and Murphy found that the "coercive postures" of the two countries were "out of sync preceding the Kremlin's fateful decision to launch a decapitation strike at Ukraine" (p. 1). While the United States directed messages at Russia

> that favored diplomatic and economic policies, augmented by a basket of legal and military activities that generally held steady throughout the year . . . Russia relied heavily on diplomatic, military, and legal instruments of coercion that were inconsistently directed against the United States. While both sides practiced multidimensional forms of coercion, they engaged asymmetrically in respective efforts to deter and compel. (Stulberg and Murphy 2022, 3)

In other words, it was very hard to tell what Russia wanted or intended by looking across the full spectrum of media messaging. This is why focusing on specific strategic narratives—and how they change—is particularly useful.

Putin deployed two distinctive conspiracy narratives in the lead-up to the 2022 invasion of Ukraine, which are evident in the speeches and articles he delivered or published in the months before the invasion. First, Putin broadcast his conviction that the Ukrainians and Russians are not separate people. In addition, he emphasized that the innocent Ukrainian people were being cynically manipulated by Western governments to both separate them from their Russian family and force them to serve as a puppet state for NATO and the West to attack along the Russian border. A second prominent conspiracy theory from Putin was that neo-Nazis were controlling the Ukrainian government.

Fiona Hill and Angela Stent (2022) address the underlying illogic of these narratives and find a critical connection between the two. Putin ordered his "special military operation" (he initially banned the use of the word "war" to describe the 2022 invasion) because "he believes that it is Russia's divine right to rule Ukraine, to wipe out the country's national identity, and to integrate its people into a Greater Russia" (p. 108). Hill and Stent point out that Putin's interpretation of history may be "historical miasmas, infused with a brew of temporal and factual contradictions," but "his narratives are a potent political weapon" (p. 110). Hill and Stent work through Putin's historical interpretation: Ukrainians are Nazis not because they follow the ideology of Hitler, but because they are what Putin terms "zealous nationalists" like the World War II Ukrainian partisan Stepan Bandera, who fought with the Germans against the Soviets (p. 111). Ukrainians are Nazis, according to Putinism, "because they refuse to admit they are Russians" (p. 114).

A 2023 Atlantic Council report by its Digital Forensic Research Lab analyzed Russian propaganda about Ukraine since 2014 and found that Russian narratives frequently had little or no relation to reality. The researchers identified five key narratives about the war: Russia is seeking peace; Russia has a moral obligation to do something about security in the region; Ukraine is aggressive; the West is creating tensions in the region; and Ukraine is a puppet of the West (2023, 1). These overlap with the four main narratives identified in this book, but they are both more specific and more divorced from reality. In particular, the idea that Ukraine is the aggressor rather than the victim of Russian aggression is simply false.

The Atlantic Council study found that it is not so much what the narratives said (which was often nonsense) that was important—it is how they signaled Russian intentions. In analyzing seven years of Russian propaganda narratives in Russian or Russian-friendly media sites and on social media, it found "the Kremlin deployed disinformation and propaganda through its media proxies, spinning yarns ranging from the misleading to the ludicrous, to weave together Putin's false case for war" (2023, 4). By looking at a range of Russian propaganda narratives in thousands of texts, the researchers found that these "lies, deceptions, and exaggerations were not in support of the Kremlin's *casus belli*; they *were* the Kremlin's *casus belli*" (p. 4; emphasis in original). In other words, an attentive follower of Russian propaganda narratives could interpret future Russian actions, perhaps better than other traditional signals such as troop movements and official announcements.

In considering how this propaganda penetrated the U.S. media system, Brandt et al. (2023) carried out a study of the popularity of Kremlin conspiracy narratives on U.S. political podcasts between February 24, 2022, and February 24, 2023. Leveraging keywords and understanding of Russian narratives from the Hamilton 2.0 Dashboard at the Alliance for Securing

148   SEEING RED

Democracy,[1] Brandt et al. tracked four prominent propaganda narratives, including the claim that Ukraine is filled with Nazis. The study also analyzed claims of U.S. support for bioweapons facilities in Ukraine, U.S. responsibility for the explosion of the Nord Stream 2 pipeline, and that the Bucha massacre of Ukrainian citizens by Russian troops was a false flag operation. After documenting the popularity of news podcasts in the United States, the researchers found only rare mentions of these Russian conspiracy theories. Across 1,885 episodes, they estimated that between 4 and 7 percent of the episodes either tacitly or explicitly endorsed Kremlin-backed narratives about Russia's war in Ukraine. They warn, however, that a lack of counter-narratives that refute even some of the most outrageous claims of Russian propaganda is problematic. In addition, even that level of resonance of Russian conspiracy theories in U.S. media is concerning.

Analyzing Putin's Statements on Ukraine, 2021–2022

In the months leading up to the massive invasion, Putin emphasized the need to liberate the Ukrainian people from their "neo-Nazi" leadership. One critical document is a 7,000-word article that appeared under Putin's name titled "On the Historical Unity Between Russians and Ukrainians" on July 12, 2021 (Putin 2021). The article includes a discussion of Russian history reaching back centuries that attempts to demonstrate the common roots of the Russian and Ukrainian people. Given that few in Russia and very few in the West would be familiar with these historical references, they form a general impression of a storied past but it is difficult to verify that they are being deployed accurately. They certainly would be challenged by Ukrainian historians.

Putin stated that "the wall that has emerged in recent years between Russia and Ukraine, between the parts of what is essentially the same historical and spiritual space, to my mind is our great common misfortune and tragedy" (2021, n.p.). Here it is clear that Putin is building on the notion of a communal "motherland" and Great Russian nation. He then turns to conspiratorial thinking, saying that this division is the "result of deliberate efforts by those forces that have always sought to undermine our unity" with the

---

[1] See https://securingdemocracy.gmfus.org/hamilton-dashboard/ (last accessed Sep 28, 2023). The Alliance for Securing Democracy is part of the German Marshall Fund.

"overarching goal being to divide and then to pit the parts of a single people against one another" (n.p.). This fits with the West is out to get Russia narrative and casts the United States, NATO, and the democratic world in general as the existential enemies of Russia and her people.

A qualitative content analysis of the historical unity article shows a strong emphasis on the idea—argued mostly through the lens of Putin's interpretation of history—that Ukraine and Russia are one nation (see Figure 6.1). There are thirty-seven mentions of this concept in Putin's article. There are also six mentions of Nazis and Nazism, split between historical references to World War II and accusations that "neo-Nazis" are rampant in contemporary Ukraine. While "Nazi" is a very evocative word in general, particularly given Russia's glorification of its role in fighting Nazis in World War II, its deployment in relation to modern Ukraine is a linguistic hook now used consistently by Putin and other Russian officials.

The fantastical elements of the article are the repeated accusations—eight in total—that Ukraine is responsible for the violence and war. There is no reference to the fact that the Russian military invaded Ukraine in 2014 and has been fighting there ever since. There are four mentions of alleged Ukrainian corruption. While there is only one direct mention of NATO, there are sixteen references that fit the strategic narrative that the West is out to destroy Russia (often linked to how Ukraine is being manipulated by the United States to establish an American military front along the Russian border). There are seventeen references to Russophobia, the unfair and unreasoning

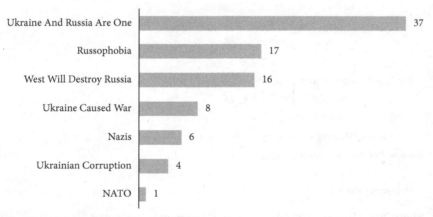

Figure 6.1 Narratives in Putin Article

hatred of Russians. Putin's article is both something old—paranoia about Western military incursions and Russophobia have been consistent parts of Russian strategic narrative for years. Yet, the element of the "Nazi" threat in Ukraine and the denial of Ukrainian ethnicity were something new for strategic narrative.

How consistent were these frames and narratives for Putin in the year after he published his historical unity article? We carried out an analysis of an additional nineteen documents posted in English on the Russian presidential website between July 13, 2021, and August 17, 2022. In the material that ranged from Putin's annual press conference to reports on phone calls with U.S. President Joe Biden, the strategic narrative that the West was out to get Russia dominated with fifty-seven mentions found via content analysis (see Figure 6.2). This analysis was carried out on the English-language documents with Provalis analytical software, highlighting mentions that ranged from a phrase to a paragraph. Thus, the unit of analysis varied slightly but was based on the minimum amount of content to make a coding decision. The items were selected out of the hundreds of documents posted over the year based on whether they had any relationship to Ukraine and the four dominant strategic narratives. Russian-language versions of the documents are available online, and one author speaks Russian, but the choice was made

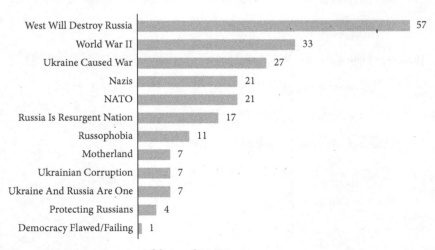

Figure 6.2 Narratives in Additional 19 Documents

STRATEGIC NARRATIVES AND THE WAR IN UKRAINE 151

to use the English documents in order to analyze language aimed at the American audience.

There was also an emphasis on the "Russia as a resurgent great nation" narrative, with seventeen mentions. There were only minor references to protecting Russians (four mentions, typically in the context of Ukraine), and only one mention that could be linked to the concept that democracy is flawed and failing. Thus, the overwhelming message was that of the West as the existential enemy of Russia. The idea of the NATO peril grew and was mentioned specifically as a threat to Russia twenty-one times throughout the documents. Russophobia is mentioned eleven times in the nineteen documents.

In these documents, Putin continued to emphasize the idea that Ukraine and Russia are one people, which was mentioned seven times. In the nineteen documents, statements that Ukraine itself was responsible for the violence were made twenty-seven times by Putin. Nazis and Nazism also were referenced, often in historical context, twenty-one times. Conspicuous by its absence was any mention of Russia's military invasion and total war on Ukraine. Instead of the current war, Putin constantly referenced World War II, which the Russians often call the Great Patriotic War (eight specific references to this phrase). Overall, there were thirty-three mentions of World War II, often in the context of commemoration, and seven references to the Russian "motherland."

While the notion of one great Slavic people and the myth that Russians and Ukrainians are one—an idea strongly rejected by Ukrainians—fits with long-term Russian narratives, the insistence on reunification strikes a new note. While suggesting that Russia protects Russians no matter where they live is a familiar Russian strategic narrative, the notion that Ukrainians are really Russians is a more recent interpretation that Putin makes clear in his July 2021 article. It is a departure from a rational, strategic narrative into more what analysts such as Pomerantsev (2014) would consider to be the construction of an aspirational world that is not based on reality.

Putin ascribes resistance to Russian rule in Ukraine to "neo-Nazi" forces and the Ukrainian leadership, as well as the machinations of the United States, NATO, and the West. He does not acknowledge that the death and violence in Ukraine are caused by the military invasion by Russia itself. It is a breathtaking example of omission and misdirection; so blatant that it's clear that Putin has no concern about ground truth. This transcends the notion of disinformation, propaganda, or even "fake news": Putin is writing about

152   SEEING RED

a world that does not exist and denying that the war is happening because Russia invaded the country.

In translating Putin's statements into strategic narratives, we should consider three issues. First, Putin is pulling at threads of collective memory and understanding of history that would resonate with much of the Russian population. For example, one of the most powerful shared memories for Russians is their victory in World War II. What is left out of this narrative, however, is that the Russians initially cooperated with the Nazis in the 1939 Molotov-Ribbentrop Pact. Second, the Russians are creating an alternative reality. Third, Putin is looking in a distorted mirror to accuse the Ukrainians of doing things that the Russians are perpetrating themselves. For example, the people carrying out the violence against Ukrainians are not Westerners or neo-Nazis—they are Russian troops, who invaded the country in 2014.

Thus, Putin is ascribing to all three of the ways that strategic narrative plays out in the Russian environment. First, he is invoking particular history and symbols that resonate with a sense of Russian nationalism. Second, he's lying, both by omission and by accusing the Ukrainian officials of being in league with the Nazi-led West and manufacturing anti-Russian sentiment. Third, he is constructing a world as he would like it to be. An important question is whether these narratives are finding any traction in the West. Below, we consider both messages about neo-Nazis and NATO, finding that complaints about NATO garner more debate and discussion than claims of neo-Nazis controlling Ukraine.

Does Anyone Aside from Putin Really Think There Are Nazis in Ukraine?

In an earlier study (Oates et al. 2022), we used a system devised by VAST-OSINT,[2] an automated data ingestion and enrichment system that gathered material from global sources, to analyze the spread of the neo-Nazi story about Ukraine. We tested the resonance of the framing of the Ukrainian Azov regiment as evidence that there were Nazis in Ukraine. Russia has exploited stories of the Azov regiment, in which some members have used symbols with links to Nazism or made statements that resonate with the far right (for a detailed history of the Azov regiment, see Umland 2019).

---

[2] Oates was an adviser to VAST.

The VAST system used a combination of natural language processing and network analysis to detect similar stories in the online sphere. First, VAST identified 28,522 online domains in mid-August 2022 that presented information on Russia's invasion of Ukraine. The system identified 1,084 domains in the Russian language and 25,343 domains in English. VAST identified a corpus of 317,625 stories across these domains. Unsurprisingly, in a general query about information on the Russian invasion of Ukraine in the U.S. media ecosystem, major news sites, particularly *The New York Times*, dominated in terms of estimated visits.

In looking specifically for stories about the Azov regiment, VAST identified clusters of stories about the regiment that were promoted by Russian outlets by starting with the keyword "Azov." The VAST system retrieved stories from January 31 to July 11, 2022. The system returned ninety-three matches of unique URLs for the query, ranging from strong hits that found matching content on twelve different websites to less resonant results that found examples of Azov Nazi stories that appeared on only one or two websites. While all of the stories identified shared the same linguistic origins, stories about the Azov regiment and Nazis appeared at different locations at different times. The average lifecycle of an online story about Azov Nazis was 6.2 days.

The most resonant story in terms of linguistic match and spread was launched on Gateway Pundit on March 3, 2022, with the headline "They May Want to Take a Step Back and Reevaluate: Israel Is Arming Neo-Nazi Group in Ukraine" (Hoft 2022b). This was first circulated on a pro-Trump website and then was repeated on ten different websites. Because the VAST database is proprietary, we will not list the specific website addresses but instead characterize the nature of the websites through human analysis. All the URLs that shared this story were right-wing websites that also were engaged with conspiracy theories (such as Biden was not elected in 2020 or that COVID vaccines are a plot to control humans). This echoes findings from Starbird (2017) and Benkler et al. (2018), with the latter's work on "networked propaganda" that found shared conspiracy theories among groups of outlets online.

Other related stories in the search claimed that the United States is a "headquarters for 'Nazi death cult' of bioweapons war criminals," more accusations that Israel is linked to Ukraine's neo-Nazi movement, that a Ukrainian TV host quoted a Nazi war criminal in an "impassioned call to kill Russian children," and many stories that mention the Azov regiment uniforms that had

154 SEEING RED

symbols associated with Nazism. Thematically, these stories often link the United States to Ukraine in general and specifically claim that the United States supports neo-Nazis in Ukraine (such as by funding or training the Azov regiment). For example, these headlines reflect these themes: "This Is the Real, Americanized, Nazi-Dominated, Ukraine" (Zuesse 2018) and "EXCLUSIVE: FBI Documents Uncovered that Tie Americans to 'Neo-Nazi' Azov Battalion in Ukraine" (Hoft 2022a).

In our study, these stories tended to recycle among right-wing or conspiratorial websites but failed to gain traction outside this bubble. This chapter does not analyze whether these right-wing websites are run by the Russian government or even funded by them. Earlier research suggests that right-wing sites often use Russian propaganda because it reflects their worldview and is a vector to attack liberal democracy (Oates et al. 2020). For example, the website for Sputnik only appears as the origin of Azov Nazi stories four times in this corpus and amplifies specific stories only five times in the period searched. The broader work of spreading these stories in the English online sphere appears to be done by the right-wing conspiratorial websites for the most part rather than Russian outlets such as Sputnik or RT.

While the VAST analysis suggests that particularly outrageous conspiracy claims tend to circulate in a limited corner of the digital space, we were interested in whether the general idea of Nazis in Ukraine held any sway among prominent U.S. right-wing sites. Using the Steno software described in Chapter 5, we scraped a range of right-wing sites for the first three months of 2022 and then created a data set including all articles that contained references to "Ukraine" and any variation of "Nazi" (including Nazis, neo-Nazi, Nazism). We analyzed forty-seven stories from Breitbart, twenty-four from Infowars, twenty-one from Fox News, seventeen from Newsmax, five from *Daily Wire*, three from One America News Network (OANN), and two from the *Daily Caller*.

The Breitbart, Fox, Newsmax, and *Daily Wire* articles did not unquestionably echo Putin's neo-Nazi narrative. Yet, the articles we analyzed often directly quoted Putin's claims about Nazis in Ukraine with little effort to provide evidence that the narrative was false. Infowars, however, displayed much closer fidelity to the Kremlin narrative. Infowars published several articles claiming that Ukraine has become increasingly fascist since the Euromaidan revolution. Despite the Ukrainian president being the Jewish descendant of Holocaust survivors, Infowars also claimed that Volodymyr Zelenskyy is

STRATEGIC NARRATIVES AND THE WAR IN UKRAINE   155

supporting Nazi military groups to fight the war with Russia. Infowars also echoed the claims about Nazis by using the story of the Azov regiment.

Our findings highlight the variation found on sites that could be described as "right-wing." As the Ad Fontes Media analysis shows (discussed in Chapter 2, see Adfontes n.d.), although both Foxnews.com and Infowars have a measurable political bias to the right, Infowars is labeled as "Hyper-Partisan Right" while the Fox News website falls between "Skews Right" and "Strong Right." The difference in their level of reliability is much greater: According to the Ad Fontes scale, Foxnews.com is labeled as "analysis or wide variation in reliability," while Infowars falls below propaganda into the category of "contains misleading information" (from analysis as of April 30, 2023, on Ad Fontes).

Infowars, which lost a libel case to the parents in the Sandy Hook school shooting by promoting the lie that the shooting was staged, promotes many conspiracies and is a hub for disinformation online. As a result, it is not surprising to find the anti-Ukraine Nazi rhetoric there, not least because our earlier research found Infowars has republished bylined material from Sputnik (Oates et al. 2021). It is impossible to tell from the content alone, however, whether this is about promoting conspiracy theories that would attract its alt-right audience or due to an admiration for Russian actions. But our research found relatively little resonance with Putin's neo-Nazi claims about Ukraine across right-wing news sites in general.

The other issue is the sheer volume of the repetition of Russian claims of neo-Nazis in Ukraine and explosion of mentions of alleged neo-Nazis in Ukraine in the mainstream U.S. media since the 2022 invasion. We used two databases (Factiva and Nexis Uni) to search the full content of *The New York Times*, *The Washington Post*, and *The Wall Street Journal* for both the decade prior to the invasion and for the period from January 1, 2022, to March 31, 2023. In the ten years prior to the invasion (January 1, 2012, to December 31, 2021), we found 156 mentions of neo-Nazis along with the words "Russia," "Ukraine," and "war" for an average of about 1.3 mentions per month across all three news outlets. In the fifteen months just before and after the 2022 invasion, we found 339 mentions at a rate of 22.6 per month.

Due to the keyword choices, most of these mentions were about neo-Nazis in Ukraine, although there were some that were not relevant (such as references to a neo-Nazi party in Sweden or mentions of neo-Nazis in the United States who supported either side in the war). There were also 168 mentions of the Azov battalion, although there was often a counterclaim that either Azov was no longer using Nazi symbolism or that it was not in any way representative of the Ukrainian army or society as a whole.

However, a common mention of neo-Nazism in the context of the Ukrainian war was quoting Putin or other Russian officials who claimed Ukraine had a "neo-Nazi" regime. These claims were often debunked as in this *Times* article on March 3, 2022 (Thompson and Alba 2022): "As the invasion neared, Russia falsely claimed that it was responding to Ukrainian aggression and liberating citizens from fascists and neo-Nazis. And since the assault began, Russia made baseless claims that Ukrainians had indiscriminately bombed hospitals and killed civilians."

At other times, however, the neo-Nazi claims are simply stated, apparently as though the claim was so ridiculous it did not need to be refuted, as in this *Post* article on February 28, 2022 (O'Grady et al. 2022): "As Moscow's vastly superior air, naval and ground forces dug deeper into the country, Russian President Vladimir Putin appeared bent on regime change, calling on Ukraine's armed forces to 'take power' from Ukraine's democratically elected leaders, whom he called 'drug addicts and neo-Nazis.'"

After the end of the period for this analysis, the *Times* ran a story on June 7, 2023, with the headline "Nazi Symbols on Ukraine's Front Lines Highlight Thorny Issues of History" (Gibbons-Neff 2023) that highlighted the conundrum for journalists covering accusations or alleged evidence of neo-Nazism in Ukraine. The article addressed the presence of military patches and other symbols that seemed to echo Nazism appearing on Ukrainian uniforms. While Ukrainian officials typically defend these symbols as independent of the Nazi past, they also work to keep them out of the international eye. What might be an unfortunate convergence of symbolism or even isolated echoes of Nazism is a dangerous issue for Ukrainians as they seek to maintain Western support: "So far, the imagery has not eroded international support for the war. It has, however, left diplomats, Western journalists and advocacy groups in a difficult position: Calling attention to the iconography risks playing into Russian propaganda. Saying nothing allows it to spread" (Gibbons-Neff 2023).

Why Not Just Blame NATO?

The research above suggests that while Russians refer to Nazis a lot, the conspiracy does not attract significant debate and discussion in the United States.

STRATEGIC NARRATIVES AND THE WAR IN UKRAINE   157

Instead, a major grievance of the Russian state about the false claim that there were 'broken promises' that NATO would not expand eastward after the collapse of the Berlin Wall is covered more seriously in the U.S. news. While most Americans are perhaps even shakier on NATO history than the history of Nazism, an argument based on a broken agreement might find more traction than a claim about neo-Nazis with no real evidence aside from isolated use of questionable Nazi symbols by one Ukrainian military group.

It's important to note the 'broken promises' story about NATO is not true because it shows how historical inaccuracies can be deployed in a propaganda narrative to propagate disinformation. In a 2009 research article entitled "The Myth of a No-NATO-Enlargement Pledge to Russia," Harvard historian Mark Kramer reviewed U.S., German, and Soviet records to find there were no promises made to the Soviets about NATO's expansion in 1990 beyond a discussion of limiting NATO presence in East Germany after German reunification. Kramer notes that much of the controversy stems from a few diplomatic conversations held in February 1990, in which Soviet officials were concerned that East Germany would become part of NATO as a result of the reunification of East and West Germany (2009, 45). Even at the time, U.S. officials pointed out that once German reunification was complete—a move that the Soviets reluctantly agreed to as the East German regime collapsed—it would be impossible to dictate international alliances within a single country and West Germany was already a NATO member.

While Mikhail Gorbachev and other Soviet leaders worried over the reunification of Germany and the enlargement of NATO within a single existing NATO member, there was no consideration of any other Eastern European countries joining NATO: "The declassified records from all sides thus confirm that at no point . . . was the question of NATO enlargement beyond Germany ever discussed" (Kramer 2009, 51). Kramer noted that no one in Moscow demanded or received an "assurance" that no additional Eastern European countries would ever be allowed to join NATO (p. 51). This was not due to cunning negotiations on the part of the West; rather, it was because it was a completely unthinkable concept for the Soviets at that time that the communist collapse would spread farther than East Germany. The Soviet collapse soon accelerated and radically changed the political landscape.

Roughly fifteen years later, Russian officials were claiming that the entry of its former satellite states in Eastern Europe would "violate a solemn 'pledge' made by the governments of West Germany and the United States in 1990 not to bring any Communist states into NATO" (Kramer, 2009, 39).

158   SEEING RED

This was complicated by inaccurate claims by many American officials, including a former U.S. ambassador to the Soviet Union in 1990, that there had been promises made about no countries east of Germany being allowed to join NATO (p. 40). While other U.S. officials pushed back against the alleged promise, Russian officials have continued to insist there were Western promises to limit NATO membership. As noted below, these claims often go unchallenged.

NATO tracks and debunks Russian disinformation about the organization, which is a military alliance between twenty-nine European countries (as of September 2023), the United States, and Canada. It was founded in 1949 as an alliance against the Soviet bloc and pledges mutual support if one member is invaded. While Ukraine has never been a serious candidate for membership, Finland and Sweden have both applied for membership since the 2022 invasion, and Finland had joined as of late 2023. It is useful that the NATO analysis divides the false claims into different categories, making it easier to map these accusations onto broader Russian strategic narratives (see Table 6.1). A review of the claims shows that they fit mostly within the "West is out to destroy Russia" strategic narrative. There is also the element of Russia as a resurgent nation in that Russia is arguing for its right to dominate the region, as well as some notion of protecting Russians outside of Russia in the concerns about NATO in former Soviet states with large ethnic Russian populations.

Two elements of the list in Table 6.1 are notable: They are consistent, and they are not based on facts. NATO provides information debunking these claims, in particular by pointing out that NATO enlargement is not an existential threat to Russia. While it is understandable that there would be contention over influence and control over former Soviet states and Eastern Europe, Russia consistently and falsely claims that there were guarantees that NATO would not expand eastward after the collapse of the Berlin Wall.

However, as Entman's theory of cascading activation suggests, it is not whether the facts support your claim, it is whether the claim resonates with your target population and is not significantly challenged by effective counterclaims. In the case of NATO, Russian claims about NATO's alleged duplicity would have fallen into a void of American indifference prior to the 2022 large-scale invasion of Ukraine. Our earlier attempt to study how Russia's framing of NATO was echoed in the U.S. media was stymied by a lack of American coverage of NATO prior to the 2022 invasion. Little was written about NATO in the U.S. news after the end of the Kosovo conflict

STRATEGIC NARRATIVES AND THE WAR IN UKRAINE 159

Table 6.1 NATO tracking Russian myths about NATO

Theme	False claims
NATO as a "threat"	NATO's presence in the Baltic region is dangerous NATO missile defense threatens Russian security NATO is aggressive and a threat to Russia NATO enlargement threatens Russia
Promises and pledges	NATO nuclear sharing and nuclear exercises violate the Non-Proliferation Treaty NATO's enhanced forward presence violates the NATO-Russia Founding Act NATO promised Russia it would not expand after the Cold War
NATO's cooperation with Russia	By suspending practical cooperation with Russia, NATO undermines security
NATO enlargement	Russia has the right to demand a guarantee that Ukraine and Georgia will not join NATO NATO has bases all around the world
NATO and its attitude to Russia	NATO whips up 'hysteria' over Russian exercises NATO is a U.S. geopolitical project NATO has tried to isolate or marginalize Russia NATO should have been disbanded after the end of the Cold War
NATO's operations	NATO's operation in Afghanistan was a failure NATO's operation over Libya was illegitimate NATO's operation over Kosovo was illegitimate

Source: North Atlantic Treaty Organization 2023.

(1998–1999) in which NATO intervened. There was some NATO news coverage during the Trump administration as he threatened to remove the United States from the alliance. But it did not rise to any prominence in the U.S. news agenda.

American interest in NATO increased sharply with the Russian invasion of Ukraine in 2022. According to Google Trends, searches for both "NATO" and "Russo-Ukrainian war" exploded in February 2022. At the same time, news interest in NATO in the United States increased significantly. A search of *The New York Times* on Nexis Uni (a database of major U.S. news sources) for "NATO" shows 8,059 stories over the ten-year period from January 1, 2011, through December 31, 2020, or about sixty-nine stories a month. In contrast, the *Times* carried 328 stories in a single month with the keyword "NATO" in February 2022. Volume remained high in the *Times* in the first year of the full-scale war: From March 1, 2022, to March 1, 2023, the *Times* published 2,207 stories with the term "NATO," at a rate of 184 per month (according to Nexis Uni).

Hill and Stent note that Putin's attacks on NATO and argument that NATO has forced Russia to invade Ukraine in order to protect Russian sovereignty have "won a variety of adherents, from prominent academics to Pope Francis, who said in June 2022 that the Ukrainian war was 'perhaps somehow provoked'" (2022, 114). This type of victim-blaming is disappointing at best and dangerous at worst, as it suggests a lack of knowledge about Russia or even the history of international relations. Another element of Russian rhetoric has been to threaten nuclear strikes, particularly in response to any actions from NATO. According to Bollfrass and Herzog, Moscow issued about twenty "nuclear signals" in the first ten weeks of the invasion of Ukraine as well as raised the alert level of the Russian nuclear arsenal (2022, 7). Although it is beyond the scope of this study, nuclear threat is another useful way to gain attention from the media and the public. It is also linked to NATO, which is focused on nuclear deterrence.

We were curious to see if blaming NATO messaging was repeated by U.S. media or whether there was a more measured debate about the role of Western influence in the global sphere. To track the resonance of the Russian narrative that blames NATO expansion for the war in Ukraine, we analyzed specific coverage that mentioned the phrase "NATO expansion" along with the keywords "Russia," "Ukraine," and "war" in news articles and opinion pieces in *The New York Times*, *The Washington Post*, and *The Wall Street Journal*. We chose these media outlets as three influential actors covering foreign affairs from the American perspective. For the period from January 1, 2022, to March 31, 2023, the search returned seventy-nine articles in the *Times*, sixty-eight in the *Post*, and nineteen in the *Journal* after filtering for duplicates and nontraditional formats such as podcast transcripts. We used both the Factiva and Nexis Uni databases to retrieve the material.

This sample represents only a small part of the widespread coverage of Russia's 2022 invasion of Ukraine. We narrowed the coverage to include only pieces that specifically mentioned "NATO expansion," as that is the crux of Putin's narrative that blames NATO for Russia's decision to invade Ukraine. We included news and opinion pieces given that both forms contribute to public knowledge, although opinion pieces are less likely to follow the balance and objectivity norms of U.S. journalism. However, we would expect elite news outlets to vet contributions for opinion pieces for accuracy and accept opinion pieces written by people with significant expertise.

We created a coding scheme to measure several aspects of the coverage, including statements that indicated NATO expansion was responsible for the Russian decision to invade Ukraine; that NATO expansion was *not* responsible for the Russian decision to invade; the paradox that the Russian invasion actually strengthened NATO; and alternative explanations for why Russia chose to invade Ukraine. We also looked for mention of specific words, such as "Nazi" and all its variants (i.e., neo-Nazi, Nazism, etc.). The coding was carried out by one author (Oates) using NVivo qualitative analysis software.

The unit of analysis was a coherent mention in a segment of text, typically a paragraph, although in coding sometimes contrasting sentences within a paragraph were coded separately (such as in the rare instances when blame was attributed to NATO, but then a counter-argument was introduced in the same paragraph to say that NATO was not the cause of the war). In other cases, two or more paragraphs were coded as a single unit because the meaning was lost if they were separated (such as the introduction of an expert and then a quote from the expert in the next paragraph). This means that one article could have many coded items.

Overwhelmingly, all three media outlets amplified Russia's claim that NATO expansion was responsible for its decision to launch a widespread invasion of Ukraine (see Figure 6.3). Across 166 stories in the three outlets, there were 325 segments that stated the Russian argument that NATO expansion triggered the need for Russia to invade Ukraine. There were only

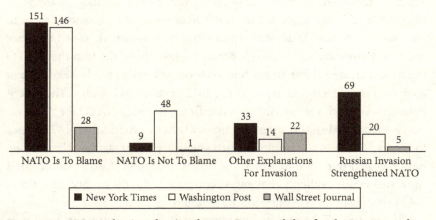

Figure 6.3 U.S. Media Articles Attributing Responsibility for the Invasion of Ukraine

162 SEEING RED

fifty-eight mentions of the idea that NATO expansion could not be held responsible. In other words, Putin's strategic narrative dominated the coverage, mentioned more than five times as often as the counter-narrative.

Here is an example of how coverage echoed Putin's fear-of-NATO narrative, from the *Times* on May 13, 2022 (Sanger 2022):

> And in expanding NATO to 32 members, soon with hundreds of additional miles of border with Russia, is the military alliance helping ensure that Russia could never again mount a vicious, unprovoked invasion? Or is it only solidifying the divide with an isolated, angry, nuclear-armed adversary that is already paranoid about Western "encirclement"?

However, other statements that mentioned Putin's NATO-blame narrative were more tempered, as in this opinion piece in the *Times* on May 4, 2022 (Bokat-Lindell 2022):

> NATO itself also needs to clarify its objectives, what it is willing to compromise on and how, argues Rajan Menon, a senior research fellow at the Saltzman Institute of War and Peace Studies at Columbia University. Does NATO want to maintain sanctions indefinitely to diminish Russia's power, or are there conditions it could meet to lift them? "It is within Putin's power to wind down this war," he writes, "but what NATO does matters as well."

The most balanced coverage overall came from the *Post*, although statements blaming NATO expansion for the war still dominated by a ratio of three to one (see Figure 6.3). Statements from Putin were repeated, joined by other Russian, European, and even U.S. officials who echoed the idea that NATO expansion created either an existential threat to Russia or at least enough of an appearance of a threat to justify the 2022 invasion of Ukraine. The lack of balance was much more striking in the *Times*: Blaming NATO for the invasion is mentioned almost seventeen times as often as claims that NATO is not to blame. The *Journal* sample is much smaller, yet it is striking that coding only revealed one time in which the notion that NATO expansion caused the invasion was explicitly challenged, compared with the twenty-eight times NATO expansion was blamed for the invasion.

Other anti-NATO coverage came from news of China's support for Russia and anti-NATO rhetoric as in this *Times* story on March 20, 2022: "China's regular denunciations of NATO make European officials bristle. In its position paper, China said 'the security of a region should not be achieved by strengthening or expanding military blocs'—a statement that supports Mr. Putin's claim that he had to invade Ukraine because of threats that included NATO expansion" (Wong and Erlanger 2022). An opinion piece in the *Times* on February 28, 2022, highlights a quote by China spokeswoman Hua Chunying that more graphically addresses the notion of threat: "When the U.S. drove five waves of NATO expansion eastward all the way to Russia's doorstep and deployed advanced offensive strategic weapons in breach of its assurances to Russia, did it ever think about the consequences of pushing a big country to the wall?" (Li 2022).

It is not at all surprising that the news outlets would repeat Putin's justification for the war and that this would focus on NATO expansion given that all the articles for this study contained the phrase "NATO expansion." What is surprising, given that a key tenet of U.S. journalism is representing different sides to a story, is how seldom in these articles that NATO expansion as the key motivation for the 2022 invasion was challenged.

However, it is not as if these three news outlets just parroted the idea that NATO expansion caused the war; the outlets also provided alternative explanations for the war or discussed Russian history and grievances with more nuance. While the *Journal* had less coverage overall mentioning NATO expansion in light of the war, it was more likely to mention alternative explanations, such as Putin's desire to hold on to power through military incursions or his fear of Ukrainian democratization (see Figure 6.3). In this sense, the *Journal* coverage was somewhat more balanced. The *Times* and the *Post* were less likely to balance their coverage with other explanations for the invasion (see Chart 6.3). The *Times* mentioned alternative explanations for Russian aggression against Ukraine thirty-three times (in seventy-nine articles) and the *Post* fourteen times (in sixty-eight articles).

While it was relatively rare in these *Times* stories to counter Putin's claims of the NATO threat with rebuttals or counter-narratives, a notable exception was the coverage of a speech by President Biden on February 15, 2022: "'The United States and NATO are not a threat to Russia,' he said, adding 'You are not our enemy'" (Troianovski and Shear 2022). A *Post* op-ed on February 18, 2022, said that preventing Ukraine from joining NATO was "only one dimension of Putin's revisionist agenda. Even if Biden and his NATO allies wanted to offer that concession, Putin won't be satiated. He will press on to undo the liberal international order for as long as he remains in power" (McFaul 2022).

164   SEEING RED

In addition, the *Times* ran a column by Hillary Clinton on March 27, 2022, that reflected that the late Madeline Albrecht, former U.N. ambassador and secretary of state, would have "rejected the criticism, renewed recently, that NATO's expansion needlessly provoked Russia and is to blame for its invasion of Ukraine." *Times* opinion writer Ross Douhat addressed the issue of Putin's reliance on the NATO threat narrative in an article that showcased four *Times* opinion writers on March 2, 2022, saying the emphasis on the threat of NATO was resurgent due to the abject failure of Ukraine accepting that they needed to be "liberated" from an alleged neo-Nazi regime: "So he [Putin] has to climb back from that second narrative to the first more reasonable, 'I don't want NATO in my backyard' narrative" (Garcia-Navarro et al. 2022).

Despite some critique of Putin's insistence that NATO was to blame for the war, one should consider why these three elite news organizations so often repeated the narrative that NATO expansion is the cause for Russia to invade Ukraine with few consistent counter-narratives or little correction. The existential fear engendered by NATO expansion through the 1990s and beyond for Russia is certainly one theory to explain Russian aggression, although not one shared by many mainstream scholars who study Russia. Rather, Putin's complaints about NATO expansion rest on false assumptions about promises that were never made and ignore the fact that at one point Russia and Putin cooperated fairly well with the West (with even some officials claiming that Russia itself should join NATO). Why are these outlets so clearly echoing this Russian strategic narrative with little balance?

There are several factors that could explain why mainstream U.S. media outlets tend to parrot a Russian strategic narrative that NATO is "to blame" for Russia's decision to invade Ukraine. Much of this could be a lack of knowledge about three key points: the diplomatic history that the West did not promise to limit NATO; that nations should have a right to self-determination; and that Putin constantly lies. In addition, these news outlets are overly reliant on a small set of commentators who amplify Putin's narratives, including those who have limited knowledge of Russia or Putin.

For example, there was much reliance on a single source who supported the "threat of NATO" justification for Russia's invasion of Ukraine: John Mearsheimer, a political scientist who authored a 2014 article entitled "Why the Ukraine Crisis is the West's Fault: The Liberal Delusions That Provoked Putin," is mentioned or quoted twenty-three times in this content across the three outlets. Meanwhile, Fiona Hill, a former U.S. National

STRATEGIC NARRATIVES AND THE WAR IN UKRAINE 165

Security Council official who is known as one of the key experts on Russia in the West, is quoted fifteen times, much less often across this coverage. Thus, Mearsheimer's views, which support Putin's argument that international alliances and actions are key in motivating countries to go to war, are amplified as a rationale for invading Ukraine. However, there are a range of scholars and analysts who could also offer insight into this specific case.

While earlier chapters of this book explored how Russians exploited discord in U.S. politics in order to sow propaganda, they can push their narrative on NATO into a void of relative ignorance. Thoughtful pieces by Hillary Clinton and forceful statements by former U.S. ambassador to Russia Michael McFaul that push back against the illogic of blaming NATO are part of the *Times* coverage as noted above (Clinton 2022; Wong and Jakes 2022). But as McFaul states, even a false narrative about NATO is successful for Putin because it puts NATO on the agenda in a way that it hasn't been before: "'Everybody's talking NATO expansion. . . . Suddenly we're debating this issue that wasn't even an issue. That's a great advantage to him [Putin]'" (Wong and Jakes 2022).

One of the most interesting points in the coverage is that by attacking Ukraine, Putin reinvigorated and strengthened NATO, to the point that now that Russia shares a much longer border with NATO because Finland joined the alliance. This does serve as a counterpoint against the argument that NATO "caused" the invasion, instead providing "the geopolitical equivalent of CPR for NATO" (Meaney 2022). The observation that the Russian invasion strengthened NATO appeared sixty-nine times in the *Times* coverage, twenty times in the *Post*, and five times in the *Journal* for a total of ninety-four mentions (see Figure 6.3). Yet, the connection was often not made for readers: Putin's key reason for invading Ukraine makes no sense because he has *strengthened* the alliance that Russia allegedly finds an existential threat. This point is often sometimes explicitly made in the articles, such as in this May 13, 2022, *Times* article (Sanger 2022) reporting that the United States

has blamed Mr. Putin for bringing NATO expansion upon himself by invading a neighbor. Jen Psaki, the White House press secretary, loosely quoted Finland's president, Sauli Niinisto, who made clear that Ukraine had forced the Finns to think differently about their security.

"You caused this," Mr. Niinisto said of Mr. Putin. "Look at the mirror."

166   SEEING RED

However, the connection was not always made so explicitly. And, as the coding results suggest, often there is no meaningful pushback against the NATO-blame narrative in many news and opinion pieces.

Nor do the stories engage with some important facts about history and even sometimes misrepresent history altogether. The content analysis found eighteen times (thirteen in the *Times* and five in the *Journal*) that diplomatic history was misrepresented, mostly by conflating the narrow promises made about East Germany in the late Soviet period with a nonexistent promise about limiting NATO expansion in general. What is perhaps most strikingly absent from the coverage is a discussion of Soviet repressive rule throughout Eastern Europe and the former Soviet republics in the wake of World War II. The articles rarely discuss the history of the alliance grounded in justifiable fears of nuclear war in the Cold War era.

While some of these errors were made in opinion pieces, media outlets should still vet opinion pieces for historical accuracy. The *Times* worked at correcting the record on NATO in general with an article on January 10, 2022, about how Russians use an inaccurate recall of history to claim that NATO promised not to expand (Baker 2022). However, Putin's NATO assertion is reported so often in so many articles that the attempt to correct the record will probably fail. There is a subtler and historically accurate discussion about how while Russia was initially receptive to American aid (and received substantial support) in its early post-Soviet years, the desire to turn against Western influence and its global dominance to take a different path became stronger over time. But that is by no means the same as promising to limit NATO expansion, which never happened in the way it is often characterized by Russian officials (and sometimes even by Americans).

Nor do the *Times* articles seriously engage with what would be a more nuanced and historically accurate argument: Russia was unable to achieve world domination through economic or political means so has chosen military adventurism. This idea arguably is far more based in reality. But instead of a discussion of the politics of limited war, the reader is generally presented with the idea that a military alliance such as NATO is such a 'threat' that a country such as Russia is 'forced' to go to war.

An attentive reader could glean important historical points from the coverage. There are four mentions in *Times* articles and one in the *Journal* about the 1994 Budapest Memorandum. Russia signed this memorandum that guaranteed territorial integrity for Ukraine, Belarus, and Kazakhstan in return for those countries decommissioning their Soviet era nuclear arms. If one wishes to make an argument based on former treaties, Russia is violating an actual treaty by invading Ukraine while they are complaining about non-existent NATO promises. However, this is rarely mentioned in the coverage.

In addition, while Putin complains about the threat of NATO, Russia invaded non-NATO states, including Georgia in 2008 and Ukraine initially in 2014. It is Russia's actions, not the NATO alliance, that are actively destabilizing the region, which makes the notion that the 'threat' of having a U.S.-led security alliance justify the invasion of non-NATO countries illogical. This lack of logic is rarely discussed in the coverage of Putin's complaints about NATO expansion.

Another reason for a lack of counter-arguments is that they may be hard to grasp and require more nuanced understanding than that offered by the theories of realism, the concept that countries rationalize going to war to maximize their status and power in the international system. One of the most frustrating and puzzling aspects of understanding why Russia invaded Ukraine is that it makes little sense. In early 2022, Putin was presiding over a fairly strong economy, high approval ratings, and gains in territory in a limited war in Ukraine in which the international community was relatively uninvolved. Even if his blitzkrieg to Kyiv had succeeded instead of showcasing the weakness of the Russian military, subduing the Ukrainian population would take enormous effort. This seems particularly pointless as Russia already had illegally seized valuable oil and gas resources in Ukraine by occupying the Crimean Peninsula.

The key explanation that is left is one so unsettling that it is understandable why media outlets failed to highlight it, although there is some mention of it: Putin became personally obsessed with conquering Ukraine to restore his sense of injured pride at not being a major player in the international sphere. This is referenced occasionally in the NATO expansion coverage, although most observers acknowledge it is impossible to assess Putin's mental state or how much he personally is responsible for the decision to invade. This also creates problems for the social-responsibility function of the mass media: Why inculcate unfathomable fears in the general public? In particular, Putin and his officials sometimes threaten to deploy nuclear weapons, which is found twenty-seven times in this coverage by searching for the word "nuclear" and its variants.

If you look at the coverage as a whole, there is a great deal of nuance and in-depth information in these three media outlets, particularly in including a range of reasons for why Russia invaded Ukraine. However, by the constant repetition of Putin's claim that NATO expansion is a key reason for invading a peaceful neighboring country, this Russian propaganda narrative is significantly amplified. While U.S. journalism calls for balance, the sheer volume of attention given to a key Russian propaganda narrative is alarming.

In addition, it would appear that the outlets need to significantly widen their base of analysts and experts for discussion, given that they rely heavily on a single academic who supports the notion that NATO is a cause of the Ukrainian invasion. It would be more useful for the media audience to focus on the responsibility that lies with the Russians for the invasion, rather than attempting to blame America and NATO for upholding the right to self-determination in Europe. In particular, highlighting how Russia's actions have made NATO more necessary than ever—a theme that is present in the coverage but not always linked to Russia's decisions to invade Ukraine—would serve readers better.

Covering Russian Lies and Calling Out Disinformation

The *Times* did cover the issue of disinformation, particularly in a March 21, 2022, story with the headline "For Putin, 'Truth' Is Just Another Front Line." This article directly addressed the paradox of trying to report on something that does not exist: "Using a barrage of increasingly outlandish falsehoods, President Vladimir V. Putin has created an alternative reality, one in which Russia is at war not with Ukraine but with a larger, more pernicious enemy in the West" (Myers and Thompson 2022). This was a useful and interesting story, but it is not the same as consistently highlighting Putin's disinformation.

This suggests that journalists might consider whether statements by the Russians about the war in Ukraine can be treated as news. Media outlets have different rules for treating statements that are considered outside the normal bounds of the political sphere (see the Chapter 2 discussion about the journalistic sphere of deviance). For example, statements by terrorist groups are often deemed illegitimate and are not covered, given that terrorists are killing innocent victims to garner attention for their political messages. News media should consider whether Putin and other Russian representatives fall into the same category as terrorists, whether the statements they make are made to inform or merely part of information warfare. If so, then elite media outlets such as the *Times*, the *Post*, and the *Journal* should limit the amplification of these statements because they are not part of the objectivity or balance called for by professional journalism.

This issue was highlighted by a statement from Senator Rand Paul, who said that while "there is no justification for Putin's war on Ukraine, it does not follow that there's no explanation for the invasion" (Blake 2022). While Rand was refuting the idea that he was calling into question Ukraine's right to self-determination, the point he highlights is that politicians—and the coverage of what they say—often conflate justification with the actual explanation of the forces at work in the Russian invasion of Ukraine. In echoing the idea that a fear of NATO encroachment is a legitimate reason to attack a neighboring country, journalists also contribute to turning *justifications* into *legitimate reasons* for readers. An article in the *Journal* quotes U.S. ambassador to Russia John Sullivan on why it is so difficult to report on Russian justifications for the war:

> As long as Russia perpetrates the fallacies that it needs to bomb Ukraine in self-defense and that the government in Kyiv is run by neo-Nazis committing genocide against ethnic Russians, there is no reason for Washington to grant access or seek it in Moscow. "It's hard to engage with people who say these things because they're so divorced from reality," he said.
>
> Sometimes leaders are mad. Sometimes they want you to think they're mad. Sometimes both.

Translating Putin's Rhetoric into Disinformation Warfare

How much do Putin's words matter? In an authoritarian media environment, the domestic media will echo these ideas throughout their coverage, which is particularly apparent on Russian state-run television. But this book is concerned with the ability of Putin's propaganda to influence American news rather than how Russians are selling the war in Ukraine to their domestic audience.

On the surface, Putin's turn toward claims of neo-Nazism and the history-defying conviction that Ukraine does not exist as a nation would not seem like the most promising choices. In the first place, Putin has developed enduring strategic narratives that have been built over decades. While each of these four narratives—failing democracy, a strong Russia, the West is out to

170 SEEING RED

get us, and protecting Russians—has some weaknesses, each also has some compelling strengths.

Playing on Russian nationalism and pride is a logical strategy and, indeed, most countries emphasize national pride as a way of asserting international authority. Attacking the United States on its record of self-serving interventionism also is a topic likely to find international support, particularly in the Global South. In the wake of Trump's rejection of democratic norms in the United States, democracy itself is ripe for attack. One aspect of Russian anti-West narratives, that NATO expansion 'caused' the war in Ukraine, has been relatively successful despite its lack of logic and truthfulness. Of course, the reality is that Russia invading Ukraine caused the war, nothing else.

There are compelling reasons why Putin chose to add certain elements to strategic narratives as he planned to launch a full-scale invasion of Ukraine. As Entman would argue in his cascading activation framework, a nation needs a strongly compelling and new meta-narrative, such as the "War on Terror," to mobilize a population to support invading another country. The Ukrainian invasion was an enormous escalation of the conflict Russia had been carrying out for eight years, and the Russian population needed a reason for that escalation. The change in narrative sent a clear signal that action would follow. Understanding strategic narrative—and how it is deployed in authoritarian states such as Russia prior to military action— would be a core benefit for security in the region. For example, how should we interpret Russian switches in narrative about the Baltic States or—even more ominously—nuclear strikes on the West?

To most of the American audience, the idea of neo-Nazis in Ukraine is absurd, not least because the Ukrainian president is Jewish. But there is logic here that would resonate with Russians, who have historic grievances against the actions of some Ukrainians during Nazi occupation. The key question about strategic narratives is not whether they are logical but whether they work.

Starbird's (2017) work demonstrating the resilience of conspiracy theories gives us important clues to understand the power of particular narratives. Putin's newer narratives about Ukraine stray into the realm of fantasy, although one can trace his tortured logic with a basic understanding of known Russian grievances about the West and Ukraine. But do they work? They have not brought him victory in Ukraine. Indeed, Hill and Stent note that strategic narratives can backfire, as the "more that Putin tries to erase the

Ukrainian national identity with bombs and artillery shells, the stronger it becomes" (2022, 114).

If Russians find these newer narratives speak to an enduring sense of grievance and nationalism, perhaps talking about how Ukrainians are neo-Nazis propped up by the U.S. state might have some traction. But is it enough to sustain a war effort on a par with the Great Patriotic War or even the War on Terror? That seems unlikely. It is even less likely to convince the world that Russia has any valid reason to attack its neighbor. The NATO grievance and claims of existential fears of the West find more resonance but ultimately are hard to sustain as an argument if you are doing the opposite of what you say. Making the claim that you need to protect yourself by attacking a neighbor should not be a compelling narrative.

On the one hand, it's fair to say that Putin's neo-Nazi narrative has not gained traction in the Western media, although the mentions of neo-Nazis in Ukraine in elite U.S. media skyrocketed as the war began. On the other hand, the Russian claim that the NATO alliance created such an existential threat to Russia that it felt compelled to attack Ukraine has garnered more significant attention and even debate in the elite U.S. media. As discussed above, these news outlets also provided excellent, in-depth coverage of Russian and American foreign affairs. Yet, should they be amplifying a key Russian strategic narrative to this extent?

This research demonstrates that Russia blaming NATO for the war—which is squarely on the shoulders of Russia itself—has gained if not credence, at least visibility in the public sphere in the United States. This matters enormously for the war of public opinion, particularly if blame is shifted to NATO then it would appear that responsibilities as well as resolutions would rest with NATO too. If members of Congress and members of the public start to support this Russian point of view, it would not be surprising to see support for the Ukrainians dwindle in a way that Russia would find greatly to its advantage. Russia may have performed poorly on the battlefield given its relative size and strength, but it would appear it is doing pretty well in the international propaganda war.

7

Conclusions

When we started this book, we set out with a fairly straightforward goal in mind: We wanted to test the presence of Russian propaganda in U.S. news. After decades of research on the Russian and Western media, we knew this was not a case of one-way influence from Russia to the United States. Rather, we found a much more complex web of disinformation that echoed between Russian strategic narratives and right-wing disinformation generated in the United States. In other words, it became a case of fellow travelers meeting in the media ecosystem rather than a foreign agent carrying out a solo mission of information warfare.

We started our discussion by talking about the two actors in this disinformation drama: Russia and the United States. In Chapter 2, we set out the significant challenges that face American journalism. Indeed, U.S. journalism is at a crisis point due to the failing economic model for news, the challenge for information dominance created by the digital sphere, and attacks on the democratic institution of the press from President Trump and others on the right. Although a crisis in American journalism is not new, Trump's election in 2016, the contentious 2020 election held while under COVID quarantine, and the Capitol insurrection all created profound challenges to U.S. democracy and media. Trust in media has declined steadily in the United States according to Gallup, falling to just 34 percent in 2022 (Brenan 2022). The United States ranks forty-two out of 180 countries on the Reporters Without Borders 2022 global media freedom index, and the organization notes while the United States was "once considered a model for press freedom and free speech, press freedom violations are increasing at a troubling rate" (Reporters Without Borders n.d.).

A failing media system in the United States opens the door to Russian propaganda. In order to highlight the flow of Russian propaganda into the U.S. media, we used the concept of strategic narratives. As strategic narratives are specific weapons in the struggle for information dominance on a global scale, it's important to define, analyze, and track them. Strategic narratives are not only the expression of how nations would wish to be viewed in the world,

Seeing Red. Sarah Oates and Gordon Neil Ramsay, Oxford University Press. © Oxford University Press 2024.
DOI: 10.1093/oso/9780197696422.003.0007

CONCLUSIONS 173

but they also signal the actions nations plan to take. Chapter 3 presented four core Russian strategic narratives: democracy is flawed and failing, the West and NATO are out to destroy Russia, Russia is a resurgent great nation, and Russia protects Russians no matter where they live. In Chapter 6, we presented newer narratives that Putin added to justify the wide-scale invasion of Ukraine in February 2022: Ukraine is awash with neo-Nazis, and that there is no such thing as Ukrainian nationhood.

Through the use of strategic narratives, we can consider how much the voice of Russia winds up in American news. Before Trump's election in 2016, there was almost no evidence of Russian influence on American news, even though RT was relatively popular for a propaganda outlet (Elswah and Howard 2020). However, significant evidence of Russian interference in the U.S. 2016 election led researchers and journalists to ask more probing questions about the role of Russian information strategy. While this book has not focused on social media, it was the Russian content and ads on social media platforms such as Facebook that attracted significant public attention in 2016. However, as analysts such as Jamieson (2018) note, the Russian hack-and-dump operation with the Democratic National Committee emails created far more damage for Clinton at a critical time in the campaign.

While the story about Clinton and the email scandal was an important moment in propaganda warfare with Russia, we were more interested in looking at the long-term effects of information warfare. Viewing isolated incidents in information warfare does not let us see the full nature of propaganda strategy. We chose to look at the possible penetration of the four key Russian strategic narratives into U.S. news. What we found was quite unnerving: The critical element was not anyone in the Kremlin, but a U.S. president aided by right-wing media outlets such as Fox News.

Along with the Russians, Trump broadcast the message that American democracy was flawed and failing. Trump attacked democratic institutions such as the media and elected officials, giving Russian outlets such as RT and Sputnik excellent fodder to promote their own anti-democratic narratives. As a result, Fox, RT, and Sputnik often promoted the same anti-democratic messages, especially when it came to talking about protests and amplifying fears about nebulous organizations such as Antifa. While Fox was attacking the Democrats and RT and Sputnik were attacking democracy writ large, the content was often very similar.

In addition, there was a curious convergence around promoting the idea of Russophobia, that there is an irrational hatred and fear of Russia in

174 SEEING RED

America. It's understandable why Russia would complain about this, but in the case of Fox and other right-wing outlets, Russophobia was a way to attack the Democrats. Again, even though the motivations might be different between Russian propaganda outlets and Fox, the content winds up looking remarkably similar.

The pivot around which this rotated was Trump. Fox supported Trump, in a way unprecedented among U.S. media outlets that allegedly adhere to the objectivity model. But Fox was not alone in this partisan rejection of journalistic practices. An array of right-wing media, such as Newsmax, also prioritized loyalty over scrutiny and were keen to continue supporting Trump even as he descended into propaganda warfare in the wake of his 2020 loss. Russian propaganda outlets promoted Trump because he espoused messages that supported their own strategic narratives, particularly the idea that democracy is flawed and failing. It was helpful that Trump also tended to broadcast positive messages about Russia. Even though Trump's motivation for praising Russia was primarily to deny Russiagate, it was still very useful for Russian propaganda. Interestingly, one of the central differences between Russian propaganda and Fox News was that Russian propaganda was more even-handed in its treatment of the two candidates in the 2020 election. As we discussed in Chapter 4, RT and Sputnik were more even-handed in their coverage of Trump and Biden than Fox.

There is no question that Trump's decision to reject the outcome of a free and fair election and encourage insurrection was one of the greatest gifts ever to Russian propaganda. As Chapter 5 demonstrates, RT and Sputnik used Trump's words and actions to show that U.S. democracy was failing. Again, we see the resonance between the way that Fox and other right-wing media covered Trump's actions and words and how Russian propaganda outlets covered him. We are aware that the motivations are different in this case: Russia wishes to end democracy, while Fox wished to support Trump. However, the outcome in terms of content is the same. This is a clear demonstration of the dangers of media outlets in a free system abandoning objectivity in the pursuit of audience share or political power. At the same time it threatened U.S. democracy from within, it created the perfect conduit for Russia to promote its own agenda in the U.S. media. During Trump's campaign against American democracy, Russia was able to join in the chorus with a full voice.

One could argue that ultimately democracy prevailed, and America demonstrated the resilience of a system with separation of powers. Despite the Capitol being overrun on January 6, 2021, order was quickly restored, although with some loss of life. The 2020 election results were validated, and President Biden was sworn in on schedule. Those who took part in the Capitol insurrection were arrested on a large scale, charged, and many have been convicted of their crimes and sentenced to long terms in prison. Trump himself faces numerous charges related to attempts to overthrow the 2020 election. This demonstrates the democratic principle that even the U.S. president is not above the law.

However, Trump's attacks on media and democracy have left significant battle scars in the United States. Many Republicans in Congress refused to validate the results of the 2020 elections or repudiate Trump or his anti-democratic movement. The majority of Republican voters continue to believe that the 2020 election was stolen (Murray 2022), and confidence in the integrity of elections now is divided sharply on partisan grounds (Kiderra 2022). It is not surprising that trust in the media now varies enormously along partisan lines: The Gallup survey cited above reported that while 70 percent of Democrats still trust the media, only 14 percent of Republicans say that they do (Brenan 2022). Despite the shock of the Capitol insurrection, Fox News host Tucker Carlson worked directly with Republicans in Congress to create an alternative representation of the events of January 6 (Mascaro and Amiri 2023). This shows a media outlet offering material assistance to a political party looking to rehabilitate its image.

Trump's ban on Facebook and Twitter was lifted by 2023, although he chose to stick with his own social media site called Truth Social for many months. He broke his silence on X (formerly Twitter) by posting his own mugshot from his arrest on state charges of election interference in the state of Georgia in August 2023. By early 2024, it was becoming more likely that Trump would run as the Republican candidate, raising the specter of new attacks on the U.S. media and free elections.

But in early 2022, the world's attention had moved from U.S. politics to Russian actions when Russia launched a large-scale invasion of Ukraine in February of that year. As Chapter 6 discusses, there was a shift in Russian strategic narratives that signaled an escalation of the attack on Ukraine. To a Western ear, conspiracy theories about neo-Nazis in Ukraine along with the bizarre notion that the Ukrainian people are really Russians might seem fantastical. A critical question is why Putin felt the need to add new narratives, given that the four existing Russian strategic narratives all could be applied to the rationale for an all-out war on Ukraine. While fears about Nazis in the near abroad would make more sense within a Russian context,

176   SEEING RED

they fall relatively flat on the international stage. Yet, an escalation of war generally calls for stronger strategic narratives that can motivate the population. At the same time, Russia has found more acceptance and less critical coverage of their complaints about NATO encroachment in leading U.S. newspapers.

Lessons Learned

What have we learned through this study? We began this research before COVID, before the 2020 election, before the Capital insurrection, and prior to Russia's full-scale invasion of Ukraine. The world has changed a great deal, but it's interesting to note that Russia has employed the same strategic narratives to a large degree throughout these massive shifts in geopolitics. In that way, it's relatively easy to study Russian propaganda because the core of it remains rather stable. This is in contrast to messaging in the United States, where over the same time period there were three presidential administrations and unprecedented use of disinformation by the Trump White House. Trump is the one U.S. president whose rhetoric has matched that of the Russian state in many ways.

While Russian propaganda and U.S. news could resemble each other, the reasons for this affinity are quite different. We were able to trace the coverage of the 2020 election and its violent aftermath in Russian content back to a key set of strategic narratives that attack democracy and promote Russian interests. At the same time, Fox content often also attacked American democratic institutions, supported Trump, and denigrated Biden. Its motivations were different from Kremlin strategists, but the coverage often looked the same. Thus, while Russia was attacking American democracy from afar, Fox was attacking American democracy from within. Fox and its audience would no doubt vehemently disagree with this conclusion. Rather, they would argue that they were trying to preserve America as they understood it by promoting Trump and denigrating the Democrats. But by attacking the institutions of democracy, specifically by undermining free media and elections, they were doing the same thing as our Russian adversaries.

This pattern continued with the news coverage of Stop the Steal. Again, disinformation and propaganda in the U.S. media system were anchored around Trump. Given that Trump was directly attacking American democracy,

Russian propaganda eagerly amplified these messages. As a result, this was a promising era for Russian propaganda, as the strategic narrative that democracy was flawed and failing was being played out within America itself. Given that the Russians have wished to undermine American democracy for decades, this juncture when messages from an American president and Russian propaganda dovetailed was indeed a successful moment for Russian strategic narratives.

Given the deep crisis in American democracy, it would seem that Russia would be content with its place in the world. However, Putin started sending signals in the summer of 2021 of a change in the narrative as it related to its ongoing invasion of Ukraine. Putin clearly signaled heightened justification for attacking Ukraine through emphasizing narratives about neo-Nazis and the complete destruction of the Ukrainian people. In other words, he articulated his desire to wipe Ukraine from the face of the Earth. By evoking the history of Nazism, he pulled on an important thread within Russian culture, but not one that had deep resonance on the world stage. Through the development and amplification of these narratives directly from the Russian president, we had a strong signal of an escalation of the war.

As a yardstick of state intentions, strategic narratives have proven to be useful tools. The theoretical work established by scholars such as Miskimmon et al. (2017), Szostek (2017), and others has allowed us to see the critical underpinnings of rhetorical strategy from countries. It's easy to be overwhelmed by public diplomacy and propaganda and hard to see how stories coalesce into compelling strategic narratives. However, when we flip the paradigm to look at the flow of content through the lens of strategic narrative, we are able to not only measure state intentions but also to visualize how these messages penetrate other media ecosystems. We also have a very effective measurement of change and intention in state information strategy, which is a useful signal of intended state action.

That is not to say that strategic narratives are a perfect science. Just as with framing theory, trying to delineate exactly what is a frame, what is a story, and what is a narrative is difficult. Ultimately, it is a balance between deductive reasoning that comes from understanding complex case studies, such as Russian politics and American elections, and inductive findings from the content itself. One way to characterize the study of strategic narratives is that it is a deeply iterative process. There were many occasions when we expected to find particular frames, stories, and narratives within

178 SEEING RED

the content, yet we were baffled. At other times, there were associations and patterns that emerged from the content that challenged our deductive reasoning.

Refining the Toolkit of Propaganda Analysis

It was not by design that this book used several different methods of analyzing content, both by humans and computers. Rather, we used an array of tools in an attempt to find what was best. If there is a particular methodological finding to report from this book, it is that we are still striving toward a system that usefully balances human content analysis with computer-aided systems. We explored analyzing text through the custom Steno software, Provalis QDA Miner, a system devised by MarvelousAI, the VAST commercial system, and others. While each of these systems contributed to the study, none could provide the full scope of data and tools to address our research. The availability of a range of automated analytical products provides opportunities for researchers, yet there is still a need for better-integrated tools to generate findings from large volumes of digital news.

As content analysis scholars, we returned to our roots in Chapter 6 with a qualitative analysis of Putin's speeches. While this is a relatively small amount of content—only 20 documents in the final analysis—Putin's words were central to establishing new strategic narratives and reinforcing old ones just before and after the wide-scale invasion of Ukraine. We also employed a close analysis of 166 articles from *The New York Times*, *The Washington Post*, and *The Wall Street Journal* to analyze how agenda-setting newspapers in the United States cover the framing of NATO as an existential threat to Russia. This helped us understand how regular news logic can wind up amplifying Russian propaganda—such as blaming NATO for the war in Ukraine—due to a repetition of Russian talking points without adequate challenge or contextualization. We used both automated content analysis and a qualitative review to show that the Russian conspiracy theory that neo-Nazis are running Ukraine is present in the U.S. media ecosystem but does not seem to attract serious engagement.

Overall, we found that while computational methods can definitely augment human content analysis, the power of these methods means that clear hypothesis formation and research design remain more important than ever. Any automated content analysis will stand or fall on the "garbage in/garbage

CONCLUSIONS 179

out" principle, and at present human expertise and oversight remain the most practical way to ensure quality control in content analysis.

Propaganda and News in 2024 and Beyond

In the post-Trump era, how much does the U.S. media system remain vulnerable to Russian propaganda? On the one hand, the Dominion lawsuit has revealed that Fox News promoted disinformation when it came to the 2020 election aftermath. There is also compelling evidence that Fox was pushing an anti-democratic narrative as it promoted Trump from the 2016 election forward. This raises a critical question about future American elections. Is the U.S. media system so broken that a major American news outlet such as Fox can carry out Russian-style propaganda? If so, has the U.S. media descended into a system in which both internal and external foes of democracy can manipulate it to destroy democracy itself?

Russia's 2022 invasion of Ukraine had significant consequences for the Kremlin's use of news media to project strategic narratives. RT America was dropped by U.S. satellite and cable providers, as well as digital platforms, at the beginning of March 2022 and promptly ceased production (Darcy 2022). The European Union banned the broadcast arms of RT and Sputnik on March 2, 2022, while the United Kingdom requested that social media platforms block access to content from the Russian outlets (Martin 2022). Russia's tit-for-tat banning of public access to Twitter, Facebook, and Instagram also closed off routes of information flow into and out of the country.

At first glance, this would suggest a reduction in the effectiveness of Russia's dissemination of propaganda. But there are still myriad ways for content produced by RT and Sputnik to reach audiences in those countries where access to the outlets is restricted. Russian officials continued to use Western social media to post disinformation and project the Russian state's view of the world. YouTube was still accessible in Russia in 2023, and while the platform blocked Russian state-funded media after the 2022 invasion, the Kremlin has been caught trying to post content and evade the ban (Thomas 2022). In the United States, Infowars continued to host content from RT in April 2023, over a year after the initial invasion (Infowars.com 2023).

With opportunities to push narratives at Western audiences more limited, the Russian state appears to have pivoted in its use of news media, stoking anti-Western sentiment in Africa and Asia. A "flood" of pro-Russian

180 SEEING RED

content has been detected in African media (Peltier et al. 2023), while RT is opening new bureaus on the continent (Reporters Without Borders 2023b). The RT and Sputnik Arabic social media accounts dramatically increased their output after the 2022 invasion of Ukraine (OECD 2022), while RT's broadcast content is frequently disseminated across the Middle East (Borshchevskaya 2023).

All this suggests that the Russian state continues to prioritize news media as a conduit for propaganda to achieve its strategic goals, and any reduction in its efforts to target U.S. audiences will be temporary. Future U.S. elections are likely to see a concentrated effort by the Kremlin to support those candidates most sympathetic to Moscow's strategic narratives. The presence of Trump as the front-runner for the Republican nomination in 2024 meant that Russia again had a candidate whose worldview aligned with its own. Any partisan division over support for Ukraine among politicians (Roche 2023) and the public (Dunn 2023) is fodder for Russia to weaponize for information warfare.

The 2024 elections may mark something of an "all or nothing" moment for Russia, given the poor military performance of the Russian armed forces and the growing pressure on a Russian economy under extensive sanctions. The June 2023 mutiny by mercenary chief Evgeni Prigozhin, who was conveniently killed in an airplane explosion two months later, exposed the weakness of Russian military control. Ukraine is heavily reliant on aid from its allies to sustain the conflict, and the United States was by far the largest single donor of military, financial, and humanitarian aid to Ukraine in the first year after the 2022 invasion (Drenon 2023). In invading Ukraine, Russia created the proxy conflict with the United States that it claimed to fear. An opportunity to use tried-and-tested tactics to carry on pushing strategic narratives, plus an incentive to support candidates whose opposition to continued funding of Ukraine's war effort, is likely to be irresistible to the Kremlin. This is one of the compelling reasons for Russia to continue to interfere in U.S. elections.

In the case of Ukraine, this would depend on a number of factors, such as whether funding the war becomes a clear point of division during the campaign and its aftermath. By 2023 some high-profile Republican politicians began to stoke opposition to continued aid to Ukraine, echoing Russian strategic narratives as they did so (Smith 2023). In addition, Trump consistently criticized spending on the war (Porter 2023). There may, therefore, be a clear link between the outcome of the 2024 election and Russia's ability to achieve victory in the war.

The emergence of a group of politicians whose views on various subjects including Ukraine are similar to those of the Kremlin will be a welcome

CONCLUSIONS   181

development for the Russians. But propaganda needs to be disseminated regardless of where it comes from. This book is about how Russian state-funded media and U.S. media can converge in how they portray the world, so a critical question is: Will U.S. media continue to be fertile ground for Russian propaganda into 2024 and beyond?

Due to two significant measures—economics and partisanship—it is likely that the problem of propaganda will get worse rather than better. The U.S. news media will go into the next election cycle in a perilous position. Some broadcast media are suffering slumps in profits (Mullin 2022), and local newspapers are continuing to disappear (as outlined in Chapter 2). Not all news media suffer equally in this environment, though. Partisan media have been able to better weather the economic storm battering traditional journalism, producing cheaper content that confirms, rather than challenges, audience opinion. Fox took a major financial hit due to its abandonment of journalistic values to cover electoral fraud, but this has been described as the network's "cost of doing business" (Levine 2023), and the network successfully saw off the challenge of Newsmax in the process. The conditions for "network propaganda" (Benkler et al. 2018) remain, even after key supporters of Russian views, such as Tucker Carlson, were forced off the network.

So is the presence of propaganda alongside news the "new normal"? If news organizations are actively disincentivized from challenging their audiences' convictions or scrutinizing the behavior of the politicians they support, favorable conditions for propaganda exist. In this model, the value of information lies in the extent to which it supports an existing framework of meaning. This is almost the reverse of the libertarian model of journalism, where information has value based on whether it helps audiences approach the best available approximation of the truth.

This book has not only demonstrated the nature of Russian propaganda in American news but also shown how to identify it at scale. This gives us tools to detect—and hopefully deter—the spread of Russian propaganda disguised as American news. However, it is beyond the scope of this book to consider what effective action to disincentivize propaganda in news reporting might look like. But if the commercial digital media environment rewards—or even encourages—the presentation of information that is indistinguishable from the propaganda of foreign states actively seeking to undermine the United States, then doing nothing is not a viable option. If journalism and democracy cannot succeed without each other, their survival in the face of propaganda is under threat.

References

Aalberg, Toril, Jesper Strömbäck, and Claes H. de Vreese. 2012. "The Framing of Politics as Strategy and Game: A Review of Concepts, Operationalizations and Key Findings." *Journalism*. 13 (2): 162–178. https://doi.org/10.1177/1464884911427799.

Abernathy, Penny. 2022. "The State of Local News: The 2022 Report." Localnewsinitiative. northwestern.edu. June 29. Accessed March 27, 2023. https://localnewsinitiative.north western.edu/research/state-of-local-news/report/.

Abrams, Abigail. 2019. "Here's What We Know So Far About Russia's 2016 Meddling." Time.com. April 18. Accessed April 5, 2023. https://time.com/5565991/russia-influe nce-2016-election/.

Ad Fontes Media. n.d. "Interactive Media Bias Chart." Adfontesmedia.com. Accessed January 25, 2023. https://adfontesmedia.com/interactive-media-bias-chart/.

Allsides. n.d. "Media Bias Ratings." Allsides.com. Accessed April 3, 2023. https://www. allsides.com/media-bias/ratings.

Antle, W. James. 2020. "Public Split on Whether Joe Biden Has Been Honest About Son Hunter's Business Activities, Washington Examiner/YouGov Poll Finds." Washingtonexaminer.com. October 21. Accessed April 11, 2023. https://www.washing tonexaminer.com/news/public-split-on-whether-joe-biden-has-been-honest-about-son-hunters-business-activities-washington-examiner-yougov-poll-finds.

Associated Press. 2021. "Transcript of Trump's Speech at Rally Before US Capitol Riot." USNews.com. January 13. Accessed April 27, 2023.https://www.usnews.com/news/ politics/articles/2021-01-13/transcript-of-trumps-speech-at-rally-before-us-capi tol-riot.

Atkeson, Lonna Rae, Wendy L. Hansen, Maggie Toulouse Oliver, Cherie D. Maestas, and Eric C. Wiemer. 2022. "Should I Vote-by-Mail or in Person? The Impact of COVID-19 Risk Factors and Partisanship on Vote Mode Decisions in the 2020 Presidential Election." *PLOS ONE*. 17 (9): 1–21. https://doi.org/10.1371/journal.pone.0274357.

Atlantic Council. February 2023. *Narrative Warfare: How the Kremlin and Russian News Outlets Justified a War of Aggression Against Ukraine*. Washington, D.C.: Atlantic Council. https://www.atlanticcouncil.org/wp-content/uploads/2023/02/Narrative-Warfare-Final.pdf.

Bagdikian, Ben. 2004. *The New Media Monopoly*. Boston: Beacon Press.

Baker, Peter. 2022. "In Threatening Ukraine, Russia Pushes for a Realm Free from NATO." *The New York Times*. January 10. Accessed April 26, 2023. https://www.nytimes.com/ 2022/01/09/us/politics/russia-ukraine-james-baker.html.

Baragona, Justin. 2020. "Right-Wing Media Stars Begin Pushing Conspiracy That Dems Infected Trump." Thedailybeast.com. October 6. Accessed March 27, 2023. https:// www.thedailybeast.com/rush-limbaugh-and-newsmax-tv-host-greg-kelly-push-con spiracy-that-democrats-infected-trump.

Barnett, Brooke, and Laura Roselle. 2008. "Patriotism in the News: 'Rally Round the Flag.'" *Electronic News*. 2 (1): 10–30. https://doi.org/10.1080/19312430701807713.

184 REFERENCES

Bauder, David. 2021. "Journalists Recount Harrowing Attacks amid Capitol Riot." APNews.com. January 8. Accessed April 5, 2023. https://apnews.com/article/donald-trump-new-york-journalists-media-social-media-cba6bd7b93be0ade1da714a32c33d74c.

Benkler, Yochai, Robert Faris, and Hal Roberts. 2018. *Network Propaganda: Manipulation, Disinformation, and Radicalization in American Politics.* Oxford: Oxford University Press.

Benkler, Yochai, Robert Faris, Hal Roberts, and Ethan Zuckerman. 2017. "Study: Breitbart-Led Right-Wing Media Ecosystem Altered Broader Media Agenda." CJR.org. March 3. Accessed March 31, 2023. https://www.cjr.org/analysis/breitbart-media-trump-harvard-study.php.

Bennett, W. Lance. 2016. *News: The Politics of Illusion.* 10th ed. Chicago: University of Chicago Press.

Blake, Aaron. 2022. "What Rand Paul's Russia Exchange with Antony Blinken Was Really About." *The Washington Post.* April 27. Accessed October 16, 2023. https://www.washingtonpost.com/politics/2022/04/27/paul-nato-blinken/.

Blinova, Ekaterina. 2020. "What's Really Behind Trump's Legal Team's Strategy & Do His Lawyers Believe in Victory?" Sputniknews.com. November 17. Accessed March 27, 2023. https://sputniknews.com/20201117/whats-really-behind-trumps-legal-teams-strategy--do-his-lawyers-believe-in-victory-1081194580.html.

Boczkowski, Pablo J., and Eugenia Mitchelstein. 2013. *The News Gap: When the Information Preferences of the Media and the Public Diverge.* Cambridge, MA: MIT Press.

Boghardt, Thomas. 2009. "Soviet Bloc Intelligence and Its AIDS Disinformation Campaign." *Studies in Intelligence.* 53 (4): 1–24.

Bokat-Lindell, Spencer. 2022. "Is More War the Only Path to Peace in Ukraine?" *The New York Times.* May 4. Accessed October 16, 2023. https://www.nytimes.com/2022/05/04/opinion/peace-ukraine.html.

Bollfrass, Alexander K., and Stephen Herzog. 2022. "The War in Ukraine and Global Nuclear Order." *Survival: Global Politics and Strategy* 64 (4): 7–32. https://doi.org/10.1080/00396338.2022.2103255.

Borger, Julian. 2020. "'Wildly inappropriate': VOA Purge Continues as Foreign Journalists' Visas Not Renewed." Theguardian.com. July 10. Accessed April 5, 2023. https://www.theguardian.com/media/2020/jul/10/wildly-inappropriate-voa-purge-continues-as-foreign-journalists-visas-cancelledv.

Borshchevskaya, Anna. 2023. "Russia's Disinformation Machine Has a Middle East Advantage." Foreignpolicy.com. March 23. Accessed April 30, 2023. https://foreignpolicy.com/2023/03/23/russia-ukraine-war-disinformation-middle-east-rt-sputnik-arabic/.

Bossie, David. 2020. "Trump Clearly Defeats Biden in First Presidential Debate." Foxnews.com. September 30. Accessed May 1, 2023. https://www.foxnews.com/opinion/david-bossie-trump-clearly-defeats-biden-in-first-presidential-debate.

Bradshaw, Samantha, and Philip N. Howard. 2019. "The Global Disinformation Disorder: 2019 Global Inventory of Organised Social Media Manipulation." Working Paper 2019. Oxford: Project on Computational Propaganda.

Brandenburg v. Ohio. 1969. 492 U.S. 444 (U.S. Supreme Court. 1969). https://supreme.justia.com/cases/federal/us/395/444/.

Brandt, Jessica, Bret Schafer, Valerie Wirtschafter, and Peter Benzoni. September 2023. *Echoes Across the Airwaves: How Kremlin Narratives About Ukraine Spread (or Don't)*

REFERENCES 185

on U.S. Political Podcasts. Washington, D.C.: Brookings Institution. https://www.brookings.edu/articles/echoes-across-the-airwaves.

Brenan, Megan. 2022. "Americans' Trust in Media Remains Near Record Low." Gallup.com. October 18. Accessed May 1, 2023. https://news.gallup.com/poll/403166/americans-trust-media-remains-near-record-low.aspx.

British Broadcasting Corporation. 2022. *BBC Group Annual Report and Accounts 2021/22.* BBC.co.uk. Accessed March 24, 2023. https://downloads.bbc.co.uk/aboutthebbc/reports/annualreport/ara-2021-22.pdf.

Bucay, Yemile, Vittoria Elliott, Jennie Kamin, and Andrea Parik. 2017. "America's Growing News Deserts." CJR.org. May 8. Accessed April 27, 2023. https://www.cjr.org/local_news/american-news-deserts-donuts-local.php.

Burunov, Oleg. 2020. "CIA Head Gina Haspel 'Should Be Fired' over Election Software 'Glitches,' Trump Lawyer Says." Sputniknews.com. November 16. Accessed March 27, 2023. https://sputniknews.com/20201116/cia-head-gina-haspel-should-be-fired-over-election-software-glitches-trump-lawyer-says-1081181430.html.

Cappella, Joseph, and Kathleen Hall Jamieson. 1997. *Spiral of Cynicism: The Press and the Public Good.* New York: Oxford University Press.

Card, Dallas, Amber E. Boydstun, Justin H. Gross, Philip Resnik, and Noah A. Smith. 2015. "The Media Frames Corpus: Annotations of Frames Across Issues." *Proceedings of the 53rd Annual Meeting of the Association for Computational Linguistics and the 7th International Joint Conference on Natural Language Processing (Volume 2: Short Papers):* 438–444. https://aclanthology.org/P15-2072/.

Carlson, Matt. 2016. "The Question of Objectivity in the 2016 Presidential Election." In *US Election Analysis 2016: Media, Voters and the Campaign,* edited by Darren Lilleker, Daniel Jackson, Einar Thorsen and Anastasia Veneti. Bournemouth, UK: Centre for the Study of Journalism, Culture & Community, Bournemouth University, 11.

Carlson, Matt, Sue Robinson, and Seth C. Lewis. 2021. *News After Trump: Journalism's Crisis of Relevance in a Changed Media Culture.* Oxford: Oxford University Press.

Carlson, Tucker. 2022. "Everything That Tulsi Gabbard Said About Biolabs in Ukraine Is True." Foxnews.com. March 14. Access April 22, 2022. https://www.foxnews.com/opinion/tucker-everything-tulsi-gabbard-said-true.

Carnevale, Anthony P., and Emma Wenzinger. 2022. *Stop the Presses: Journalism Employment and the Economic Value of 850 Journalism and Communication Programs.* Washington, D.C.: Georgetown University Center on Education and the Workforce. http://cew.georgetown.edu/journalism.

Centers for Disease Control and Prevention. N.d. "CDC Museum COVID-19 Timeline." CDC.gov. Accessed March 10, 2023. https://www.cdc.gov/museum/timeline/covid19.html.

Chegodaeva, Sofia. 2020. "Senate Majority Leader Rep. Mitch McConnell Congratulates Biden on Winning Presidential Election." Sputniknews.com. December 15. Accessed March 27, 2023. https://sputniknews.com/20201215/senate-majority-leader-rep-mitch-mcconnell-congratulates-biden-on-winning-presidential-election-1081469878.html.

Cillizza, Chris. 2020. "Donald Trump Is Now Openly Begging for Votes." CNN.com. October 14. Accessed March 22, 2023. https://www.cnn.com/2020/10/14/politics/2020-election-donald-trump-suburban-women-voters/index.html.

Clark, Neil. 2020. "Masking Their Deficiencies—Why Biden and the Democrats Deserve to Lose in November." Sputniknews.com. September 2. Accessed March 22, 2023.

186 REFERENCES

https://sputniknews.com/columnists/202009021080350348-masking-their-deficiencies---why-biden-and-the-democrats-deserve-to-lose-in-november/.

Clinton, Hillary. 2022. "Madeline Albright Warned Us, and She Was Right." *The New York Times*. March 27. Accessed April 26, 2023. https://www.nytimes.com/2022/03/25/opinion/madeleine-albright-secretary-of-state.html.

CNN. 2023. "CNN Worldwide Fact Sheet." CNNpressroom.blogs.CNN.com. February 2023. Accessed March 31, 2023. https://cnnpressroom.blogs.cnn.com/cnn-fact-sheet/#.

Cochrane, Emily. 2020. "Republican Congressional Leaders Remain Silent on Biden Victory as Trump Refuses to Concede." *The New York Times*. November 8. Accessed March 9, 2023. https://www.nytimes.com/2020/11/08/us/elections/republican-congressional-leaders-remain-silent-on-biden-victory-as-trump-refuses-to-concede.html.

Cohen, Marshall, Oliver Darcy, and Zachary Cohen. 2020. "How Team Trump Used Fox News as a Laundromat for Unverified Russian Information About Top Democrats." CNN.com. October 10. Accessed March 22, 2023. https://www.cnn.com/2020/10/11/politics/fox-news-ratcliffe-russia-intelligence/index.html.

Comcast Corporation. 2022. *Annual Report 2022*. Cmcsa.com. https://www.cmcsa.com/static-files/156da323-653e-4cc6-9bb4-d239937e9d2f.

Committee to Protect Journalists. N.d. "58 Journalists Killed in Russia Between 1992 and 2023." New York: Committee to Project Journalists. Accessed April 27, 2023. https://cpj.org/data/killed/europe/russia/?status=Killed&motiveConfirmed%5B%5D=Confirmed&type%5B%5D=Journalist&cc_fips%5B%5D=RS&start_year=1992&end_year=2023&group_by=location.

Corporation for Public Broadcasting. 2023. *Combined Financial Statements and Report of Independent Certified Public Accountants*. CPB.org. Accessed March 24, 2023. https://cpb.org/sites/default/files/aboutcpb/financials/audited/cpb_combinedstatements_fy2022.pdf.

Cortes, Corinna, and Vladimir Vapnik. 1995. "Support-Vector Networks." *Machine Learning*. 20: 273–297. https://doi.org/10.1007/BF00994018.

Crilley, Rhys, Marie Gillespie, Bertie Vigden, and Alistair Willis. 2022. "Understanding RT's Audiences: Exposure Not Endorsement for Twitter Followers of Russian State-Sponsored Media." *The International Journal of Press/Politics*. 27 (1): 1–23. https://doi.org/10.1177/1940161220980692.

Cummings, William, Joey Garrison, and Jim Sergent. 2021. "By the Numbers: President Donald Trump's Failed Efforts to Overturn the Election." Usatoday.com. January 6. Accessed March 9, 2023. https://eu.usatoday.com/in-depth/news/politics/elections/2021/01/06/trumps-failed-efforts-overturn-election-numbers/4130307001/.

Cunningham, Finian. 2020a. "Russia's Threat . . . of Peace." Sputniknews.com. October 26. Accessed March 22, 2023. https://sputniknews.com/columnists/202010261080881386-russias-threat-of-peace/.

Cunningham, Finian. 2020b. "Trump and Dems Take Turns Playing 'Russian Card'—Which Only Proves It's the Joker." RT.com. August 28. Accessed March 22, 2023. https://www.rt.com/op-ed/499346-trump-dems-russian-card/.

Darcy, Oliver. 2022. "RT America Ceases Productions and Lays Off Most of Its Staff." CNN.com. March 3. Accessed April 30, 2023. https://edition.cnn.com/2022/03/03/media/rt-america-layoffs/index.html.

Davis, Mark. 2019. "A New, Online Culture War? The Communication World of Breitbart.com." *Communication Research and Practice*. 5 (3): 241–254. https://doi.org/10.1080/22041451.2018.1558790.

REFERENCES 187

Department of Digital, Culture, Media and Sport. 2012. *Leveson Inquiry—Report into the Culture, Practices and Ethics of the Press.* London: HMSO.

Deutsche Welle. 2016. "Don't Politicize Teen 'Rape,' Berlin Asks Moscow." DW.com. January 27. Accessed April 17, 2023. https://www.dw.com/en/germany-warns-russia-against-using-teen-rape-case-for-political-ends/a-19007807.

Drenon, Brandon. 2023. "How Much Money Has the US Given to Ukraine?" BBC.com/news. February 21. Accessed April 30, 2023. https://www.bbc.com/news/world-us-canada-64656301.

Dunaway, Johanna, and Regina G. Lawrence. 2015. "What Predicts the Game Frame? Media Ownership, Electoral Context, and Campaign News." *Political Communication.* 32 (1): 43–60. https://doi.org/10.1080/10584609.2014.880975.

Dunn, Amina. 2023. "As Russian Invasion Nears One-Year Mark, Partisans Grow Further Apart on U.S. Support for Ukraine." Pewresearch.org. January 31. Accessed April 30, 2023. https://www.pewresearch.org/short-reads/2023/01/31/as-russian-invasion-nears-one-year-mark-partisans-grow-further-apart-on-u-s-support-for-ukraine/.

Eady, Gregory, Tom Paskhalis, Jan Zilinsky, Richard Bonneau, Jonathan Nagler, and Joshua A. Tucker. 2023. "Exposure to the Russian Internet Research Agency Foreign Influence on Twitter in the 2016 US Election and Its Relationship to Attitudes and Voting Behavior." *Nature Communications.* 14, Article number 62: 1–11. https://www.nature.com/articles/s41467-022-35576-9.

Edmondson, Catie, Marc Santora, Jenny Gross, Neil Vigdor, and Michael Cooper. 2020. "More Republicans Assail Trump's False Claims of Election Fraud, While Others Defend Them." Nytimes.com. November 6. Accessed March 9, 2023. https://www.nytimes.com/2020/11/06/us/elections/more-republicans-assail-trumps-false-claims-of-election-fraud-while-others-defend-them.html.

Edmondson, Catie and Edward Wong. 2020. "With Push from Trump, Senate Moves to Install Contentious Filmmaker at U.S. Media Agency." Nytimes.com. May 8. Accessed April 5, 2023. https://www.nytimes.com/2020/05/08/us/politics/michael-pack-voa.html.

Ekimenko, Svetlana. 2020. "Independent Probe Claims FBI Showing 'Proactive Interest' in Pursuing Allegations of Voter Fraud." Sputniknews.com. November 30. Accessed March 27, 2023. https://sputniknews.com/20201130/independent-probe-claims-fbi-showing-proactive-interest-in-pursuing-allegations-of-voter-fraud-1081314312.html.

Elswah, Mona, and Philip M. Howard. 2020. "'Anything That Causes Chaos': The Organizational Behaviour of Russia Today (RT)." *Journal of Communication.* 70 (5): 623–645. https://doi.org/10.1093/joc/jqaa027.

Entman, Robert M. 1993. "Framing: Toward Clarification of a Fractured Paradigm." *Journal of Communication* 43 (4): 51–58. https://doi.org/10.1111/j.1460-2466.1993.tb01304.x.

Entman, Robert M. 2003. "Cascading Activation: Contesting the White House's Frame After 9/11." *Political Communication* 20 (4): 415–432. https://doi.org/10.1080/10584600390244176.

Federal Communications Commission. 1974. *Fairness Report.* 39 Fed. Reg. 26372 (1974).

Feierstein, Mitchell. 2020. "US Political Discourse Is so Toxic & Divided That Friends of 30 Years No Longer Talk to Me. The America I Loved Has Gone Forever." RT.com. October 1. Accessed March 22, 2023. https://www.rt.com/op-ed/502235-us-politics-toxic-civil-war/.

188 REFERENCES

Fleitz, Fred. 2020. "Report Claims Hillary OK'd Effort to Defeat Trump in 2016 with False Russia Collusion Charge." Foxnews.com. October 1. Accessed March 22, 2023. https://www.foxnews.com/opinion/hillary-clinton-trump-russia-collusion.

Flint, Joe. 2023. "Surge in Newsmax Ratings Shook Fox News, Then Faded." *The Wall Street Journal*. March 16. Accessed April 20, 2023. https://www.wsj.com/articles/surge-in-newsmax-ratings-shook-fox-news-then-faded-59e1e373.

Flood, Brian. 2020. "Twitter Slaps Trump Tweet with Another Disclaimer Claiming 'Voting by Mail Is Safe and Secure.'" Foxnews.com. October 7. Accessed March 22, 2023. https://www.foxnews.com/media/twitter-slaps-trump-tweet-with-another-disclaimer.

Fox Corporation. 2022. *Annual Report 2022*. Media.foxcorporation.com. Accessed March 31, 2023. https://media.foxcorporation.com/wp-content/uploads/prod/2022/09/19142833/FOX-2022-Annual-Report_Final_Web.pdf.

Gaber, Ivor, and Rodney Tiffen. 2018. "Politics and the Media in Australia and the United Kingdom: Parallels and Contrasts." *Media International Australia*. 167 (1): 27–40. https://doi.org/10.1177/1329878X18766721.

Galeotti, Mark. 2017. *Controlling Chaos: How Russia Manages Its Political War in Europe*. Berlin: European Council on Foreign Relations.

Gao, Pengjie, Chang Lee, and Dermot Murphy. 2018. *Financing Dies in Darkness? The Impact of Newspaper Closures on Public Finance*. Washington, D.C.: Brookings Institution.

Garcia-Navarro, Lulu, Thomas L. Friedman, Ross Douthan, and Yara Bayomy. 2022. "Four Times Opinion Writers on War in Ukraine: 'It Is Very Clear Putin Has No Plan B.'" Nytimes.com. March 2. Accessed on April 26, 2023.https://www.nytimes.com/2022/03/02/opinion/war-ukraine-putin.html.

Gatov, Vasily. 2015. "Russia's Stalinist Diplospeak." Thedailybeast.com. July 25. Accessed April 17, 2023. https://www.thedailybeast.com/russias-stalinist-diplospeak.

Geydarova, Asya. 2020. "General Services Administration Tells Biden Transition Can Formally Begin." Sputniknews.com. November 23. Accessed March 27, 2023. https://sputniknews.com/20201123/general-services-administration-reportedly-tells-biden-transition-can-formally-begin-1081254104.html.

Gibbons-Neff, Thomas. 2023. "Nazi Symbols on Ukraine's Front Lines Highlight Thorny Issues of History." *The New York Times*. June 7. Accessed 28, 2023. https://www.nytimes.com/2023/06/05/world/europe/nazi-symbols-ukraine.html.

Giles, Keir. 2016. *Handbook of Russian Information Warfare*. Rome: NATO Defense College.

Gorbachev, Max. 2020. "More Voters Believe Joe Biden Was Engaged in Corruption as Situation Heats Up Before Election." Sputniknews.com. October 30. Accessed March 22, 2023. https://sputniknews.com/20201030/more-voters-believe-joe-biden-was-engaged-in-corruption-as-situation-heats-up-before-election-1080931762.html.

Gottfried, Jeffrey, Michael Barthel and Amy Mitchell. 2017. "Trump, Clinton Voters Divided in Their Main Source for Election News." Pewresearch.org. January 18. Accessed April 5, 2023. https://www.pewresearch.org/journalism/2017/01/18/trump-clinton-voters-divided-in-their-main-source-for-election-news/.

Graber, Doris, and Johanna L. Dunaway. 2005. *Mass Media and American Politics, seventh edition*. Washington, DC: CQ Press.

Grieco, Elizabeth, Nami Sumida, and Sophia Fedeli. 2018. "About a third of large U.S. newspapers have suffered layoffs since 2017." Washington, D.C.: Pew Research Center. July 23. Accessed April 27, 2023.https://www.pewresearch.org/short-reads/

2018/07/23/about-a-third-of-large-u-s-newspapers-have-suffered-layoffs-since-2017/.

Groeling, Tim. 2008. "Who's the Fairest of Them All? An Empirical Test for Partisan Bias on ABC, CBS, NBC, and Fox News." *Presidential Studies Quarterly*. 38 (4): 631–657. https://doi.org/10.1111/j.1741-5705.2008.02668.x.

Hallin, Daniel, and Paolo Mancini. 2004. *Comparing Media Systems: Three Models of Media and Politics*. Cambridge, UK: Cambridge University Press.

Halverson, Jeffrey R., H. L. Goodall Jr., and Steven R. Corman. 2011. *Master Narratives of Islamist Extremism*. New York: Palgrave Macmillan.

Harcup, Tony and Deirdre O'Neill. 2017. "What Is News? News Values Revisited (Again)." *Journalism Studies*. 18 (12): 1–19. https://doi.org/10.1080/1461670X.2016.1150193.

Harris, Shane, Ellen Nakashima, Greg Miller, and Josh Dawsey. 2020. "White House Was Warned Giuliani Was Target of Russian Intelligence Operation to Feed Misinformation to Trump." Wahsingtonpost.com. October 15. Accessed March 22, 2023. https://www.washingtonpost.com/national-security/giuliani-biden-ukraine-russian-disinformation/2020/10/15/43158900-0ef5-11eb-b1e8-16b59b92b36d_story.html.

Hearns-Branaman, Jesse Owen. 2016. *Journalism and the Philosophy of Truth: Beyond Objectivity and Balance*. London: Routledge.

Heese, Jonas, Gerardo Pérez-Cavazos, and Caspar David Peter. 2022. "When the Local Newspaper Leaves Town: The Effects of Local Newspaper Closures on Corporate Misconduct." *Journal of Financial Economics*. 145 (2): 445–463. https://doi.org/10.1016/j.jfineco.2021.08.015.

Helmus, Todd C., Elizabeth Bodine-Baron, Andrew Radin, Madeline Magnuson, Joshua Mendelsohn, William Marcellino, Adnriy Bega, and Zev Winkelman. 2018. *Russian Social Media Influence: Understanding Russian Propaganda in Eastern Europe*. Santa Monica, CA: RAND Corporation.

Herd, Graeme P. 2016. "Russian Information Operations Seek Strategic Realignment in Europe." *The Concordian: Journal of European Security and Defense Issues* (Special Edition): 6–13.

Herman, Edward S., and Noam Chomsky. 1988. *Manufacturing Consent: The Political Economy of the Mass Media*. New York: Pantheon.

Higgins, Tucker. 2020. "Obama Response to 2016 Russian Election Meddling Had 'Many Flaws,' Senate Report Finds." CNBC.com. February 6. Accessed April 5, 2023. https://www.cnbc.com/2020/02/06/obama-response-to-2016-russian-meddling-had-many-flaws-senate-report.html.

Hill, Fiona, and Angela Stent. 2022. "The World Putin Wants: How Distortions About the Past Feed Delusions About the Future." *Foreign Affairs* 103 (5): 108–123.

Hinck, Robert S., Skye C. Cooley, and Randolph Kluver. 2020. *Global Media and Strategic Narratives of Contested Democracy: Chinese, Russian, and Arabic Media Narratives of the U.S. Presidential Elections*. New York: Routledge.

Hinck, Robert S., Randolph Kluver, and Skye Cooley. 2018. "Russia Re-Envisions the World: Strategic Narratives in Russian Broadcast and News Media During 2015." *Russian Journal of Communication* 10 (1): 21–37. https://doi.org/10.1080/19409419.2017.1421096.

Hoffman, Frank G. 2007. *Conflict in the 21st Century: The Rise of Hybrid Wars*. Arlington, VA: Potomac Institute for Policy Studies.

Holmstrom, Miranda. 2015. "The Narrative and Social Media." *Defence Strategic Communications: The Official Journal of the NATO Strategic Communications Centre of Excellence*. 1 (1): 118–133.

190 REFERENCES

Horwitz, Jeff. 2021. "The Facebook Whistleblower, Frances Haugen, Says She Wants to Fix the Company, Not Harm It." WSJ.com. October 3. Accessed April 28, 2023. https://www.wsj.com/articles/facebook-whistleblower-frances-haugen-says-she-wants-to-fix-the-company-not-harm-it-11633304122.

Howard, Philip N., Bharath Ganesh, Dimitra Liotsiou, John Kelly, and Camille François. 2018. *The IRA, Social Media and Political Polarization in the United States, 2012–2018*. Oxford: Oxford Internet Institute.

Hsu, Tiffany. 2022. "The Sandy Hook Defamation Cases Have Put Alex Jones's Finances Under Scrutiny." Nytimes.com. August 5. Accessed April 8, 2023. https://www.nytimes.com/2022/08/05/us/alex-jones-finances.html.

Infowars.com. 2023. "Russia Won't Play by the 'Rules' Imposed by West—Putin." Infowars.com. April 29. Accessed April 30, 2023. https://www.infowars.com/posts/russia-wont-play-by-rules-imposed-by-west-putin/.

Inskeep, Steve. 2021. "Timeline: What Trump Told Supporters for Months Before They Attacked." NPR.org. February 8. Accessed March 8, 2023. https://www.npr.org/2021/02/08/965342252/timeline-what-trump-told-supporters-for-months-before-they-attacked.

Iyengar, Shanto. 1996. "Framing Responsibility for Political Issues." *Annals of the American Academy of Political and Social Science*. 546: 59–70. https://www.jstor.org/stable/1048170.

Jamieson, Kathleen Hall. 2018. *Cyberwar: How Russian Hackers and Trolls Helped Elect a President—What We Don't, Can't, and Do Know*. New York: Oxford University Press.

Justwan, Florian, and Ryan D. Williamson. 2022. "Trump and Trust: Examining the Relationship Between Claims of Fraud and Citizen Attitudes." *PS: Political Science & Politics*. 55 (3): 462–469. https://doi.org/10.1017/S1049096522000221.

Kaczynski, Andrew, Chris Massie, and Nathan McDermott. 2017. "80 Times Trump Talked About Putin." CNN.com. March 2017. Accessed April 17, 2023. https://edition.cnn.com/interactive/2017/03/politics/trump-putin-russia-timeline/.

Kalmoe, Nathan P., and Lilliana Mason. 2019. *Lethal Mass Partisanship: Prevalence, Correlates, and Electoral Contingencies*. Washington, D.C.: National Capital Area American Political Science Association American Politics Meeting.

Kanno-Youngs, Zolan. 2020. "Warnings of Russian Efforts Against Biden Were Blocked." Nytimes.com. September 3. Accessed March 22, 2023. https://www.nytimes.com/2020/09/02/us/politics/trump-biden-russia-election.html.

Karni, Annie, and Maggie Haberman. 2020. "Fox's Arizona Call for Biden Flipped the Mood at Trump Headquarters." Nytimes.com. November 16. Accessed March 9, 2023. https://www.nytimes.com/2020/11/04/us/politics/trump-fox-news-arizona.html.

Kessler, Glenn, Meg Kelly, Salvador Rizzo, Leslie Shapiro, and Lee Dominguez. 2021. "A Term of Untruths." Washingtonpost.com. January 23. Accessed April 8, 2023. https://www.washingtonpost.com/politics/interactive/2021/timeline-trump-claims-as-president/?itid=lk_inline_manual_10.

Kessler, Glenn, and Salvador Rizzo. 2020. "President Trump's False Claims of Vote Fraud: A Chronology." Washingtonpost.com. November 5. Accessed March 8, 2023. https://www.washingtonpost.com/politics/2020/11/05/president-trumps-false-claims-vote-fraud-chronology/.

Kiderra, Inga. 2022. "Partisan Gap on Trust in U.S. Elections Has Grown Even Wider, Survey Finds." San Diego: University of California San Diego. Accessed May 1, 2023. https://today.ucsd.edu/story/yankelovich-center-survey-trust-in-us-elections-2022.

REFERENCES   191

Kivimäki, Veli-Pekka. 2014. "Russian State Television Shares Fake Images of MH17 Being Attacked." Bellingcat.com. November 14, 2014. Accessed April 17, 2023. https://www.bellingcat.com/news/2014/11/14/russian-state-television-shares-fake-images-of-mh17-being-attacked/.

Kolga, Marcus. 2019. *Stemming the Virus: Understanding and Responding to the Threat of Russian Disinformation*. Ottawa, ON: Macdonald-Laurier Institute.

Kovach, Bill, and Tom Rosenstiel. 2001. *The Elements of Journalism: What Newspeople Should Know and the Public Should Expect*. New York: Three Rivers Press.

Kramer, Mark. 2009. "The Myth of a No-NATO-Enlargement Pledge to Russia." *The Washington Quarterly* 32 (2): 39–61. DOI: 10.1080/01636600902773248.

Lachlan, Kenneth A., Patric R. Spence, and Matthew Seeger. 2016. "Terrorist Attacks and Uncertainty Reduction: Media Use After September 11." *Behavioural Sciences of Terrorism and Political Aggression*. 1 (2): 101–110. https://doi.org/10.1080/1943447090 2771683.

Laruelle, Marlene. 2019. "Mirror Games? Ideological Resonances Between Russian and U.S. Radical Conservatism." In *Contemporary Russian Conservatism: Problems, Paradoxes, and Perspectives*, edited by Mikhail Suslov and Dmitry Uzlaner. Leiden, The Netherlands: Brill, 177–204.

Laruelle, Marlene. 2021. *Is Russia Fascist?: Unraveling Propaganda East and West*. Ithaca, NY: Cornell University Press.

Lawrence, Regina G. 2001. "Game-Framing the Issues: Tracking the Strategy Frame in Public Policy News." *Political Communication*. 17 (2): 93–114. https://doi.org/10.1080/105846000198422.

Leskovec, Jure, Lars Backstrom, and Jon Kleinberg. 2009. "Meme-Tracking and Dynamics of the News Cycle." Proceedings of the 15th ACM SIGKDD International Conference on Knowledge Discovery and Data Mining. Paris, France.

Letterman, Clark. 2018. *Image of Putin, Russia Suffers Internationally*. Washington, D.C.: Pew Research Center.

Levine, Sam. 2023. "'Dominion wins but the public loses': Fox Settlement Avoids Paying the Highest Price." Theguardian.com. April 18. Accessed April 30, 2023. https://www.theguardian.com/us-news/2023/apr/18/dominion-wins-but-the-public-loses-fox-settlement-avoids-paying-the-highest-price.

Li, Yuan. 2022. "Why the Chinese Internet Is Cheering Russia's Invasion." Nytimes.com. February 28. Accessed April 26, 2023. https://www.nytimes.com/2022/02/27/business/china-russia-ukraine-invasion.html.

Liedke, Jacob, and Jeffrey Gottfried. 2022. "U.S. Adults Under 30 Now Trust Information from Social Media Almost as Much as from National News Outlets." Washington, D.C.: Pew Research Center. October 27. Accessed April 28, 2023. https://www.pewresearch.org/short-reads/2022/10/27/u-s-adults-under-30-now-trust-information-from-social-media-almost-as-much-as-from-national-news-outlets/.

Lokot, Tetyana. 2021. *Beyond the Protest Square: Digital Media and Augmented Dissent*. Lanham, MD: Rowman & Littlefield.

Looney, Dennis, and Natalia Lusin. 2018. *Enrollments in Languages Other Than English in United States Institutions of Higher Education*. New York: Modern Languages Association of America.

Malic, Nebojsa. 2020. "Battle for the Soul of America? That's Turning Out to Be True, but Not in the Way Joe Biden Intended." RT.com. November 2. Accessed March 22, 2023. https://www.rt.com/op-ed/505303-battle-soul-america-election/.

192 REFERENCES

Martin, Alexander. 2022. "Ukraine Invasion: Facebook and Instagram to Block RT and Sputnik in the UK Following Government Request." News.sky.com. March 4. Accessed April 30, 2023. https://news.sky.com/story/ukraine-invasion-facebook-and-instag ram-to-block-rt-and-sputnik-in-the-uk-following-government-request-12557469.

Mascaro, Lisa, and Farnoush Amiri. 2023. "McCarthy Defends Giving Tucker Carlson Jan. 6 Trove Access." APNews.com. February 28. Accessed May 1, 2023. https://apnews. com/article/jan-6-capitol-riot-mccarthy-tucker-carlson-50a41c27108279a448682 3a5db284dc1.

McFaul, Michael. 2022. "Vladimir Putin Does Not Think Like We Do." *The Washington Post*. February 18. Accessed October 16, 2023. https://www.washingtonpost.com/opini ons/2022/01/26/vladimir-putin-does-not-think-like-we-do/.

Meaney, Thomas. 2022. "The Return of 'the West.'" *The New York Times*. March 13. Accessed October 16, 2023. https://www.nytimes.com/2022/03/11/opinion/nato-rus sia-the-west-ukraine.html.

Mearsheimer, John J. 2014. "Why the Ukraine Crisis Is the West's Fault: The Liberal Delusions That Provoked Putin." *Foreign Affairs* 93 (5): 77–89.

Meister, Stefan. 2016. "The 'Lisa Case': Germany as a Target of Russian Disinformation." NATO.int. July 25. Accessed April 17, 2023. https://www.nato.int/docu/review/ articles/2016/07/25/the-lisa-case-germany-as-a-target-of-russian-disinformation/ index.html.

Miskimmon, Alister, Ben O'Loughlin, and Laura Roselle, eds. 2017. *Forging the World: Strategic Narratives and International Relations*. Ann Arbor: University of Michigan.

Mitchell, Amy, Jeffrey Gottfried, Michael Barthel, and Nami Sumida. 2018. "Distinguishing Between Factual and Opinion Statements in the News." Pewresearch. org. June 18. Accessed March 22, 2023. https://www.pewresearch.org/journalism/ 2018/06/18/distinguishing-between-factual-and-opinion-statements-in-the-news/.

Moore, Martin. 2018. *Democracy Hacked: Political Turmoil and Information Warfare in the Digital Age*. London: Perlego Books.

Moore, Martin, and Thomas Colley. 2022. "Two International Propaganda Models: Comparing RT and CGTN's 2020 US Election Coverage." *Journalism Practice*. Online Publication: 1–23. https://doi.org/10.1080/17512786.2022.2086157.

Morris, Jonathan, S. 2005. "The Fox News Factor." *International Journal of Press/Politics*. 10 (3): 56–79. https://doi.org/10.1177/1081180X05279264.

Morrow, Allison. 2022. "How Much Is Vladimir Putin Worth? Almost No One Knows for Sure." Edition.CNN.com. February 28. Accessed April 5, 2023. https://edition.cnn. com/2022/02/28/business/vladimir-putin-wealth-sanctions/index.html.

Mueller, Robert S. III. 2019. *Report on the Investigation into Russian Interference in the 2016 Presidential Election*. Vol. 1. Washington, D.C.: U.S. Department of Justice. Accessed April 12, 2023. https://www.justice.gov/archives/sco/file/1373816/download.

Mullin, Benjamin. 2022. "Profits Slump at CNN as Ratings Plummet." Nytimes.com. August 2. Accessed April 30, 2023. https://www.nytimes.com/2022/08/02/business/ media/cnn-profit-chris-licht.html.

Murphy, Chris. 2020. "Sen. Murphy: The American People Need to Know the Facts About Russia's Interference in the US Election." CNN.com. October 26. Accessed March 22, 2023. https://www.cnn.com/2020/10/26/opinions/russian-interference-election-mur phy/index.html.

Murray, Mark. 2022. "Poll: 61% of Republicans Still Believe Biden Didn't Win Fair and Square in 2020." NBCnews.com. September 27. Accessed May 1, 2023. https://www.nbcnews.com/meet-the-press/meetthepressblog/poll-61-republicans-still-believe-biden-didnt-win-fair-square-2020-rcna49630.

Myers, Stephen Lee, and Stuart A. Thompson. 2022. "For Putin, 'Truth' Is Just Another Front Line." *The New York Times*. March 22. Accessed April 26, 2023. https://www.nytimes.com/2022/03/20/world/asia/russia-putin-propaganda-media.html.

Nagourney, Adam, and Jim Rutenberg. 2020. "Trump, Attacking the Democratic Process, Falsely Says He Won." Nytimes.com. November 4. Accessed March 9, 2023. https://www.nytimes.com/2020/11/03/us/elections/trump-attacking-the-democratic-process-falsely-says-he-won.html.

Nelson, Jacob L., and Seth C. Lewis. 2022. "The Structures That Shape News Consumption: Evidence from the Early Period of the COVID-19 Pandemic." *Journalism* 23 (12): 2495–2512. https://doi.org/10.1177/14648849221095335.

New York Times. 2023. "Redacted Documents in Dominion Fox News Case." Int.nyt.com. Accessed March 23, 2023. https://int.nyt.com/data/documenttools/redacted-documents-in-dominion-fox-news-case/dca5e3880422426f/full.pdf.

Newman, Nic, Richard Fletcher, Craig T. Robertson, Kirsten Eddy, and Rasmus Kleis Nielsen. 2022. *Reuters Institute Digital News Report 2022*. Oxford: Reuters Institute for the Study of Journalism.

Nimmo, Ben. 2015. *Anatomy of an Info-War: How Russia's Propaganda Machine Works, And How to Counter It*. Brussels: Central European Policy Institute.

Noam, Eli. 2018. "Beyond the Mogul: From Media Conglomerates to Portfolio Media." *Journalism* 19 (8): 1096–1130. https://doi.org/10.1177/1464884917725941.

North Atlantic Treaty Organization (NATO). 2023. NATO-Russia Relations: The Facts. April 20. https://web.archive.org/web/20231218051122/https://www.nato.int/cps/en/natohq/topics_111767.htm#Myth. Last accessed February 13, 2024.

Nussbaum, Matthew. 2018. "A Look Back at Trump's Statements on Whether Russia Meddled in the Election." Politico.com. July 13. Accessed April 11, 2020. https://www.politico.com/story/2018/07/13/trump-statements-russia-meddling-719281.

Nye, Joseph. 1990. "Soft Power." *Foreign Policy*. 80 (Autumn): 153–171. https://doi.org/10.2307/1148580.

Oates, Sarah. 2007. "The Neo-Soviet Model of the Media." *Europe-Asia Studies*. 59 (8): 1279–1297. https://www.jstor.org/stable/20451453.

Oates, Sarah, Joseph Barrow, and Bobbie Foster. 2018. *From Network to Narrative: Understanding the Nature and Trajectory of Russian Disinformation in the U.S. News*. Paper presented at International Journal of Press/Politics Conference, Oxford.

Oates, Sarah, and John Gray. 2019. *#Kremlin: Using Hashtags to Analyze Russian Disinformation Strategy and Dissemination on Twitter*. Paper presented at the American Political Science Association Annual Meeting, Washington, D.C. https://papers.ssrn.com/sol3/papers.cfm?abstract_id=3445180.

Oates, Sarah, Olya Gurevich, Christopher Walker, Danielle Deibler, and Jesse Anderson. 2020. *Sharing a Playbook?: The Convergence of Russian and U.S. Narratives About Joe Biden*. Paper presented at the American Political Science Association Annual Meeting. https://preprints.apsanet.org/engage/apsa/article-details/5f56826c11e5c800121844be.

Oates, Sarah, Doowan Lee, and David Knickerbocker. 2022. *Data Analysis of Russian Disinformation Supply Chains: Finding Propaganda in the U.S. Media Ecosystem in Real*

194 REFERENCES

Time. Paper presented at the American Political Science Association Annual Meeting, Montreal, Canada. https://papers.ssrn.com/sol3/papers.cfm?abstract_id=4218316.

Oates, Sarah, Lynda Lee Kaid, and Mike Berry. 2010. *Terrorism, Elections, and Democracy: Political Campaigns in the United States, Great Britain, and Russia*. Basingstoke: Palgrave Macmillan.

Oates, Sarah, and Wendy W. Moe. 2017. "Donald Trump and the 'Oxygen of Publicity': Branding, Social Media, and Traditional Media." In *The Presidency and Social Media: Discourse, Disruption, and Digital Democracy in the 2016 Presidential Election*, edited by Dan Schill, John Allen Hendricks, and Thomas E. Patterson, Abingdon, UK: Routledge.

Oates, Sarah, Gordon Ramsay, Olya Gurevich, Danielle Deibler, and David Rubenstein. 2021. *Nyetwork News: The Convergence of the Russophobia Narrative in Russian Propaganda and Fox News in Election 2020*. Paper presented at the American Political Science Association Annual Meeting (virtual). https://dx.doi.org/10.2139/ssrn.3934064.

Oates, Sarah, and Sean Steiner. 2018. "Projecting Power: Understanding Russian Strategic Narrative." *Russian Analytical Digest*. 229 (October 2018): 2–5. https://css.ethz.ch/content/dam/ethz/special-interest/gess/cis/center-for-securities-studies/pdfs/RAD 229.pdf.

OECD. 2022. "Disinformation and Russia's War of Aggression Against Ukraine." OECD. org. November 3. Accessed April 30, 2023. https://www.oecd.org/ukraine-hub/pol icy-responses/disinformation-and-russia-s-war-of-aggression-against-ukraine-37186bde/.

O'Grady, Siobhán, John Hudson, David L. Stern, and Ellen Nakashima. 2022. "Ukrainians Resist Russian Onslaught as Tanks and Planes Dig Deeper Toward Kyiv." *The Washington Post*. February 25. Accessed October 21, 2023. https://www.washingtonp ost.com/national-security/2022/02/25/russia-ukraine-friday-invasion-overview/.

O'Hare, Rachel Buchanan. 2020. *American Journalism and the Deviant Voter: Analyzing and Improving Coverage of the Electorate in the Trump Era*. Doctoral Dissertation. College Park, University of Maryland.

Orttung, Robert W., and Elizabeth Nelson. 2019. "Russia Today's Strategy and Effectiveness on YouTube." *Post-Soviet Affairs*. 35 (2): 77–92. https://doi.org/10.1080/1060586X.2018.1531650.

Patterson, Thomas E. 1993. *Out of Order*. New York: Knopf.

Patterson, Thomas E. 2000. *Doing Well and Doing Good: How Soft News and Critical Journalism Are Shrinking the News Audience and Weakening Democracy—And What News Outlets Can Do About It*. Cambridge, MA: Joan Shorenstein Center for Press, Politics and Public Policy.

Patterson, Thomas E. 2016. *News Coverage of the 2016 General Election: How the Press Failed the Voters*. Cambridge, MA: Harvard Kennedy School.

Paul, Christopher, and Miriam Matthews. 2016. *The Russian "Firehose of Falsehood" Propaganda Model: Why It Might Work and Options to Counter It*. Washington, D.C.: RAND Corporation.

Paul, Kari. 2020. "Facebook and Twitter Restrict Controversial *New York Post* Story on Joe Biden." Theguardian.com. October 14. Accessed March 22, 2023. https://www.theg uardian.com/technology/2020/oct/14/facebook-twitter-new-york-post-hunter-biden.

Paul, Kari. 2023. "RT Videos Spreading Ukraine Disinformation on YouTube Despite Ban—Report." Theguardian.com. February 23. Accessed April 5, 2023. https://www. theguardian.com/media/2023/feb/22/rt-ban-youtube-videos-google-disinformation.

REFERENCES 195

Peltier, Elian, Adam Satariano, and Lynsey Chutel. 2023. "How Putin Became a Hero on African TV." Nytimes.com. April 13. Accessed April 30, 2023. https://www.nytimes.com/2023/04/13/world/africa/russia-africa-disinformation.html.

Pew Research Center. 2004. "Cable and Internet Loom Large in Fragmented Political News Universe." Pewresearch.org. January 11. Accessed March 31, 2023. https://www.pewresearch.org/politics/2004/01/11/cable-and-internet-loom-large-in-fragmented-political-news-universe/.

Phillips, Kristine, and Kevin Johnson. 2020. "Paul Manafort Was 'A Grave Counterintelligence Threat,' Republican-Led Senate Panel Finds." Usatoday.com. August 19. Accessed March 22, 2023. https://eu.usatoday.com/story/news/politics/2020/08/18/senate-details-paul-manafort-ties-russian-intel-officer-kilimnik/3390437001/.

Picard, Robert G., and Victor Pickard. 2017. *Essential Principles for Contemporary Media and Communications Policymaking.* Oxford: Reuters Institute for the Study of Journalism.

Pickard, Victor. 2020. *Democracy Without Journalism? Confronting the Misinformation Society.* Oxford: Oxford University Press.

Plokhy, Serhii. 2017. *Lost Kingdom: The Quest for Empire and the Making of the Russian Nation.* London: Basic Books.

PolitiFact. N.d. "Donald Trump." Politifact.com. Accessed April 5, 2023. https://www.politifact.com/personalities/donald-trump/.

Pomerantsev, Peter. 2014. *Nothing Is True and Everything Is Possible: The Surreal Heart of the New Russia.* New York: PublicAffairs.

Porter, Tom. 2023. "Trump Says US Is Giving Ukraine too Much Support, as New Skeptical Republicans Take Office and Swing Control of the House." Businessinsider.com. January 3. Accessed April 30, 2023. https://www.businessinsider.com/trump-says-us-is-giving-ukraine-too-much-money-renews-nato-criticism-2023-1?r=US&IR=T.

Pulitzer.org. N.d. "Public Service." Pulitzer.org. Accessed March 28, 2023. https://www.pulitzer.org/prize-winners-by-category/204.

Putin, Vladimir. 2021. "On the Historical Unity of Russians and Ukrainians." Moscow: Administration of the President of Russia. July 12. Accessed April 21, 2023. http://en.kremlin.ru/events/president/news/66181.

Pynnöniemi, Katri, and András Rácz, eds. 2016. *Fog of Falsehood: Russian Strategy of Deception and the Conflict in Ukraine.* Helsinki: Finnish Institute of International Affairs. https://www.fiia.fi/wp-content/uploads/2017/01/fiiareport45_fogoffalsehood.pdf.

Radnitz, Scott. 2021. *Revealing Schemes: The Politics of Conspiracy in Russia and the Post-Soviet Region.* New York: Oxford University Press.

Rae, Maria. 2021. "Hyperpartisan News: Rethinking the Media for Populist Politics." *New Media & Society.* 23 (5): 1117–1132. https://doi.org/10.1177/1461444820910416.

Ramsay, Gordon, and Sam Robertshaw. 2019. *Weaponising News: RT, Sputnik and Targeted Disinformation.* London: King's College London.

Reimers, Nils, and Iryna Gurevych. 2019. "Sentence-BERT: Sentence Embeddings Using Siamese BERT-Networks." *Computation and Language.* https://doi.org/10.48550/arXiv.1908.10084.

Reporters Without Borders. N.d. "United States 2022 Global Score." RSF.org. Accessed May 1, 2023. https://rsf.org/en/index.

Reporters Without Borders. 2023a. "Russia." RSF.org. Accessed April 5, 2023. https://rsf.org/en/country/russia.

196 REFERENCES

Reporters Without Borders. 2023b. "RT Moves Its Pawns in Africa, Opening a Bureau in Algeria." RSF.org. April 4. Accessed April 30, 2023. https://rsf.org/en/rt-moves-its-pawns-africa-opening-bureau-algeria.

Rid, Thomas. 2020. *Active Measures: The Secret History of Disinformation and Political Warfare.* London: Profile Books.

Rizzo, Lillian. 2023. "Judge Rejects Fox Motions, Allows Dominion's $1.6 Billion Defamation Suit to Go to Trial." CNBC.com. March 31. Accessed April 19, 2023. https://www.cnbc.com/2023/03/31/fox-motions-rejected-dominion-lawsuit-trial.html.

Roche, Darragh. 2023. "Republicans' Divided Stance on Russia Is Major Boost for Putin." Newsweek.com. March 15. Accessed April 30, 2023. https://www.newsweek.com/republicans-divided-stance-russia-major-boost-putin-ukraine-1787933.

Rogers, James, and Andriy Tyushka. 2017. "'Hacking' into the West: Russia's 'Anti-Hegemonic' Drive the Strategic Narrative Offensive." *Defence Strategic Communications: The Official Journal of the NATO Strategic Communications Centre of Excellence.* 2 (Spring 2017): 35–60.

Romer, Daniel, and Kathleen Hall Jamieson. 2020. "Conspiracy Theories as Barriers to Controlling the Spread of COVID-19 in the U.S." *Social Science & Medicine.* 263 (October 2020): 1–8. https://doi.org/10.1016/j.socscimed.2020.113356.

Roose, Kevin. 2020. "Newsmax Courts Fox News Viewers with Election Denialism." Nytimes.com. November 12. Accessed March 10, 2023. https://www.nytimes.com/2020/11/12/technology/newsmax-fox-news-trump.html.

Roselle, Laura, Alister Miskimmon, and Ben O'Loughlin. 2014. "Strategic Narrative: A New Means to Understand Soft Power." *Media, War & Conflict.* 7 (1): 70–84. https://doi.org/10.1177/1750635213516696.

Rosenberg, Matthew, and Jim Rutenberg. 2021. "Key Takeaways from Trump's Effort to Overturn the Election." Nytimes.com. February 1. Accessed March 8, 2023. https://www.nytimes.com/2021/02/01/us/politics/trump-election-results.html.

RT.com. 2020a. "'Why wouldn't they overturn an election?' Trump Claims Huge Step of Nullifying Biden's Victory Justified by Dems' Alleged 'Fraud.'" RT.com. November 25. Accessed February 15, 2023. https://www.rt.com/usa/507849-trump-pennsylvania-election-hearing/.

RT.com. 2020b. "Trump Says Biden Can Only Move into White House if He 'PROVES' His Votes Weren't 'Illegally Obtained.'" RT.com. November 27. Accessed March 27, 2023. https://www.rt.com/usa/508049-trump-biden-white-house-proves/.

RT.com. 2020c. "Ex-Obama Adviser Susan Rice Mourns Democracy's NEAR-DEATH Experience with Trump in Melodramatic Appeal to Georgia Voters." RT.com. December 2. Accessed March 27, 2023. https://www.rt.com/usa/508484-susan-rice-near-death-trump/.

RT.com. 2020d. "Trump Attorneys Will Expose Biden's 'Abject Fraud,' Says Lawyer on President's Team." RT.com. November 8. Accessed March 27, 2023. https://www.rt.com/usa/506122-trump-lawyer-abject-fraud-fox/.

RT.com. 2020e. "'I'm going to RELEASE THE KRAKEN': Michael Flynn's Attorney Vows to Expose Dem Collusion Behind Prominent Voting Machine Firm." RT.com. November 14. Accessed March 27, 2023. https://www.rt.com/usa/506698-powell-kraken-dominion-election-fraud/.

RT.com. 2020f. "'KrakenOnSteroids': Sidney Powell Says She 'Understands' Trump's Lawyers Distancing Themselves from Her, Vows to Fight On." RT.com. November 23.

Accessed March 27, 2023. https://www.rt.com/usa/507511-powell-kraken-steroids-trump/.

RT.com. 2020g. "Trump Lawyer Sidney Powell Hits Back at 'Rude' Tucker Carlson: Says She Offered Affidavit & Witness on Voter Fraud." RT.com. November 20. Accessed March 27, 2023. https://www.rt.com/usa/507342-sidney-powell-tucker-carlson-dominion/.

RT.com. 2020h. "Trump's Legal Team Distances Itself from Sidney Powell After She Suggests That Georgia's GOP Governor Conspired to Help Biden Win." RT.com. November 23. Accessed March 27, 2023. https://www.rt.com/usa/507510-powell-trump-legal-team/.

Rubado, Meghan E., and Jay T. Jennings. 2019. "Political Consequences of the Endangered Local Watchdog: Newspaper Decline and Mayoral Elections in the United States." *Urban Affairs Review*. 56 (5): 1552–1556. https://doi.org/10.1177/1078087419838058.

Ruiz-Gonzalez, Francisco J. 2013. *The Foreign Policy Concept of the Russian Federation: A Comparative Study*. Madrid, Spain: Instituto Espanol de Estudios.

Sanger, David. 2022. "Finland and Sweden Embraced by NATO, but Ukraine Must Wait." *The New York Times*. May 13. Accessed October 16, 2023. https://www.nytimes.com/2022/05/12/us/politics/nato-finland-sweden-ukraine.html.

Schradie, Jen. 2019. *The Revolution That Wasn't: How Digital Activism Favors Conservatives*. Cambridge, MA: Harvard University Press.

Schudson, Michael. 2008. *Why Democracies Need an Unlovable Press*. Malden, MA: Polity Press.

Seib, Philip. 2004. *Beyond the Front Lines: How the News Media Cover a World Shaped by War*. London: Palgrave.

Serebriakova, Aleksandra. 2020. "Putin Congratulates Biden on Election Victory." Sputniknews.com. December 15. Accessed February 15, 2023. https://sputniknews.com/20201215/putin-congratulates-biden-on-election-victory-1081463006.html.

Serwer, Adam. 2023. "Why Fox News Lied to Its Viewers." TheAtlantic.com. February 19. Accessed March 31, 2023. https://www.theatlantic.com/ideas/archive/2023/02/fox-news-dominion-lawsuit-trump/673132/.

Shearer, Elisa, and Katerina Eva Matsa. 2018. "News Use Across Social Media Platforms 2018." Washington, D.C.: Pew Research Center. September 10. Accessed April 27, 2023. https://www.pewresearch.org/journalism/2018/09/10/news-use-across-social-media-platforms-2018/.

Siebert, Fred S., Theodore Peterson, and Wilbur Schramm. 1956. *Four Theories of the Press: The Authoritarian, Libertarian, Social Responsibility and Soviet Communist Concepts of What the Press Should Be and Do*. Chicago: University of Illinois Press.

Singman, Brooke. 2020a. "Ratcliffe Says ODNI Has Provided Nearly 1,000 Documents to DOJ to Support Durham Probe." Foxnews.com. October 7. Accessed March 22, 2023. https://www.foxnews.com/politics/declassification-documents-durham-probe.

Singman, Brooke. 2020b. "Biden Mum on Hunter Biden Emails, Alleged Knowledge of Son's Overseas Business Dealings." Foxnews.com. October 19. Accessed March 22, 2023. https://www.foxnews.com/politics/joe-biden-response-hunter-biden-emails-business-dealings.

Smith, Anthony D. 1998. *Nationalism and Modernism*. London: Routledge.

Smith, David. 2023. "Rightwing Republicans Rail Against US Aid for Ukraine: 'We've done enough.'" Theguardian.com. March 4. Accessed April 30, 2023. https://www.theg

198 REFERENCES

uardian.com/us-news/2023/mar/04/cpac-rightwing-republicans-ukraine-support-marjorie-taylor-greene.

Smyth, Regina. 2020. *Elections, Protest, and Authoritarian Regime Stability: Russia 2008–2020*. New York: Cambridge University Press.

Society of Professional Journalists. 2014. "SPJ Code of Ethics." SPJ.org. Accessed March 26, 2023. https://www.spj.org/ethicscode.asp.

Sputnik International. 2020a. "'Shoddy, Poorly Written' Lawsuits by Trump Campaign Yet Another Way to Suppress Vote—Experts." Sputnikews.com. November 6. Accessed March 27, 2023. https://sputniknews.com/20201106/shoddy-poorly-written-lawsuits-by-trump-campaign-yet-another-way-to-suppress-vote---experts-1081073758.html.

Sputnik International. 2020b. "Ousted Election Security Chief Calls Giuliani Presser 'Most Dangerous' Television in US History." Sputniknews.com. November 20. Accessed March 27, 2023. https://sputniknews.com/20201120/ousted-election-security-chief-calls-giuliani-presser-most-dangerous-television-in-us-history-1081216650.html.

Starbird, Kate. 2017. "Examining the Alternative Media Ecosystem Through the Production of Alternative Narratives of Mass Shooting Events on Twitter." *Proceedings of the International AAAI Conference on Web and Social Media*. 11 (1): 230–239. https://doi.org/10.1609/icwsm.v11i1.14878.

Steiner, Sean P., and Sarah Oates. 2019. "Reading the RT Leaves: Foreign Policy Lessons from Russian International Media Coverage of Venezuela." *Kennan Cable* 43. Wilson Center, Washington, D.C. https://www.wilsoncenter.org/publication/kennan-cable-no-43-reading-the-rt-leaves-foreign-policy-lessons-russian-international.

Stulberg, Adam, and Dennis Murphy. 2022. "Deciphering Russia's Playbook: Lessons from the Lead-Up to Putin's War in Ukraine." Washington, D.C.: PONARS Eurasia at the George Washington University Elliott Scholl of International Affairs. October. Accessed April 21, 2023. https://www.ponarseurasia.org/deciphering-russias-playbook-lessons-from-the-lead-up-to-putins-war-in-ukraine/.

Sutter, Daniel. 2001. "Can the Media Be So Liberal: The Economics of Media Bias." *Cato Institute Journal*. 20 (3): 431–452.

Szostek, Joanna. 2017. "Defence and Promotion of Desired State Identity in Russia's Strategic Narrative." *Geopolitics* 22 (3): 571–593. https://doi.org/10.1080/14650045.2016.1214910.

TASS. 2020. "Press Review: Trump Campaigns Down to the Wire and Armenia Requests Russian Aid." TASS.com. November 2. Accessed March 22, 2023. https://tass.com/pressreview/1218929.

Thomas, Elise. 2022. "Russia Today Digs Deep to Stay on YouTube." Isdglobal.org. July 5. Accessed April 30, 2023. https://www.isdglo.bal.org/digital_dispatches/russia-today-digs-deep-to-stay-on-youtube/

Thompson, Stuart A. 2022. "How Russian Media Uses Fox News to Make Its Case." *The New York Times*. April 15. Accessed February 18, 2024. https://www.nytimes.com/2022/04/15/technology/russia-media-fox-news.html.

Thompson, Stuart A. and Davey Alba. 2022. "Fact and Mythmaking Blend in Ukraine's Information War." *The New York Times*. March 3. Accessed October 21, 2023. https://www.nytimes.com/2022/03/03/technology/ukraine-war-misinfo.html.

Tolz, Vera, Stephen Hutchings, Precious N. Chatterje-Doody, and Rhys Crilley. 2020. "Mediatization and Journalistic Agency: Russian Television Coverage of the Skripal Poisonings." *Journalism*. 22 (12): 2971–2990. https://doi.org/10.1177/1464884920941967.

REFERENCES 199

Translators Without Borders. N.d. "Language Data for Ukraine." Translatorswithoutborders.org. Accessed April 17, 2023. https://translatorswithout borders.org/language-data-for-ukraine.

Transparency International. 2023. "CPI for Eastern Europe & Central Asia: Growing Security Risks and Authoritarianism Threaten Progress Against Corruption." Transparency.org. January 31. Accessed April 5, 2023. https://www.transparency.org/en/news/cpi-2022-eastern-europe-central-asia-growing-security-risks-authoritarianism-threaten-progress-corruption.

Troianovski, Anton, and Michael D. Shear. 2022. "As Russia Welcomes Talks, Biden Warns Invasion Is Still Possible." *The New York Times.* February 16. Accessed April 26, 2023. https://www.nytimes.com/2022/02/15/world/europe/russia-ukraine-troops.html.

Tsukanov, Ilya. 2020. "'Trump Won This Election in a Landslide': Flynn Lawyer Vows to Prove Mass Vote Fraud Plot Soon." Sputniknews.com. November 14. Accessed March 27, 2023. https://sputniknews.com/20201114/trump-won-this-election-in-a-landsl ide-flynn-lawyer-vows-to-prove-mass-vote-fraud-plot-soon-1081165727.html.

Tuchman, Gaye. 1972. "Objectivity as Strategic Ritual." *American Journal of Sociology.* 77 (4): 660–679. https://www.jstor.org/stable/2776752.

Tweedie, James. 2020a. "Joe Biden Misses Obama's Call to Take the Stage Three Times at Michigan Rally." Sputniknews.com. November 2. Accessed March 22, 2023. https://sputniknews.com/20201102/joe-biden-misses-obamas-call-to-take-the-stage-three-times-at-michigan-rally---video-1080957320.html.

Tweedie, James. 2020b. "President of Soros-Linked Voting Software Firm on Biden Transition Team—Trump Lawyers." Sputniknews.com. November 15. Accessed March 27, 2023. https://sputniknews.com/20201115/president-of-soros-linked-voting-softw are-firm-on-biden-transition-team---trump-lawyers-1081174974.html.

Umland, Andreas. 2019. "Irregular Militias and Radical Nationalism in Post-Euromaydan Ukraine: The Prehistory and Emergence of the 'Azov' Battalion in 2014." *Terrorism and Political Violence.* 31 (1): 105–131. https://doi.org/10.1080/09546553.2018.1555974.

United States Senate Committee on Foreign Relations. 2018. *Putin's Asymmetric Assault on Democracy in Russia and Europe: Implications for U.S. National Security.* A Minority Staff Report. Washington, D.C.: U.S. Government Printing Office.

United States Senate Select Committee on Intelligence. 2020. *Russian Active Measures Campaigns and Interference in the 2016 U.S. Election. Volumes I-V Together with Additional Views.* Washington, D.C.: U.S. Government Printing Office. November 10. Accessed March 22, 2023. https://www.intelligence.senate.gov/publications/report-sel ect-committee-intelligence-united-states-senate-russian-active-measures.

Vaidhyanathan, Siva. 2018. *Antisocial Media: How Facebook Disconnects Us and Undermines Democracy.* New York: Oxford University Press.

Vilmer, Jean-Baptiste Jeangène, Alexandre Escorcia, Marine Guillaume, and Janaina Herrerra. 2018. *Information Manipulation: A Challenge for Our Democracies.* Paris: Centre d'analyse, de prévision et de stratégie, and Institut de recherche stratégique de l'École militaire. https://www.diplomatie.gouv.fr/IMG/pdf/information _manipulation_rvb_cle838736.pdf.

Wagnsson, Charlotte. 2023. "The Paperboys of Russian Messaging: RT/Sputnik Audiences as Vehicles for Malign Information Influence." *Information, Communication & Society* 26 (9): 1–19. https://doi.org/10.1080/1369118X.2022.2041700.

Wagnsson, Charlotte, and Costan Barzanje. 2021. "A Framework for Analysing Antagonistic Narrative Strategies: A Russian Tale of Swedish Decline." *Media, War & Conflict*. 14 (2): 239–257. https://doi.org/10.1177/1750635219884343.

Walker, Christopher. 2016. "The Authoritarian Threat: The Hijacking of 'Soft Power.'" *Journal of Democracy*. 27 (1): 49–63.

Walker, Mason. 2021. "U.S. Newsroom Employment Has Fallen 26% Since 2008." Pewresearch.org. July 13. Accessed March 26, 2023. https://www.pewresearch.org/fact-tank/2021/07/13/u-s-newsroom-employment-has-fallen-26-since-2008/.

Wells, Chris, Dhavan Shah, Josephine Lukito, Ayellet Pelled, John CV Pevehouse, and JungHwan Yang. 2020. "Trump, Twitter, and News Media Responsiveness: A Media Systems Approach." *New Media & Society* 22 (4): 659–682. https://doi.org/10.1177/1461444819893987.

Wike, Richard, Janell Fetterolf, Moira Fagan, and Sneha Gubbala. 2022. *International Attitudes Toward the U.S., NATO, and Russia in a Time of Crisis*. Washington, D.C.: Pew Research Center. Accessed April 17, 2023. https://www.pewresearch.org/global/wp-content/uploads/sites/2/2022/06/PG_2022.07.22_U.S.-Image_FINAL.pdf.

Wolff, Michael. 2008. *The Man Who Owns the News: Inside the Secret World of Rupert Murdoch*. New York: Alfred A. Knopf.

Wong, Edward, and Stephen Erlanger. 2022. "China as Peacemaker in the Ukraine War? The U.S. and Europe Are Skeptical." *The New York Times*. March 20. Accessed April 26, 2023. https://www.nytimes.com/2023/03/19/us/politics/russia-china-putin-xi.html.

Wong, Edward, and Laura Jakes. 2022. "NATO Won't Let Ukraine Join Soon. Here's Why." Nytimes.com. January 13. Accessed April 26, 2023. https://www.nytimes.com/2022/01/13/us/politics/nato-ukraine.html.

Wright, Kate, Martin Scott, and Mel Bunce. 2020. "Soft Power, Hard News: How Journalists at State-Funded Transnational Media Legitimize Their Work." *The International Journal of Press/Politics*. 25 (4): 607–631. https://doi.org/10.1177/1940161220922832.

Wring, Dominic. 2012. "'It's Just Business': The Political Economy of the Hacking Scandal." *Media, Culture & Society*. 34 (5): 631–636. https://doi.org/10.1177/0163443712442435.

Yablokov, Ilya. 2018. *Fortress Russia: Conspiracy Theories in the Post-Soviet World*. London: Polity.

Yablokov, Ilya, and Precious Chatterje-Doody. 2021. *Russia Today and Conspiracy Theories: People, Power and Politics on RT*. London: Routledge.

Yang, Yunkang, and Lance Bennett. 2021. "Interactive Propaganda: How Fox News and Donald Trump Co-produced False Narratives about the COVID-19 Crisis." In *Political Communication in the Time of Coronavirus*, edited by Peter van Aelst and Jay G. Blumler. London: Routledge, 83–100.

Zulli, Diana, Kevin Coe, and Zachary Isaacs. 2022. "News Framing in the Aftermath of the January 6 Attacks on the U.S. Capitol: An Analysis of Labels, Definitional Uncertainty, and Contextualization." *American Behavioral Scientist*, 67 (6): 1–19. https://doi.org/10.1177/00027642221096333.

Index

For the benefit of digital users, indexed terms that span two pages (e.g., 52–53) may, on occasion, appear on only one of those pages.

ABC, 30, 35–36
absentee ballots, 13, 83
Access Hollywood, 4, 60–61
Ad Fontes Media, 38, 39, 155
Afghanistan, 60, 74, 145, 158–59
Albrecht, Madeline, 164
Allsides, 38, 39
Antifa, 18–19, 74, 83, 89–90, 106–7, 108–9, 112, 173
Arab Spring, 63, 144
authoritarian media model, 112
Azov battalion (*see* Azov regiment)
Azov regiment, 152, 153–57

Baltic States, 58–59, 72–73, 170
Bandera, Stepan, 146–47
Berlin Wall, 7, 58–59, 156–57, 158
Biden
  Hunter,
    allegations of corruption in Ukraine, 91–92, 98
    laptop, 81–82, 83, 86–87, 89–90, 96–97, 98–100, 103–6, 112
  Joe, 74, 123, 150–51, 174–75
    allegations of corruption in Ukraine, 91–92, 105–6
    attacks on, 18–19, 83, 86–88, 89, 112–13, 176
    campaign coverage, 5, 86–87, 89
    conspiracy theories about, 42–43, 153
    coverage by Fox, 82–83, 103, 105, 174
    criticism of Donald Trump, 50–51
    criticism of Russia, 163
    Russian propaganda about, 83
bioweapons, alleged use of by U.S., 61, 147–48, 153–54

Black Lives Matter (BLM), 18–19, 74, 81–82, 106–7, 110
Boston Marathon, 21
Breitbart, 21, 39–40, 154–55
British Broadcasting Corporation (BBC), 28–29, 65–66
Bucha massacre, 147–48
Budapest Memorandum, 166–67
Bush, President George W., 7–8, 145

Cable News Network (*see* CNN)
Carlson, Tucker, 37, 88–89, 131, 175, 181
cascading activation theory, 145, 158–59, 170
CBS, 30, 35–36
China, 6, 103, 162–63
CIA (Central Intelligence Agency), 102, 130–31
Clinton
  Bill, 46
  Hillary, 4, 9, 93–94, 102, 165, 173
    2008 campaign, 22, 41–42
    2016 campaign, 41–42, 83–84
    comments on NATO, 164
    negative coverage of, 4, 40–41, 48
    Russian disinformation of, 44, 60–61, 90, 93, 97, 173
    Trump attacks on, 15
CNN, 30–31, 36, 37, 38–39, 47, 89, 98–99, 100–1, 109
Cold War, 4, 6–7, 16–17, 43–44, 60, 61, 65–66, 92, 158–59, 166
Communist Party of the Soviet Union, 6–7, 58
comparative models of media systems, 29–30

202 INDEX

Congress, U.S., 4–5, 28–29, 30, 74, 91–92, 94, 129, 171, 175
conspiracy theories, 2–3, 21, 25, 42–43, 51, 56, 70, 76–77, 81–82, 84–85, 105–6, 115–16, 117, 118, 127, 133, 136–37, 138, 139, 145, 146, 147–48, 153–54, 155, 170–71, 175–76
Conway, Kellyanne, 46, 65–66
Cooper, Anderson, 38–39, 88–89
Corporation for Public Broadcasting, 28–29
COVID, 2, 12–13, 18–19, 33, 35, 42–43, 46–47, 50, 51, 75, 83, 118, 172, 176
Crimea, 18, 60, 62, 65, 144, 167

Daily Caller, 154
Daily Wire, 154–55
Democratic National Committee, 8–9, 44, 74, 86, 97, 173
Democratic Party, 46, 60–61, 90, 95, 103–5
Dominion Voting Systems, 51–52, 115, 116, 119–20, 130–31, 136–38, 139, 140, 179
Donbas, 143, 144

Eastern Europe, 7, 58–59, 157–58, 166
Eastern Ukraine, 60, 62, 72, 144
East Germany, 58–59, 73, 157, 166
elections, U.S.
    Russian interference in, 44–45, 49, 90–92, 93, 94, 97, 99, 100–1, 105–6, 173, 180
    2022 midterm, 2–3
Electoral College, 120
Estonia, 71–72
Euromaidan, 62, 144, 154–55
Europe, 58, 66–67, 71, 144, 158, 162–63, 168
European Union, 17, 44, 73–74, 144, 179

Facebook, 4, 21, 173, 175, 179
Fairness Doctrine, 30, 31
Federal Communications Commission (FCC), 30
Finland, 73–74, 158, 165

Floyd, George, 18–19, 106
Flynn, Michael, 129, 131
Fortress Russia, 67, 72–73

Georgia
    Republic of, 7–8, 62, 72–73, 158–59, 167
    U.S. State, 120, 124, 175
Germany, 58, 71, 73, 157–58
Giuliani, Rudy, 96–97, 98, 99–100, 103, 105, 129, 131
Gorbachev, Mikhail, 58–59, 157
Graham, Lindsey, 129
Great Patriotic War (*see* World War II)

Hannity, Sean, 38–39, 131
Hawley, Josh, 129
Hill, Fiona, 146–47, 164–65

Infowars, 21, 51–52, 129, 154–55, 179
Ingraham, Laura, 37, 132
Iraq, 31–32, 74, 145

Jones, Alex, 129
journalism, horse race, 32, 83–84, 86
journalistic standards, 23–24, 39, 138–39

Kazakhstan, 166–67
Khrushchev, Nikita, 58
Kosovo, 7, 73, 158–59

Latvia, 71–72
Lavrov, Sergei, 65, 94
libertarian media model, 4, 29, 30, 40, 49, 51–52, 112
Limbaugh, Rush, 30–31
Lisa F. case, 71
Lithuania, 71–72

machine classifiers, 93, 94, 112–13, 114
mail-in ballots, 18–19, 113–14, 118, 119
Malaysia Airlines Flight 17, 18, 60, 65, 66
Manafort, Paul, 91, 95–96
McConnell, Mitch, 127
McFaul, Michael, 165
Mearsheimer, John, 164–65
media, European, 64
media, trust in, 19, 20, 21, 39, 48, 172, 175
media ecosystem, U.S., 19–22, 178

INDEX 203

media freedom, Russia, 43
media models
  authoritarian (*see* authoritarian
    media model)
  libertarian (*see* libertarian
    media model)
media outlets, local, 19–20, 34, 45–46
Meta (*see* Facebook)
Molotov-Ribbentrop Pact, 58, 152
MSNBC, 36, 37, 47, 98–99
Mueller, Robert, 4–5, 74, 78, 91, 97, 101–2
Murdoch, Rupert, 37–38, 138–39

National Security Council, 164–65
NATO (North Atlantic Treaty
    Organization), 5, 62, 66, 146, 152,
    160, 161, 162, 165, 166, 167, 169,
    170, 171, 172–73
  American interest in, 159–60
  criticism by China, 162–63
  expansion of, 72–74, 75–76, 161, 162, 165
  history of, 7, 62, 73, 74, 156–58, 166–67
  role in Russian strategic narratives, 12,
    62–63, 66–67, 69–70, 145, 148–49,
    152, 162
  Russian disinformation about, 5, 12, 17,
    25, 62–63, 158, 160, 166–67
  Russian grievances against, 7, 62–63,
    68, 69–70, 72–74, 75–76, 142, 145,
    146, 151–52, 156–57, 175–76
  U.S. news coverage of, 25, 73–74, 142, 158–
    60, 161–62, 163–65, 166–68, 178
Navalny, Alexei, 93, 94
Nazis, 107, 149–50, 151–52, 156, 161, 162,
    164, 169
  alleged in Ukraine, 25, 76–77, 142, 143–
    44, 146–48, 149–50, 151, 153, 154,
    155, 156, 169–70, 171, 175–76
  Azov regiment, 152, 153–54, 155–56
  history of, 25, 142, 143–44, 149, 151,
    152, 153–57, 171, 175–76, 177
  in Russian strategic narrative, 76,
    143–44, 147–48, 169–70, 172–73,
    175–76, 177
  symbols, 156–57
  U.S. news coverage of claims, 142, 153–
    56, 171, 178
  World War II, 70, 76–77, 149, 152

NBC, 30, 35–36, 65–66
Neo-Nazis (*see* Nazis)
Newsmax, 25, 38, 39, 51, 115, 117, 121,
    122, 134–37, 138, 139, 140, 154–
    55, 174, 181
newspapers, 19, 20, 33, 45–46, 89, 99,
    175–76, 178, 181
  British, 68–69, 138
New York Times, 11, 24–25, 34, 42, 45–46,
    89, 96–97, 98–99, 100–1, 103, 105,
    107, 108–9, 110, 130–31, 138, 139,
    142, 153, 155, 159–60, 162, 163–
    65, 166–67, 168–69, 178
Nixon, Richard, 46
Nord Stream, 147–48
NTV (Russian commercial television), 17
nuclear weapons, 92, 160, 166–67

One America News Network (OANN),
    139, 154
Obama, Barack, 22, 41, 46
objectivity, 2, 3, 11, 20–21, 25, 31–33,
    36–37, 39, 42, 137, 140–41, 160,
    168–69, 174
Operation Infektion, 61–62

Paul, Rand, 169
Pence, Mike, 120
Powell, Sidney, 129, 130–31
Prigozhin, Evgenii, 180
Project Veritas, 129
Proud Boys, 110
Putin, Vladimir, 7, 8, 11, 59–60, 94, 123,
    142, 150–51, 156, 163, 167, 172–
    73, 175–76
  attitude toward NATO, 160, 161–62,
    163, 164, 165, 166–67
  attitude toward Ukraine, 72, 76, 145,
    146–47, 148–49, 151, 170–71
  authoritarian control, 60
  Crimea, 60
  erosion of media freedom under, 43
  historical unity article, 149–51
  international relations, 7, 62
  mental state, 167
  Nazis and neo-Nazi claims, 76–77, 142,
    143–44, 146–47, 148, 149, 151–52,
    155–56, 171

204 INDEX

Putin, Vladimir (*cont.*)
  popularity, 60
  praise from Donald Trump, 78
  propaganda, 147, 169
  resonance with Trump
    messaging, 25–26
  response to Euromaidan, 144
  strategic narratives, 25, 54, 57, 63,
    65, 67, 77, 94–95, 143–44, 152,
    164, 169–70, 177, 178
  traits shared with Donald Trump, 10
  U.S. news coverage of, 5, 168–69
  World War II, 70, 149, 151, 152

Radio Liberty, 6–7, 61
Republican Party, 2, 5, 22–23, 78, 91–92,
  121, 129, 139
  2020 convention, 50, 180
  voters, 118, 175
Republicans
  2020 campaign, 50, 107
  fusion with Russian messaging, 95
  lack of trust in media, 20
  Stop the Steal conspiracy narrative,
    119, 175
  use of Russophobia narrative, 91
Rice, Susan, 125
Rubio, Marco, 100–1
Russia
  domestic media, 17–18, 71, 130, 132–33
  media freedom, 43
  media history, 43
  Tsarist rule, 58, 76
Russiagate, 18–19, 78, 91, 92, 93–94, 95–
  96, 97, 174
Russia "hoax," 83, 91, 95, 101–2
Russian ads, U.S. 2016 campaign, 75
Russian history, contemporary, 59
Russian Ministry of Foreign Affairs, 65
Russian Revolution (1917), 58
Russians, ethnic in Ukraine, 72, 76

Sandy Hook Elementary School shooting,
  21, 155
Smartmatic, 119–20
Sochi Olympics, 67–68
social media
  ban on Trump, 175

Russian influence of, 4, 9, 44–45, 74, 90,
  172, 179–80
  Trump use of Twitter, 71, 78, 127–28
  use in foreign influence, 78
Soviet Union, 71–72, 157
  Eastern Europe, 58–59, 72–73, 157, 166
  media, 6–7, 17, 69
  NATO, 73, 157, 166
  propaganda, 23, 61, 63, 64
  transition to Russian Federation, 7, 17,
    43, 59, 157
  Ukraine, 76
  World War II, 58, 70, 143–44, 146–47
Stalin, Josef, 58
Stop the Steal, 1, 5, 6, 23, 25, 45, 49, 75,
  114, 122–23, 133, 176–77
Sweden, 73–74, 78–79, 155–56, 158
Syria, 7–8, 62, 67, 70

TASS, 88
Trump supporters, 2, 20, 22, 45–46, 47,
  48, 82, 91, 107, 115, 121, 129,
  139, 140
trust in media (*see* media, trust in)
Truth Social, 175
Tsarist Russia, 57–58, 76

Ukraine
  2014 invasion, 60–61, 64, 72, 75–76,
    144, 145, 149–50, 152, 167
  2022 invasion, 1, 5, 11, 17, 43, 62, 73–74,
    75–76, 94–95, 142, 143–44, 145,
    146–48, 153, 158–60, 162, 167,
    170, 177, 178, 179, 180
  Azov regiment (*see* Azov regiment)
  Biden conspiracy about, 105–6
  Bucha massacre, 147–48
  Budapest Memorandum, 166–67
  claims of bioweapons in, 147–48
  claims of Nazis in, 1, 25, 76–77, 142,
    143–44, 146, 147–48, 149–50, 151–
    56, 170, 171, 175–76, 177, 178
  effect of Russian propaganda on
    international support, 68–69
  ethnic Russians in, 72, 76
  European Union membership, 73–74
  history of, 76
  NATO membership in, 73–74, 158

INDEX 205

Putin's statements about, 146, 148–50, 151–52
Russian fears about, 75–76
Russian strategic narratives about, 65, 68–69, 70, 72, 75, 76, 77, 80, 142, 143, 144, 145, 147, 160, 169–71, 177
Trump impeachment, 74, 91–92, 94
U.S. news coverage of, 5, 142, 154–55, 160, 161–62, 163, 164–65, 168–69, 178
U.S. podcasts about, 147–48
Unsafe Streets narrative, 83, 107–8, 110
U.S. Senate Committee on Foreign Relations, 65–66, 67
U.S. Senate Select Committee on Intelligence, 91–92, 97, 99, 100–2

Voice of America, 6–7, 48, 61
voting machines, 115, 119–20, 128–29, 130–31, 132, 138, 139

Wall Street Journal, 11, 24–25, 81, 89, 98–99, 100–1, 110, 142, 155, 160, 178
Washington Post, 11, 24–25, 45–47, 81, 89, 98–99, 100–1, 142, 155, 160, 178
Western media systems, 15–16, 26, 143–44
West Germany, 73, 157–58
White House, 7–8, 42–43, 46, 50, 74, 81, 90–91, 101, 105, 111–12, 145
WikiLeaks, 4
World War II, 16, 58–59, 70, 72–73, 76–77, 146–47, 149, 151, 152, 166, 171

Yanukovych, Viktor, 144
Yeltsin, Boris, 58–59
Yugoslavia, 7, 73

Zelenskyy, Volodymyr, 76–77, 91–92, 154–55